BLOODY
MEADOWS

Dedicated to all Victims of War,
Past, Present and Future

BLOODY MEADOWS

INVESTIGATING LANDSCAPES OF BATTLE

JOHN AND PATRICIA CARMAN

SUTTON PUBLISHING

First published in the United Kingdom in 2006 by
Sutton Publishing Limited · Phoenix Mill
Thrupp · Stroud · Gloucestershire · GL5 2BU

British Library Cataloguing in Publication Data
A catalogue record for this book is available from the British Library.

ISBN 0-7509-3734-3

Typeset in 11/15pt Sabon.
Typesetting and origination by
Sutton Publishing Limited.
Printed and bound in England by
J.H. Haynes & Co. Ltd, Sparkford.

CONTENTS

LIST OF ILLUSTRATIONS, TABLES AND FIGURES

COLOUR PLATES

Battlefield Landscapes (between pages 114 and 115)

BLACK AND WHITE ILLUSTRATIONS

Battlefield Features

FIGURES

ACKNOWLEDGEMENTS

Fieldwork in 1998 and 2000 was generously funded by grants from the McDonald Institute for Archaeological Research, University of Cambridge. An Overseas Conference grant from the British Academy – given to enable John Carman to attend the annual meeting of the European Association of Archaeologists in Lisbon in 2000 – also assisted with the costs of travel to Portugal in connection with fieldwork in 2000. A further Overseas Conference grant from the British Academy assisted with the costs of attendance at the eighth annual meeting of the European Association of Archaeologists in Thessaloniki in 2002 where a report on work was presented. Clare Hall generously supported several attendances at overseas conferences at which presentations related to the project were given, and we are particularly grateful to Professor Gillian Beer, then President of Clare Hall, and Edward Jarron, Bursar, for their support and help.

The origins and work of the Bloody Meadows Project have been reported upon at a number of conferences and in other talks, beginning with the Theoretical Archaeology Group conference in Liverpool in 1996, and we are grateful to Sarah Tarlow and Suzie West for the chance to participate in their session. Subsequent opportunities presented themselves at meetings of the European Association of Archaeologists, especially the third held in Ravenna in 1997, the fifth held in Bournemouth in 1999, and the eighth held in Thessaloniki in 2002. We are grateful to Mark Pearce, Julian Thomas and Christopher Fowler, and Stephanie Koerner – session organisers respectively – for their interest in our work. We are particularly grateful to John Schofield, Bill Johnson and Colleen Beck for the opportunity to present some preliminary theoretical ideas at the fourth World Archaeology Conference in Capetown, South Africa in 1999; and to Anthony Harding for allowing a paper that took his conference on ancient warfare, held in Durham in 1996, beyond the realm of the prehistoric.

Other conferences specifically devoted to warfare include *Dressing up for War* held in Barcelona in 1999, *Fields of Conflict* held in Glasgow in 2000, the Sheffield Archaeological Society and Prehistoric Society conference on

Prehistoric Warfare held in Sheffield in 2001, the second *Fields of Conflict* conference held in Åland, Finland in 2002 and the third held in Nashville, Tennessee, USA in 2004. We are grateful to the organisers of all these – especially Phil Freeman and Tony Pollard, Mike Parker Pearson, Vivecka Löndahl and Douglas Scott – for providing space for us to present; and to Phil Freeman and Doug Scott again for kindly delivering our papers at the second and third *Fields of Conflict* conferences which we could not attend in person. Thanks are due also to Andrew Gardner and Steve Townend for inviting us to participate in their session at *TAG in Ireland* in 2001, and to Andrew and Simon James for their invitation to take part in their session on violence in the Roman world at TRAC 2003. Other papers were presented at sessions at TAG in Lampeter in 2003 and at the annual IFA conference in 2004, and we are grateful to the organisers for all their help.

Outings in sessions not specifically devoted to issues of warfare include participation in the Anglia Polytechnic University conference on *Visual Culture and Tourism* held in Cambridge in 2000, in the series of public talks *Not the Elgin Marbles* held at York University in 2002, the CELAT conference *Objets Mobilés* held in Quebec, Canada in 2003, and the first CHAT conference at Bristol in 2003. Also at York, a paper was presented as a York Medieval Studies Seminar in 2000. Particular thanks go to Jane Grenville and Laurajane Smith for organising and chairing the York presentations, to Daniel Arsenault for inviting us to go to Quebec and overseeing our stay there, and to Dan Hicks in Bristol. In addition, papers were presented within Cambridge University at the third Cambridge Heritage Seminar on *Heritage That Hurts* in 1998, to the McDonald Institute in 1998, as Graduate Seminars in the Department of Archaeology in 2000 and 2003, and to the Cambridge University Archaeological Field Club in 2000 and 2002.

We are grateful to all those who have heard us talk upon the work of the Project and all those to whom we have talked over meals or drinks. We are very grateful for particular help to Anthony Harding, Larry Zimmerman, Laurajane Smith and Jane Grenville. We are extremely grateful to Glenn Foard for early advice on the battlefield of Northampton and access to his work on that site. In addition, the support given by a number of friends and colleagues who have shown interest in the project beyond the call of the duties of friendship must be recorded: Chris Evans, Mary-Cate Garden, Helen Geake, Kristian Kristiansen, Marco Madella, Carol McDavid, Phil Mills, Ulla Rajala, Marie Louise Sørensen and Corinne Roughley have all listened politely while we rambled on about our travels and travails. Particular thanks go to some anonymous guides and respondents we have encountered in our travels, and who have been instrumental in helping make some kind of sense of the battlefields we have visited. In addition to these direct personal contacts, we need to acknowledge the help given to us by members of email lists to requests for advice: Paul Courteney, Paula D. Girschick, Maggie Goodall, David Harvey and David Petts, among others whose advice we did not take up, all gave us very useful pointers. Finally, thanks must go to the managers and staff of Suttons for their help in seeing this work into print, and to Dr Helen Geake and the Cambridge University Photographic and Illustration Service for assistance with preparation of photographs.

John and Patricia Carman
Cambridge, December 2005

ONE

RESEARCHING BATTLEFIELDS

The aim of the Bloody Meadows Project is to contribute to current debates upon the place of war in the world by developing an understanding of changes in warfare practice and ideology over the long term. In operation, it is an exercise in the comparative study of battlefields from all periods of history and in all parts of the world. Treating battlefields as landscapes, and drawing upon recent approaches adopted in landscape archaeology, the project focuses on the battlefield as a *place*. Battles as events are a main focus of military history in all periods, and battlefields are also increasingly being taken up as part of a nation's 'official' cultural heritage and as the focus of research by archaeologists and others who also seek to elucidate the sequence of events at such sites. By placing the focus upon the battle*field* itself, however – and by looking at those from all periods – it becomes possible to gain an insight into the underlying cultural imperatives guiding the practice of war, and to discover aspects of war-making in the past that challenge modern perceptions and expectations. From this emerges the possibility of reaching new understandings of war as a cultural phenomenon.

The approach taken to battlefields by the Bloody Meadows Project is to treat them as particular types of landscape because there is more to the human response to landscape than treating it as a purely 'natural' phenomenon (Bender, 1993; Tilley, 1994). It is learned sets of taken-for-granted ideas, understandings and responses that provide the framework within which landscapes are experienced, turning landscape from a mere 'natural' backdrop into a cultural artefact. These culturally informed ideas, understandings and responses in turn structure the military use or non-use of landscape. Being part of a commonly held cultural frame of reference, attitudes towards landscape, expectations of landscape, and thus understanding of landscape – all of which differ for different peoples in different times and different places – are not usually part of express military discourse and are thus not open to examination. The consequence is that to understand the underlying attitudes towards battlefields held by different peoples at different times requires an investigation of the place itself as well as of the battle as an event. In doing so, we must move beyond the conventional

1

discourses of military history and indeed military archaeology, which so often consider landscape only in terms of its direct effect on the events of battle.

The Bloody Meadows Project therefore takes an explicitly *comparative* approach to the study of battlefields: rather than devoting efforts to one or a few sites, the aim is to discover how one battlefield differs from another and how they differ across time and across space. The search is not for the decisive, the spectacular or the distinctive, but for the typical 'norm' in any period. There is an acute awareness throughout that fighting set-piece battles at particular places is not the only way of conducting wars, and the institution of 'battle' as we know it may be a relatively late invention in human history (perhaps no earlier than the Bronze Age of Egypt, *c.* 1500 BC). The Bloody Meadows Project is therefore concerned with understanding battle as a particular cultural form, and we work from the premise that battlefields have something to tell us about the nature of human violence as expressed in war, and this makes them important as *culturally constructed locales.*

The contribution of such a study to understanding war as a cultural activity lies in the culturally driven assumptions that lie behind the choice of place in which to fight in particular historical periods. Work from 1998 to 2002 (and reported upon in detail for the first time here) has highlighted the range of different landscapes in which battles are fought: but while similar types of place may be chosen in one period of history, these will differ significantly and noticeably from those chosen in other periods. The choice of battleground, we believe, therefore reflects unstated ideas about how war should be conducted, and these ideas vary across history. By studying the places themselves where these acts took place we can develop an insight into the minds of soldiers in the past, which challenges our own assumptions about the place of war in our society and forces us to look again at our own assumptions and expectations.

The project has its origin in some of the shared interests of the authors. One of these concerns the nature of heritage places of all kinds. Another concerns the place of war in human history. A third concerns the attempt to develop a specifically archaeological contribution to one of the important debates of our time (Carman, 1997b, 1–23). Coming as we do out of archaeology, we are concerned ultimately with the way humans interact with each other and with their physical surroundings, as represented to us by the traces left upon those physical surroundings. Not all such traces are tangible, although these intangible traces may themselves subsequently be represented by physical marks. This is what happens when we return to a place or an object and mark it as a special kind of object or place, by putting a barrier around it, by putting a marker on it, or by (at a place) building a memorial. The relevance of this to the category of place called the 'battlefield' will be evident: the mass act of violence constituting the battle may leave little in the way of clear traces, but they are frequently marked out as special, particularly by the construction of monuments to the event and those who died during it.

The very specific focus of the project arose initially out of the interest of one of us (JC) in the way in which particular heritage objects are selected, categorised and given value (an issue addressed in terms of the legal frameworks available in Carman, 1996). The desire was felt to take this theme further – in particular to take it more deeply into specific categories – and also to develop a fieldwork project that would allow some contact with fresh air rather than the stuffy gloom of the academic law library. Accordingly, a suitable category of heritage object was sought for examination, and one that would also provide the opportunity to do more in the way of research than merely note its existence and the bureaucratic arrangements for its treatment, or simply add to its number by identifying new sites that fit the category. At the same time, and in order especially to avoid duplicating the work of others, the category needed to be one not yet being systematically addressed either in terms of heritage or some other possible research question. It needed to be a category sufficiently large – and preferably with some international recognition – to allow a reasonable amount of specific fieldwork time, but not one so broad as to cover almost anything or any place marked as 'heritage'.

The happy accident of the production of the English Heritage *Register of Historic Battlefields* (1995) coincided with the period of this search for a focus of fieldwork. Its production combined with both our interests in war as a contemporary and historical problem – especially in the light of the return of war to Europe after the end of the Cold War – and also with the simultaneous rise of battlefield archaeology as a distinct specialism (Doyle and Bennett, 2002; Freeman and Pollard, 2001). A focus on battlefields appeared to be a good way of meeting the needs of the desired fieldwork project and at the same time incorporating a concern with human violence. A project that also expressly combined issues of heritage with research into an aspect of the past would represent a new kind of project: we know of no others that combine these two aspects from the outset and where the two interact so closely.

Some Inspirational Texts on War

The Face of Battle (Keegan, 1976) represented a new turn in the traditional military historian's approach to battle as a historical event. The book concentrates on understanding the reality for combatants at three well-known and well-recorded battles from the past, which were fought within a relatively small distance from one another: Agincourt (1415), Waterloo (1815) and the first day of the Somme (1916). Opening with a sustained critique of the accepted manner of writing military history – and especially the 'battle piece' – the book goes on to examine in some detail the sequence of the events of each battle in terms of their experiential aspects: the effects of particular weapons on the human frame, the means of keeping men in the fighting line or of urging them to the attack, and the aftermath. Instead of a distanced, 'general's-eye view' and rationalistic account of battle, the book offers the possibility of constructing a view 'from the inside' and of understanding the experience of war at the sharp end. In terms of the interests of the authors of the Bloody Meadows Project, Keegan's work opened up the possibility of taking an overtly 'materialist' approach to battle (see also Carman, 1997b, 1–23) – in the simple sense of looking at its physical characteristics and consequences, rather than dealing with battle as the outcome of purely cerebral activity. Keegan's directly comparative approach across several centuries also strikes a chord with our own interest in taking a long-term perspective on battles (Carman, 1997c, 220–39).

The Western Way of War (Hanson, 1989) offered something similar to Keegan's in terms of ancient Greek hoplite warfare. Taking the elements of Greek warfare apart, the book explores the contexts within which Greek city-state wars took place, the place of the hoplite in Greek society, the relationship of men to their weapons and their fellows, the devices used to overcome fear, the organisational systems of command and control, the specific phases of combat, and the aftermath. It also, however, went one step further in attempting to use this as a window to consider the approach to war generally taken in the Western world. Arguing that the single, decisive clash of arms represented by hoplite battle has been taken in the West as the model for how war ought to be, Hanson points up the inappropriateness of such an understanding to modern conditions in an age of long-range weapons of mass destruction. He thus uses an understanding of war in historical times as a means to critique our own age. Keegan develops this theme in his own History of Warfare (1993), which seeks to draw on history for alternative but subordinate models of war which contain elements that may be more appropriate for an age where placing limits on war may be the more rational course. Both of these works thus contain the seeds of investigating the ideology of warfare by an examination of its specific form in particular historical periods.

Archaeological Perspectives on the Battle of the Little Bighorn (Scott *et al.*, 1989) is not (as it is sometimes taken to be) the first application of archaeology to a site of military action. It was, however, the inspiration for the current phase of military archaeology. Taking advantage of the cutting of the grass at the Custer Memorial site, Scott and his colleagues used metal detectors to trace the fall of bullets and the ejection of cartridges across the space of the fight between units of the 7th US Cavalry and Lakota and Cheyenne warriors. Differences in weapons used by one group of participants from those used by others allowed the researchers to identify Native American shot from that of the soldiers, and the distribution especially of cartridge cases across the space identified the movement of men and formations through the space. From this, a model of the sequence of events emerged which confirmed Native American accounts frequently dismissed. Other work on soldier burial sites allowed also the identification of individuals, the opportunity to infer the location of the bodies of missing soldiers, and the chance to develop a picture of the 'typical' soldier for the late nineteenth century in North America. The techniques applied and the results achieved have since been taken as a model for similar work in the USA and other parts of the world (as represented in, for instance, Freeman and Pollard, 2001). The work at the Little Bighorn has accordingly made the historic battlefield a suitable object of archaeological enquiry.

Elliot's *Twentieth-Century Book of the Dead* is a strange but interesting work, described by its author as 'a *necrology* . . . [meaning] a naming or listing of the dead' (1972, 11). As such, the book seeks to chart and quantify the various ghastly ways in which human beings have slaughtered each other over a particular period of history. In the case of this work, the title is somewhat of a misnomer, since the 'twentieth century' covered ends in 1970, thus comprising a mere 70 per cent of the total. A distinctive feature of the book is its focus less upon the direct experience of individuals than upon charting the types of 'man-made death' by orders of magnitude: typically, deaths due to direct military action are far fewer than those caused by public terror, guerrilla action, habitual 'ethnic' violence, and privation such as hunger and exposure. Indeed, it is shown that those caused by privation – both deliberate and collateral – by far exceed all the others. The book goes on to analyse the processes by which these deaths were made and draws some preliminary moral consequences from the lessons learned. This last clearly makes a connection with the origins of the Bloody Meadows Project, but there is another aspect of Elliot's approach which has a more direct link. As Elliot puts it: 'Much of what is written about violence is based on theories and attitudes extraneous to violence, and I cannot think of

5

anything more lacking and more necessary to the study of violence than a discipline based on the facts of violence' (1972, 15). A crucial fact at the centre of military activity is the place where that activity was carried out. To the extent that the Bloody Meadows Project is a contribution to the discipline of 'necrology', it lies in the focus upon the place of military activity as a constitutive fact of violence.

Like Elliot's necrology, *Postmodern War* (Gray, 1997) and *Violent Cartographies* (Shapiro, 1997) are works coming from disciplines beyond and separate from both archaeology and military history. They represent the return to war as a topic in the social sciences (in these cases sociology and geography), and a new critical approach to the study and understanding of war in our own age. *Postmodern War* (Gray, 1997) charts the rise of the cyborg-soldier as a part of twentieth-century existence and the domination of a discourse of war in modern Western society. Like *Violent Cartographies* (Shapiro, 1997) and Keegan's *History of Warfare* (1993), it thus seeks to reveal the cultural basis for the modern project of making war appear a realm of rational decision-making and one subject to human control. As Shapiro explains his own purpose: 'I have had to mount a resistance to many familiar languages of analysis, in particular the rationalistic discourses that dominate "security studies". [The aim] is to juxtapose such rationalism to a more ethnographic mode of thinking, to make rationalistic and logistical thinking appear to be a peculiar preoccupation rather than an edifying pedagogy' (1997, xi). Gray (1997) chooses to address the components of modern war systems, unpacking the illogic and untruth that lie at the heart of military organisation and planning. He ends by suggesting alternative futures: one dominated by the out-of-control war machine, the other by the concomitant rise of soldiers who are themselves opposed to wars. Shapiro (1997) addresses the rhetoric of military activity, mapping in a series of chapters the ways in which – at least in the American imagination – enemies have their humanity stripped from them, creating a moral space in which the military preference for violence can prevail. In thus taking a critical perspective upon war in our own time, these works – and others like them – inspire the possibility of a critical examination of war in the past, one not limited to the professional expectations of military history held by the soldier nor to dominant traditions of enquiry. Instead, it opens up the possibility of examining aspects of war in the past in their own terms. It is this that the Bloody Meadows Project aims to do in relation to the places where military violence was carried out.

A SHORT HISTORY OF BATTLEFIELD RESEARCH

While battles as events have been the focus of historical interest since the discipline of history was first invented, a specific interest in battlefields took longer to develop. Foard (1995, 343–82) records the early efforts of Edward Fitzgerald from 1842, whose work at Naseby in England includes the recording of field names and other topographical features, drawing the contemporary appearance of the landscape, noting where local people had found artefacts from the battle, and recording where local tradition placed particular events of the battle. Fitzgerald's work went on to include the digging of test-pits and finding a mass grave (Foard, 2001). At about the same time, Richard Brooke was pursuing his interest in the battlefields of the Wars of the Roses, inspired in him by his birth near the site of the battle of Stoke. His *Visits to the Fields of Battle in England of the Fifteenth Century* (Brooke, 1854) is largely a discussion of the historical sources he drew upon and concerns the events of the fight and the names of the prominent killed and wounded. He does, however, provide useful sketch maps of each site, some of which are of more practical use today than more modern ones.

Subsequent interest has largely remained in the realm of Brooke's primary concern, of identifying the places where battles took place, rather than using them as research objects in their own right. Once identified, the tendency is to assume that the landscape as seen today is similar, if not identical, to that on the day of the battle. Accordingly, Keegan – although aiming to gain an insight into the experience of battle in particular historical periods, which might have included gaining an insight into how the space of the battle might be 'read' by participants – makes no attempt to confirm that the location of the woods at Agincourt has not altered since the early fifteenth century (1976, 88) and the topography of battlefields is not discussed anywhere in his text. Similarly, as Foard (2001) makes clear in his criticism of both the standard form of battlefield 'guide' and the English Heritage *Register* (1995) which so closely resembles such guides, most publications on battlefields continue to 'place stylised battle formations and key topographical features . . . almost arbitrarily against a modern map base'. Frequently, however, students of military history have taken the trouble to visit the sites of the battles they discuss and to relate the topography to contemporary accounts: accordingly, both Oman (1902) and Weller (1962) travelled extensively through Spain and Portugal to visit the sites of the battles of the Peninsular campaign, and Oman in particular took care to relate General Napier's recollections of the war to what he saw. Authors of the volumes contained in such popular series as 'British Battles' (e.g. Naylor, 1960; Tomasson and Buist, 1962; Woolrych, 1966) have also been assiduous in relating action to landscape features, and the best battlefield guides (among them Burne, 1950; Seymour, 1975) have done the same. However, the primary focus has always been upon the literary evidence for battle action, rather than what the place itself could provide.

However, a group of unrelated twentieth-century researches have moved closer to a direct concern with the battlefield itself, and while all have much to teach us in pursuing this field, only the last has led to the recent explosion of interest in battlefield archaeology. The first exercise in battlefield archaeology in the twentieth century took place in the late 1950s and early 1960s, when the then military government of Portugal sought, among other things, to celebrate Portugal's military past by promoting the deeds of its medieval chivalry. Excavations in advance of building a monument and a museum at the site of the battle of Aljubarrota, where Portugal first emerged as an independent state, revealed a mass grave (do Paço, 1962, 115–63) and battlefield features. Not widely published, and incompletely at that, this exercise in battlefield archaeology has gone largely unnoticed by the battlefield archaeology community. A decade later in England, work at Marston Moor (Newman, 1981) and roughly contemporary geological work at Maldon (Petty and Petty, 1993, 159–69) testify to the importance of topographical research and careful reconstruction of the historic landscape by revealing how accounts based upon the modern appearance can be highly misleading. At Marston Moor, the realisation that the sunken road which played such a large part in nineteenth- and twentieth-century accounts of the battle was a feature added in the eighteenth century (and therefore was not present on the day of the battle) altered understanding of contemporary accounts. At Maldon, confirmation that a significant change in sea level had occurred from the tenth century to the twentieth forced a reassessment of the one contemporary account of the battle, and the removal from the battle sequence of several events added later to allow the modern appearance of the site to fit the ancient account. Most recently, the combination of careful recording of artefact scatters, topographic research, and the search for remains of the dead at the Little Bighorn site in the USA (Scott et al., 1989) finally brought battlefield archaeology attention, and these techniques have since been applied in the USA at Palo Alto, Texas (Haecker and Mauck, 1997), in the UK at Towton (Fiorato et al., 2000) and elsewhere (for examples, see Doyle and Bennett, 2002; Freeman and Pollard, 2001).

The Bloody Meadows Project is therefore at once an heir to a developing tradition of battlefield research while at the same time aiming to make a distinct contribution of its own. Unlike other battlefield researchers, we do not focus on individual sites. Similarly, we do not focus upon the discovery of artefacts or artefact scatters at sites, but rather upon the shape of the land itself. We are also interested in relating sites to one another in an expressly comparative process, rather than identifying the thought processes of individual commanders in specific circumstances. We are also not exclusively concerned with understanding battle in the past, but with understanding the places where battles have taken place in the present: this is a concern with the historic battlefield as heritage object.

BATTLEFIELDS AS HERITAGE OBJECTS

The term 'heritage' as used here covers all those ways in which the past – especially the material remains of the past – is used in the present. The field of heritage as thus defined has grown into a major area of research over the past twenty years. It comprises, among other areas, concerns with the manner in which research into the past – especially archaeology – is carried out, with the dissemination and especially popular presentation of the past, with the relations of archaeologists with others, with issues of identity and the politics of the past, and especially with the ethics of researching into the past in an age of competing interests (see for instance Carman, 2002; Skeates, 2000). Our own interests have concerned especially the manner in which particular objects are selected to be treated as part of a collective community history – a 'heritage' – and what kinds of treatments they are subject to once selected. Previous publications in this field have been concerned with the distinguishing characteristics of heritage objects in terms of how they differ from other kinds of object (Carman, 2002, 30–57) and, especially in relation to the category of the *archaeological site*, how these relate to the study of the human past (Carman, 1999c).

As a category of heritage object, battlefields appear to us to have distinct qualities which make them interesting. At one level, as *sites*, they share the attributes of all such places. Sites are spatial phenomena that are deemed to be bounded – that is, we understand and apprehend them to be limited in physical extent rather than spilling out into the surrounding vistas. Accordingly, battlefield spaces can in some measure be considered as separate from the land surrounding them, and many are treated in this way. The concept of site is, however, complicated by the fact that as a focus of scholarly attention – and especially in archaeology – it represents two different phenomena, often conflated. The site as a focus of activity in the past represents one such phenomenon. The site as a focus for attention (and especially study) in the present is the other. The fact that they may be located at the same point in space is at once a convenience for the modern student but also serves to hide the fact of the fundamental difference of the two concepts of site. It also serves to make the idea of placing a boundary around the space of scholarly attention – whether in the form of a physical barrier or a merely conceptual border – seem both normal and unexceptional. The battlefield thus appears to us as a place with clear edges to it and clearly separable from the land around it. This capacity to be separated out makes the treatment of the site as a heritage object – its 'management' – relatively easy: it can be classed as different from all the objects surrounding it and it can be fixed at a certain stage in its life cycle, to keep it as it is for posterity.

At the same time as they can be considered as sites, battlefields also fall into the category of *landscape*, which is a category much more difficult to delineate (Carman, 1998, pp. 31–4). Landscapes flow and are not bounded except by the barriers to human vision represented by the curvature of the earth, atmospheric conditions, and the position of obstacles opaque to light. Landscapes are also generally considered to be the containers for other types of phenomena – including sites. As landscapes, battlefields cannot be conveniently bounded and cannot have edges placed to them. Instead, they merge with the movements that brought troops to the place of battle from other more distant locations, and with the movements of troops – both victorious and defeated – away from the battle once it was over. Landscapes are also prone to change over time: their shape has been made by myriads of processes over the long term, some geological, some biological, some agricultural, some industrial. Accordingly, unlike the site which is a point in space and can be frozen in a moment of its history, the landscape is always subject to alteration, if not the alteration of this particular feature, then by changes to an adjacent or more distant one. This makes the management of landscapes very difficult: what is preserved (if anything) is not the condition of the space at a particular moment but the general 'character' of the space through time.

In terms of the management of a historic battlefield in the present, the differences between a site and a landscape are highly pertinent. As a site, a battlefield will be treated in one set of ways. As a landscape, it will be treated in other ways. Its apprehension as a site or as a landscape will thus determine what possibilities exist for its future; and will indeed inform the decision-making process in terms of what its future *should* be. The manner of marking a site is quite different from that of marking a landscape. A site can usually be marked in a physical manner, by placing an object on or near it. As a bounded entity, it can be fenced or edged around, or markers can be placed around the edges to make them evident. A landscape, however, cannot be so marked. Any marking is usually much more intangible, and often conceptual only, as in the designation of an area of land as in some way special. This may be as an Area of Outstanding Natural Beauty or as a Heritage Coastline or some other form of words to emphasise the distinctive quality of the space, but without (necessarily) supplying it with a clear boundary.

Many historic battlefields are clearly marked, especially by the erection of monuments or other features. Some – particularly those from more recent times – are maintained as cemeteries with all the monumental attributes of funerary space. Others are marked as historical places for passers-by to note by the presence of obelisks, plaques and information boards. Others are maintained as fully fledged 'heritage sites', sometimes including museum facilities, guided walks and other paraphernalia of the presented past (Stone and Molyneaux, 1994). An aspect of interest here is the type of use they are put to and at whose service the marking of the place as 'special' lies. Some are maintained at the service of the descendants – whether biological or institutional – of those who fought there. Others are maintained at the service of the nation in whose territory they lie. Others yet are maintained at the service of those in whose name the battle was fought, or maintained for different purposes entirely. In recording and noting such matters as these, the uses to which historic battlefields are now put – and from this what uses are considered appropriate for them – will become evident.

One of our interests is in whose name – and for what purpose – battlefields are marked and maintained. We are also concerned with understanding why some are marked and maintained while others are not. We are interested too in the type of marking involved – whether physical or conceptual – and to what extent such sites are considered to be either sites or landscapes. Out of such concerns we hope to be able to say something about the management of battlefield sites that will be of use to those responsible for their future.

TOWARDS AN APPROACH TO BATTLEFIELDS

The Bloody Meadows Project emerged out of the range of interests and their history outlined here. The question requiring a clear answer from the outset was how we were to research battlefields. We needed to establish the questions we specifically wished to address, and they needed to be questions that battlefields themselves could answer. Standing in the centre of an empty piece of modern landscape and expecting it to tell us things was all very well, and would no doubt be highly enjoyable, but we needed to be more systematic than that in our approach to our object of enquiry. Out of visits to a number of sites and a critical reading of key military texts some ideas emerged which subsequently became hardened into a workable methodology. These are the topics of the next chapter.

Two

UNDERSTANDING BATTLEFIELDS

As outlined in Chapter One, the Bloody Meadows Project seeks to explore the phenomenon of the 'historic battlefield' in both its historic and its contemporary guises. The former is an exercise in understanding how places were chosen as battle sites in the past and the consequences for the place of that choice. The latter is an exercise in understanding the ongoing and modern interest and significance of such places, with a view to their future treatment. This chapter will discuss the thinking behind the approach to these questions developed for the Bloody Meadows Project and outline the mechanics of the approach itself.

ABOUT BATTLES

Fighting battles is the way Western societies conduct their wars. Our histories are dotted with such encounters, a few capable of being considered significant or 'decisive' (Creasy [1851], 1908; Fuller, 1970), or more commonly dismissed as 'indecisive' (Weigley, 1991). Battles are the usual focus – and certainly the main punctuation points – of military history (Keegan, 1976; Nosworthy, 1992, 1995; Weigley, 1991) to the almost complete exclusion of other aspects of military organisation and activity. The ideal of battle is 'a paradox of the highest order, a deliberate attempt to harness, to modulate, and hence to amplify the wild human desire for violence through . . . order and discipline' (Hanson, 1989, 16). Battle in the Western tradition is at heart held to be the starkly simple infliction of mass violence, 'bereft of heroics and romanticism' (Hanson, 1989, 17), to achieve a particular aim.

Battle as Culture

The violence of battle takes the form of 'institutionalised combat', something which needs to be clearly distinguished from 'an impromptu scrap' (Jones, 1980, 98). The difference is that the former 'has rules, and the rules must be followed, otherwise the participants lose, rather than gain, prestige' (Jones, 1980, 98). Battles – in order to be battles, rather than ambushes, skirmishes, riots, massacres or other kinds of violent events – have to be intensely rule-directed. The purpose of the Bloody Meadows research is to identify those rules as they apply in particular times and places, and how they change through time and across space. This idea is very similar to the charge made by Gray (1997) and others, that war represents a kind of discourse: that is, a way of speaking about and acting towards things. Discourses too have rules that must be followed and an appropriate language in which to 'speak'. The language of war is that of blood and flesh (Clausewitz [1832], 1976, 149), but Sun Zi (Chaliand, 1994, 221–38) identified five factors of importance in war, of which only three were under human control: from the beginning of the study of war the crucial distinction was always between what was inevitably 'natural' and what was deemed to be 'rational' or controllable (Gray, 1997, 94).

The rule-bound nature of warfare practice – in the present as in the past – both derives from and simultaneously determines the very definition of 'battle' itself. A battle is held to be not the same as a skirmish, which is a mobile encounter between forces who never become fully engaged (English Heritage, 1995, 3). Nor is a battle a siege, which involves cutting off a fortified castle or settlement from outside help in order to force its surrender: for Weigley (1991, 55) the drawn-out formal siege of the seventeenth century is 'ritualistic' in form, while the battle is simply 'bloodshed'. But there are sufficient ritual aspects to battle for this particular distinction to be considered an unnecessary one. English Heritage has determined that, for a battle to be included in its official *Register* (1995), it must not represent a 'lesser form of engagement', such as a skirmish; it must have involved recognised military units, and thus not riotous crowds or other disorganised groups; it must have had political, military historical or 'biographical' significance; and it must have been fought over a definable geographical space. Similarly, the functions of battle are closely defined: 'the purpose of the engagement [is] the destruction of the enemy' (Clausewitz [1832], 1976, 230); it is 'a moral conflict . . . [requiring] the moral collapse of one of the two contending parties' (Keegan, 1976, 296); it is also thereby designed to curb 'the horrors of war [by] achieving decisiveness in the conduct of war' (Weigley, 1991, 73). Battles are also always mutually agreed: 'There can be no engagement unless both sides are willing' (Clausewitz [1832], 1976, 245); '*all* battles take place by mutual agreement, although such agreement is usually informal in the modern era' (Keeley, 1996, 60); battle 'requires . . . a mutual and sustained act of will by two contending parties'

(Keegan, 1976, 296). Keeley (1996) in particular points to the highly ritualised elements of modern battle: the complex 'choreography' required in acts of surrender by individuals and units, such as white flags, raised hands, proffered or cast-away weapons, the use of certain key words, and sometimes carefully arranged ceasefires (Keeley, 1996, 61); legal and other limitations upon who may be killed by what weapons and under what conditions, rendering the slaughter of prisoners illegal (Keeley, 1996, 62); and the obsession of soldiers throughout recorded time with the capture of enemy standards and correctly worn regalia (Keeley, 1996, 62–3). Clausewitz – the arch-exponent of war as a rational activity – was also highly aware of the ritualised and dance-like movements of early modern warfare: 'The troops move calmly into position in great masses deployed in line and depth . . . [and are] left to conduct a firefight for several hours, interrupted now and then by minor blows – charges, bayonet assaults, and cavalry attacks. . . . Gradually, the units engaged are burned out, and when nothing is left but cinders, they are withdrawn and others take their place' ([1832], 1976, 226). With a historian's hindsight, Weigley (1991, 168) sees the same: 'Battles [of the eighteenth century] were tournaments between serried ranks of colorfully [*sic*] uniformed toy soldiers come to life, advancing toward each other to the beating of drums . . . [so] the notion of battlefields as paradegrounds is not altogether deceptive.'

Table 2.1   *Characteristics of battle*

Organised Violence	Clear Function and Purpose	Ritualised Elements
Recognised military units	Destruction of the enemy	Mutual agreement to fight
Definable geographical space	Moral collapse of one contending party	Limits on behaviour
	Limitation of violence	Closely ordered movement
	Achievement of decision	

These aspects of battle, as set out and summarised in Table 2.1, may seem to us to be grounded in an obvious rationality. But this is much more the effect of an accumulated historical focus on the battle as the epitome of war, and even of philosophical attention in coming to terms with war, than with the objective reasonableness of battle's practices for all times and places. Battle does not emerge on to the historical stage until the Bronze Age of Egypt (Dupuy and Dupuy, 1970, 3–4; Laffin, 1995, 274; Montgomery, 1968, 45): it becomes something relatively common only as written history develops; indeed, battle is the subject of much early history. The normality of battle to us therefore depends upon its familiarity to us. But we may ask: how reasonable is it really for closely organised and heavily controlled groups of specific individuals to come together at a specific place at a specific time, to stand under what may be a long and lethal bombardment, not to run away and hide, but at a determined time to approach close to others who share the intention of mass slaughter? If Weigley (1991, 73) is right, and violent battles of annihilation serve to curb the other horrors of war, then they do so by a form of magic which has little to do with reason. Instead, they are to do with common understandings about what is appropriate and right. These rules – frequently unwritten, but in modern times transposed into actual laws – concern and determine the nature of battle in any particular period, and indeed the appropriateness of battle itself as a mode of behaviour. The rules concern when it is appropriate to fight: for what reason, over what dispute, and after which declarations of animosity and intent. They concern who it is appropriate to fight: certain categories of foe are not worthy of meeting in battle; these must represent at least one's equals in some sense. They concern who may be involved in the fighting, who must be involved in the fighting and who must remain a non-combatant. They concern how to fight: which weapons may be used and whether one attacks or defends, stands or moves. All these rules relate to those concerning who may or must fight, and extend beyond mere functionality to questions of social status. In particular, the rules concern where it is appropriate to fight: at what kind of place, on what type of ground, or even that it shall be at a specific location sanctioned by law or custom.

'Terrain' and its Uses: the Military Discourse of War

As outlined above, battle is the particular concern of military history, and military history has a particular trajectory of its own and a particular purpose: it is derived originally from studies of war by professional military personnel, and its purpose is to assist the professional soldier in the performance of his duties (Keegan, 1976, 15–22). The discourse of war that has arisen out of this – one also shared in political and strategic studies – is quite distinctive and highly powerful, and can be thought of as containing three elements.

Linear Narrative

The first element is a focus upon linear narrative (Brodie, 1973; Cline, 2000; Fuller, 1970; McPherson, 1990; Wedgwood, 1957; Weigley, 1991), and especially upon the narrative of individual events. Military histories – and there is some very fine military history – seize upon the violent encounters that make up the waging of war, usually to consider them in terms of their level of 'decisiveness' (Creasy [1851], 1908; Fuller, 1970; Weigley, 1991). McPherson justifies his narrative version of the history of the American Civil War by reference to a narrative's ability to 'do justice [to the] dynamism, [the] complex relationship of cause and effect, [and the] intensity of experience' of a nation at war (1990, ix). He cites as an example the value of a narrative – as opposed to a thematic approach – in demonstrating the importance of the Battle of Antietam, 1862, which came at the same time as events in the diplomatic, domestic political and economic fields which were all affected by the outcome to the battle (McPherson, 1990, ix). Wedgwood's history of the Thirty Years War is also written in narrative form, justified by the way in which it reveals 'the dismal course of the conflict, dragging on from one decade to the next and from one deadlock to the next, [providing] an object lesson on the dangers and disasters which can arise when men of narrow hearts and narrower minds are in high places' (1957, 10). Keegan – paradoxically also focusing on the single military event in his own work – points out that this approach has led 'whole squads of modern military historians [to indulge in] an endless, repetitive examination of battles that . . . can be said to have done nothing but make the world worse [and to ascribe to] strategically piffling, pointless bloodbaths . . . the cachet "decisive" on the grounds that they must have decided something' (1976, 62). Keegan is highly critical of the so-called 'battle piece', the traditional 'rhetoric of battle history' narrative (1976, 36), composed of 'disjunctive movement . . . uniformity of behaviour . . . simplified characterization [and] simplified motivation' among large numbers of individuals (1976, 65–6).

In essence, military history offers the argument that wars, campaigns and battles can all be reduced to a story of the same basic form. Initial background information concerns the reasons for fighting, the forces available and their relative position in space. Movements to bring the forces closer together are then described and what happens at the point of contact. The third and final phase concerns the outcome: victory for one side, defeat for the other, and the consequences for victor and defeated. The focus is upon the *reasons* for conflict, the *means* applied, and the *outcome*: this is war as a rational means-ends relationship.

Functionalist Interpretations

The second element in the discourse of war derives from the first, since a focus on cause and effect relationships leads to a view of war and the practices of warfare as practical means to practical ends; and this in turn leads to a particular interpretive stance. The focus of attention is placed upon those who organise and lead in war, and who are assessed for their skills as commanders – especially in terms of how they mobilise resources to achieve ends (Montgomery, 1968). In the same vein, landscape features present on a battlefield are treated as having varying levels of functional utility: as objects that are useful to a soldier; as objects that have no utility to a soldier; and as objects that actively present threats to a soldier. The literature of the study of war is accordingly littered with commentary upon landscape representing threat or opportunity: classic writers such as Clausewitz ([1832], 1976, 348–54) and Sun Zi (Chaliand, 1994, 221–38; Tao, 2000, 116–23) refer to it as 'terrain'; while Montgomery (1968, 307) writes upon 'obstacles'. The typical – and expected – shape of a battlefield is accordingly of a space containing distinct features.

Warfare as a means-end relationship requires tools to achieve its object. Among these are the people who do the fighting, the strategies and tactics they apply, the equipment they carry, and the ground on which they stand or over which they march. In interpreting war in the past, all these have rational and functional roles to play. Their presence and absence from the battlefield, their effects upon the fighting, the outcomes they produce: all can be explained in utilitarian terms. Among historians of war in the ancient world, Hanson is critical of 'classical' military historians who have focused on 'deployment, drill, weapons and tactics' (1989, 24), taking a distanced viewpoint 'as if they were suspended above the killing on the battlefield in an observation balloon looking downward, detached from if not uninterested in the desperate individuals below' (1989, 23).

'Ritual' Versus 'Real' War

This dominant and very 'functionalist' reading of warfare in the historic period reflects a deeper set of assumptions in the treatment of war which are evident in studies of prehistoric periods. Turney-High's (1949) distinction between 'primitive' and 'true' war (although also adopted in part more recently by Keegan (1993)) has in general given way to a distinction between 'real' and 'ritual' war in the distant past (Carman and Carman, 2001, 275–81; Halsall, 1989, 155–77). This distinction is evident also in Keeley's (1996) *War Before Civilization*, which has challenged the general assumption of a 'peaceful' past, maintaining for example the highly functionalist 'defensive' purpose of large hilltop bank-and-ditch enclosures against those who argue for a more symbolic role for these constructions. In considering what he calls 'postmodern war'

Chris Hables Gray (1997) also argues for the maintenance of a distinction between 'ritual' war and 'ancient' war – the latter more akin to our own highly organised and highly technological warfare.

However, Hanson (1989, 1991) is at pains to point out that ancient Greek hoplite warfare was not a matter of the rational consideration of strategy and tactics, but a brutal and essentially irrational ritual of community. Keegan (1993) brings the argument up to date, by suggesting that the modern Western form of war is the product of particular cultural factors, rather than inherently 'natural' or rational.

Battlefield Landscape and Architecture

As a result of this kind of discourse, the ground over which battles on land are fought is conventionally treated by military historians as an inconvenience to be overcome or a resource to be used. The idea has begun to extend beyond history to the emerging field of 'military geography' (Doyle and Bennett, 2002), but this way of thinking about the land on which soldiers fight has an ancient pedigree. Kautilya (India, fourth century BC) emphasises the importance of possessing the advantage of strength, time and place: '[space] means the earth . . . there are such varieties of land, as forests, villages, mountains, level plains, and uneven grounds. . . . That part of the country in which [our] army finds a convenient place for its manoeuvre . . . is the best; that part [convenient to the enemy] is the worst' (Chaliand, 1994, 322). For Sun Zi (China, fourth century BC), 'earth' is the third of the five constant factors to be taken into account in war, and comprises 'distances, great and small; danger and security; open ground and narrow passes; the chances of life and death' (Chaliand, 1994, 222); his practical advice covers how to manoeuvre in mountains, how to cross rivers and marshes, and the use of high ground (Chaliand, 1994, 233–4). The *General Maxims* of Flavius Vegetius (Rome, fourth century AD) include the belief that 'The nature of the ground is often of more consequence than courage.' Recommendations include advice to 'cover one of your flanks either with an eminence, a city, the sea, a river or some protection of that kind', and always to 'choose the proper ground for [cavalry]' (Chaliand, 1994, 216). Leo VI (Byzantium, ninth century AD) exhorts commanders not to 'go near the foothills of mountains' in case the enemy occupies them (Chaliand, 1994, 356), while Al-Rawandi (Persia, thirteenth century AD) advises that 'if the enemy has more horsemen, a narrow terrain . . . must be chosen' (Chaliand, 1994, 442). Under this influence, Clausewitz ([1832], 1976, 348–54) thought terrain an important enough factor to be accorded two entire chapters, indicating how 'geography and the character of the ground. . . . have a decisive influence on the engagement':

> Geography and ground can influence military operations in three ways: as an obstacle to the approach, as an impediment to visibility, and as cover from fire. . . . We shall find . . . that there are three distinct ways in which an area may differ from the concept of a flat and open plain: first in the contours of the countryside, such as its hills and valleys; second in such natural phenomena as forests, swamps and lakes; and third in the factors produced by agriculture. . . . It is . . . easiest to wage war in flat and only moderately cultivated areas. But this holds true only in general and altogether disregards the value of natural obstacles to defence (Clausewitz [1832], 1976, 348–9).

He nevertheless concludes that the 'only thing that really counts' is *victory in battle. . . .* [determined by] the relative quality of the two armies and their commanders. Terrain can only play a minor role' (Clausewitz [1832], 1976, 354). Keegan (1993, 68–70) takes a wider perspective, pointing out that 'about seventy per cent of the world's . . . dry land is either too high, too cold or too waterless for the conduct of military operations. . . . [Intense] military activity has been concentrated into a fraction even of that space where conditions do favour the movement and maintenance of armed forces. Battles not only tend to recur on sites close to each other . . . but have also frequently been fought on exactly the same spot over a very long period of history.' For all these students of war – ancient and modern – topography generally represents one of the naturally occurring limitations upon successful war-making capacity.

There are, however, hints of a possible alternative approach in Garlan's (1975, 58) discussion of the immunity given to certain types of place in ancient Greek warfare, especially temples and religious shrines. The phenomenon of 'ritual wars' – 'rather like long-term tournaments or competitions . . . [taking] place periodically within a religious context of a mythical or cultural nature, according to rules which restrict the object and the extent of the conflict' (Garlan, 1975, 26) – also suggests the periodic return to a designated 'battle site', a place of deliberate cultural choice rather than one determined by external environmental factors. This idea is given further support by 'repeated engagements, generation after generation, in the identical Argive, Corinthian, and Mantinean plains. . . . [and] the striking proximity of battle-sites in Boiotia – a veritable "blood alley" of sorts – over a 200-year period; there, only a very few miles separate [battlefields]' (Hanson, 1991, 254). Ober (1991, 188) sees in Greek hoplite warfare 'a system of war that was more ritualistic than rational in its set forms'. There are also hints in Sun Zi of a more 'metaphorical' and rather less functionalist understanding of natural features in the colourful use of imagery: 'The general who is skilled in defence hides in the deepest recesses of the earth; he who is skilled in attack flashes forth from the heavens' (Chaliand, 1994, 226); 'just as water retains no constant shape, so in warfare there are no constant conditions' (Chaliand, 1994, 230); 'Let your rapidity be that of the wind, your compactness that of the forest. In raiding and plundering be like fire, in immovability like a mountain' (Chaliand, 1994, 231). Ancient Greek immunities and rituals, and ancient Chinese metaphors, all imply the cultural importance of places and natural features in warfare: rather than these things acting as impediments to action, useful resources or simply topographical background, they are capable of being invested with a kind of meaning. It is this meaning that our research into historic battlefields of all periods aims to understand.

One of us (JC; Carman, 1999b) has provisionally suggested that battles from the earliest to the late medieval periods were generally fought on relatively flat and unfeatured ground: by 'unfeatured' is meant ground that contains no major natural features or built structures which play a significant part in the action of the battle. This does not mean that such features did not exist at the battle site: lines of stream, linear embankments or ditches, or rising ground and even buildings may well have been present. But it does not automatically follow that soldiers fighting battles at that place would necessarily have taken notice of them or used them to allow or impede movement, for concealment or as cover. It is clear that the Greeks so far as possible always made the deliberate 'choice of level battlefields' (Hanson, 1991, 6), comprising 'usually a flat terrain' to accommodate up to 50,000 fighters (Lazenby, 1991, 88); this was because 'hoplites could do battle properly only in a wide, clear, flat space that was free of even minor obstacles. . . . The set forms of hoplite battle . . . [thus] defy geomorphic logic' (Ober, 1991, 173) and one can expect the practical advice of commentators as to the 'proper' use of terrain to have been lost on them. However, from the point of view of a modern scholar of warfare, the type of landscape over which battles were fought can perhaps give insights into the attitudes of those fighting the battle to that landscape.

Modern students are hampered, however, by the fact that ancient depictions of battle do not usually include a representation of the local topography (Montgomery, 1968, 37). Instead, we have images of groups of fighting men: anonymous, often closely packed, but highly mobile. Clearly, the emphasis is being placed upon these formations composed of human beings, dressed and equipped alike and all moving in unison. These formations are people as part of a machine: what Haraway (1985, 95–107) calls 'cyborgs'. If the topography of a battlefield, including any built structures it contains, can be seen as the static architecture of that space, then the linear or rectangular forms composed of mass humanity which traverse that space may be seen also as a kind of architecture: not static architecture, but mobile. In moving there, three things come together in the battlefield space: groups of people organised in various ways; things these people carry with them in the form of equipment and weapons; and the physical form of the battlefield space itself. In making the thing called 'battle' these three things – people, technology and landscape – interact. The forms of interaction which take place on any particular battle site can give us a means of understanding the attitudes and ways of thinking of the people involved.

INVESTIGATING BATTLEFIELDS

These theoretical considerations are designed to provide a framework within which individual battle sites can be considered as places of cultural significance. The purpose of this approach is to find out what they may be able to tell us about the people who went there in the past and those people's attitudes to each other and that place. The discussion so far has outlined a number of different aspects of battle sites that may be questioned and drawn upon as a means to greater understanding of ancient warfare, summarised in Table 2.2 (see p. 25). These can then be applied to individual battles in an attempt to gain a deeper insight into them and to allow comparison. The key element is always the landscape of the battle itself, which we approach by drawing upon the recent application of ideas from phenomenology in archaeology.

A 'Phenomenological' Approach to Historic Battlefields

Tilley has perhaps given the clearest justification for such a 'phenomenological' approach to studying landscapes in archaeology.

> [What] is clear [from the ethnographic record] is the symbolic, ancestral, and temporal significance of landscape [to peoples]. The landscape is continually being encultured, bringing things into meaning as part of a symbolic process by which human consciousness makes the physical reality of the natural environment into an intelligible and socialised form. . . . It [is

accordingly] evident . . . that the significance of landscape for different populations cannot be simply read off from the local 'ecological' characteristics of a 'natural' environment (Tilley, 1994, 67).

Cultural markers [such as monuments are used] to create a new sense of place. . . . An already encultured landscape becomes refashioned, its meanings now controlled by the imposition of [a new] cultural form (Tilley, 1994, 208).

These comments of Tilley's specifically refer to the relationship of prehistoric monuments to mostly empty rural landscapes in Britain. Following his lead, and that of others, a phenomenological approach to the study of landscapes as taken by archaeologists has generally been limited to the monumental 'ritual' landscapes of later European prehistory. The approach is, however, also of more general relevance to any encultured space, especially any marked as a particular kind of space. The typical interpretive device in battlefield research is the battlefield plan – an objective view from above, divorced from the action. But, as Tilley also emphasises, place is not something that can be understood 'object-ively': 'Looking at the two-dimensional plane of the modern topographic map with sites [or artefact scatters] plotted on it, it is quite impossible to envisage the landscape in which these places are embedded. The representation fails, and cannot substitute for being there, being *in place*. [The] process of observation requires time and a feeling for the place' (1994, 75). The same is true of the traditional battlefield plan: it cannot substitute for actually being there.

Nor can it substitute for movement through the space. We therefore draw upon the ideas of archaeologists of prehistory who are developing ways of utilising the idea that the way of moving through particular kinds of spaces can be considered a form of ritual or performance (Carman, 1999b, 242; Pearson, 1998, 34–41). For example, Barrett writes of prehistoric monuments in Wiltshire, England, that 'for the distinctions [between people] to have operated . . . it was necessary for people to *move* between these [architectural] regions; to enter and leave each other's presence, to observe passively or to act, to lead processions or to follow. The practice of social life is thus . . . performed' (Barrett, 1994, 29). Here, ritual activity is considered as a form of 'acted out' discourse (Barrett, 1991, 5; Thomas, 1991, 34), focusing on the physicality and (apparent) 'objectivity' of actions (Barrett, 1991, 4–6). Participants in rituals are guided through a series of specific meaningful actions, leading them to make the approved connections between them (Thomas, 1991, 34). Taking such ideas further, Thomas (1991) and Pearson (1998, 32–41) argue that the focus of early Bronze Age 'beaker' burial ritual in Britain was on the body of the deceased. Objects that were put into the ground 'constituted material signifiers whose role was to ensure that the intended reading of the dead person was made by the audience [at] the funeral' (Thomas, 1991, 34). Here, the space of the grave itself acted as the 'stage' of a theatrical performance (Pearson, 1998, 36–7). Mourners thus became active participants in the funerary ritual (Thomas, 1991, 39) – players in the drama as well as spectators (Pearson, 1998). The often slow and deliberate movements of bodies of troops across the space of a battlefield – frequently in defiance of common sense – have obvious ritual connotations. So do aspects such as drill, the proper use of equipment, standardised formations, and the focus on the capture of enemy standards and correctly worn regalia (Keeley, 1996, 62–3).

Putting these two styles of approach together – gaining a feeling for the place as a place, and a focus on how one moves through it in performance – one can perhaps gain a particular sense of what a particular historic battlefield represents in terms of experience and meaning. The purpose of the Bloody Meadows Project is thus not so much an attempt to recreate what a particular battlefield was like on the day of battle – or indeed the events of the battle – but rather to establish a meaning for the historicity of the place in the present. Hence our simultaneous concern both for an understanding of the nature of war in the past and preservation and public interpretation in the present.

It is for these reasons that the Bloody Meadows Project looks very specifically at the *kind* of place where the battle was fought. The majority of archaeologists working on battlefields spend their time looking at the ground, trying to find the material left behind by the action. We instead spend time looking up and around us, at the shape of the space itself. A close focus on the shape of the space allows differences of choice across space and through time to become evident. In taking such an approach, and in being deliberately aware of both past and present in a particular place, we walk the line that lies between the past and the present, where neither dominates the other. Instead, they interact in interesting and challenging ways. It is not a search for an experience of being in the past, but rather an experience *in the present* which reflects and derives from the contribution of history to a particular place. In the case of a historic battlefield, it is not an experience of ancient slaughter, but an experience of a particular place in the present as read through its history as manifested in material form. This history inevitably includes the event of the battle that was fought there, but not exclusively.

Investigating Battlefields as Historic Places

The primary data source used in the project is the physical landscape of the place where warfare was practised. Drawing upon the work of previous scholars – who have identified the locations of many battlefields from the past – we focus upon the landscape itself to ask specific questions, including:

- how clearly bounded is the battlefield space (does it have clear boundaries, such as impassable ground or a water obstacle)?
- is it high or low ground relative to the surrounding space?
- what kind of use (other than for war) was the site put to, if any?
- is it near or distant from settlement?
- is it visible from settlement?
- does the ground contain particular types of landscape features – natural or built – which play a part in the battlefield action?
- what features present in the landscape (if any) played no part in the battlefield action?
- was the battlefield subsequently marked by a monument or memorial in any way?

The answers can be ordered as set out in Table 2.2.

Table 2.2 *Parameters for studying battlefields*

Rules of War	Battlefield Architecture
Agreement to fight: Y/N	Features present:
	Type of feature used:
Mutual recognition as 'legitimate' enemies: Y/N	Type of feature not used:
	Use of terrain:
Level of violence: High, Medium, Low	as cover:
	to impede visibility:
Marking of battle site:	to impede movement:
	Structured formations: Y/N
Participants:	

Functional Aspects
Dysfunctional Aspects

In Table 2.2, the *rules of war* cover such things as the degree of mutual agreement needed before fighting could commence, whether the two sides were required to see each other as 'legitimate' enemies or whether anyone could participate in a battle, some assessment of the level of violence employed, and how (if at all) the battle site was remembered afterwards. They are a measure of how 'formal' battle was regarded and how it was distinctive from other forms of conflict at that time.

The *characteristics of the battlefield landscape* are addressed in order to identify features present in the battlespace and how they were used by combatants. This gives some insight into attitudes to the battlefield as a place. The query as to whether structured formations were present (such as ordered columns or lines of troops) gives a clue to how participants moved through the battlefield space: if the landscape is seen as architecture, so too can the forces engaged be seen as a kind of 'mobile architecture'. The point is not merely to note those features present and used by combatants, as military historians might, but also and especially those features present but not used, and those present today but not on the day.

The two final sections attempt to summarise our expectations as filtered through an understanding of 'good military practice' derived from military writings (as in the concept of 'inherent military probability' discussed by Keegan (1976, 33–4)). It is, we believe, the *dysfunctional* behaviour (that is, the apparent mistakes or omissions) which can give a clue to cultural attitudes and expectations of the battlefield space which differ from our own. In applying this analysis to distinctive examples of warfare from various periods, the differences between periods become evident.

In approaching the landscapes that are our object, we use what we have called 'the archaeologist's eye' – that is, the capacity of a trained landscape archaeologist to interpret space and to identify (especially manufactured) features in landscapes otherwise unfamiliar to them – to reach an understanding of the spaces of battle. By approaching such sites with a structured set of questions and by recording data in a standard format (see Table 2.2 and Chapter Three) it becomes possible to recognise what such sites have in common and how they differ from one another. This in turn – by tabulating the results (Chapter Four) – allows the identification of the types of location favoured as battle sites in particular periods of history, and these can be related to other aspects of the battle as recorded by historians – including the type of participants, the nature of the conflict of which the battle is a part, and the flow of the action. Overall, it presents an opportunity to gain a direct insight into the ideological factors guiding warfare practice in that period and to compare them with those guiding warfare practice in a different period.

BATTLEFIELDS AS HERITAGE

The definition of 'heritage' is contested. In particular, it can be considered either as a body of objects, monuments and places; or as a set of practices and a process.

In archaeological circles, and as a body of collected materials, the heritage is frequently defined in legal terms: it can in particular be items 'governed by legislation' (Cleere, 1989, 10) or 'things preserved by legislation' (Lipe, 1984, 3). Its definition can be limited to 'archaeological sites and monuments' (Reichstein, 1984, 37) or more narrowly only 'to all identified sites' (Darvill, 1987, 25). It may 'predominately consist of the physical evidences . . . left on a landscape by past societies' (Scovill *et al.*, 1977, 45) or can be extended to 'all evidences of past human occupation which can be used to reconstruct the lifeways of past peoples' (McGimsey and Davis, 1977, 109). The category of heritage can also be held to be limited only to the remains of a particular nation's past (Daniel and Renfrew, 1988, 194) and as a consequence fall prey to criticisms of the contemporary combination of 'Enterprise and Heritage' as dangerously insular and retrospectively nostalgic (Robins, 1991, 21–44; Walsh, 1992). In general, however, a heritage is thought of as items 'associated with global, national or local identity and/or promoted as educational or diverting entertainment' (Hodder *et al.*, 1995, 237).

By contrast, and as a set of practices and a process, heritage can be considered as involving a series of necessary stages. First, certain kinds of things are identified as heritage. They are then specifically designated as something special, often in legal terms: as a 'national monument', a 'historic landmark', or a 'World Heritage Site', for instance. Once so designated, they will be subject to procedures designed to ensure their preservation for the future. Very often, but not always, the final stage and the purpose of the heritage process will be to make them available to the broader public as objects to see, places to visit or amenities to enjoy. Alternatively, and sometimes simultaneously, the purpose of preservation will be to ensure the existence of the object or place for future scholars to study.

Historic battlefields can, one way or another, be seen as heritage objects or become subject to these various processes (Table 2.3). In some countries (such as the USA) certain historic battlefields are protected by law, while others are taken into the care of state or other preservation agencies. In England, they may be included on the English Heritage *Register of Historic Battlefields* (1995) and become worthy of note and subject to a minimal amount of protection from change or damage. Accordingly, as heritage places, battlefields are the subject of efforts in preservation, of public access and of interpretation. As such, they exist as contemporary sites of interest and amenity. Simultaneously as sites of research they are deemed to contribute something to our knowledge of the past. The Bloody Meadows Project combines these interests in one effort at investigation.

Table 2.3 *Battlefields as heritage places*

Heritage Object	Heritage Processes
Historic place or archaeological site	Identified as place of historical activity
Erection of monument	Designated as 'historic battlefield' or 'national monument'
National significance	Preserved or managed
Legal or official recognition and protection	Available for researchers or visitors

The Marking of Battlefields

Many battlefields are marked by the erection of monuments of stone or concrete which are solid and enduring. Others are marked in different ways: by more ephemeral signs of memory, such as the names given to places and features, or local traditions which ascribe particular events to particular points in the landscape. Others again are marked by the actions of officialdom in recognising the site as of particular historical interest and importance: the traditional manner is to place an interpretive sign at a prominent view-spot and perhaps to construct a circular walk or drive to visit the locations deemed important to an understanding of the events of the battle and its landscape context. Officialdom may also – as in the case of the English Heritage *Register* – mark the site out on a map, providing it with a convenient border and edge, allowing preservation and management within and less control without.

All such methods of marking battle sites, and others, indicate the way in which the site is perceived in the present; and to whom, and in what way, it is conceived to be important. The purpose of investigating these aspects of battlefields is to gain an insight into the contemporary meanings ascribed to such places. The reason for combining such interests with research into the battle site as a historic landscape in its own right is to relate the two: to find out if particular kinds of historic places are treated in one set of ways, while others are treated the same or differently, and to what extent, by whom and for what purpose.

Battlefields as Cemeteries and Memorials

The archaeological study of monuments to the dead and how war is commemorated is an area that has come to the fore in recent years. Much of this has focused on monuments to the wars of the last century – especially the First and Second World Wars. According to some, the memorialisation of the dead of the First World War was a process of depersonalisation at the service of a sense of national unity (Parker Pearson, 1982): lists of named casualties gave way to monuments commemorating an anonymous 'The Glorious Dead' or simply 'The Fallen'; and annual acts of remembrance denied the opportunity for a consideration of the experience or purpose of war (Bushaway, 1992, 136–67). On the other hand, it has been pointed out that the majority of war memorials constructed after the First World War 'were initiatives which came from the people rather than the politicians. . . . [Their] erection was instigated by the bereaved public' (Tarlow, 1999, 162–3). They represented a response to the loss that had been suffered by large numbers of the population who wished to find some way of marking and coming to terms with that loss. This emphasis on bereavement represents another strand to some recent archaeological work: a focus not only on the physical aspects of remains, but also on the emotional content of particular kinds of object (see also Tarlow, 1999). In looking at monuments to the dead from this point of view, the question of who they were for comes particularly to the forefront and opens up a sensitivity to the meanings they carry.

Battlefield Preservation

The idea of preserving battlefields as important historic places is a relatively new one in Europe. In England, for example, English Heritage (1995) has published a *Register of Historic Battlefields* listing those considered worthy of preservation; and there are plans to produce similar registers elsewhere in the UK and in Ireland. As Foard (2001) among others makes clear, however, such documents treat battlefields not as archaeological phenomena – to be treated as the equivalent of (or at least as similar to) ancient monuments and sites – but as historical phenomena, where the primary sources are written and where the location is of secondary concern. Accordingly, the fact that a battlefield included in the *Register* should be taken into account for development control purposes under relevant official guidance does not equate with full legal protection.

This situation contrasts with the position in, for example, the USA, where battlefields considered worthy of note are taken into full legal protection and stewardship by responsible agencies under the aegis of the American Battlefield Protection Program [*sic*] of the Federal National Park Service (see: www.cr.nps.gov/abpp). A series of Federal laws relating to the preservation and protection of historic battlefields have been passed, primarily to provide funding programmes for suitable initiatives, and the most important battle sites of American history – especially those from the Revolutionary and Civil wars – have been taken into state care by the National Park Service under various designations. These include:

- Battlefield
- National Battlefield
- National Battlefield Park
- National Battlefield Site
- National Cemetery
- National Military Park

Investigating Battlefields as Places in the Present

The interest of the Bloody Meadows Project in the way battlefields are subsequently marked – whether soon after the battle or a considerable time later – is reflected particularly in the research question: Was the battlefield subsequently marked by a monument or memorial in any way? We take note of all such markers on or near the site itself, contemporary with the battle or later, and are particularly interested in asking:

- where is it in relation to the battle site?
- what form does it take?
- who or what does it commemorate?
- who raised it?
- when was it raised?
- is there any indication of the specific audience it is intended to address?
- what does it say about the relations of commemorator or commemoratee to the battle site?
- are links made with other sites or to other events?

We are always fully conscious that marking a site is not the only measure of its importance or interest. Failure to mark a site can itself constitute a statement: sometimes this will be a representation of a lack of recognition of any importance or significance the site may carry for certain people, but other times a more positive omission with a purpose to it. By looking closely at such sites and the monuments and other marks they bear it is possible to come to an understanding of the meanings they carry in our own time.

These are also reflected in the purposes for which such sites are used. Battlefields from the past rarely offer much in the way of an obvious physical legacy. Where earthwork defences were constructed, or the fighting resulted in significant changes to the shape of the land, these traces may persist to become part of later uses. In those cases where archaeological investigation has been carried out, the archaeology has most often consisted of human remains buried at the site. More recent researches have revealed the presence of scatters of material across the battlespace – most typically for battles of the firearms era, bullets and bullet casings (Haecker and Mauck, 1997; Scott *et al.*, 1989); for earlier periods, attachments to clothing which may have been torn off in the struggle (Sutherland, 2000, 155–68). Since such remains are generally invisible to the naked human eye, however, the landscape of such places has been seen as 'empty' of archaeology and therefore available for other uses. These uses may extend to the provision of park and amenity spaces, the historical significance of the location giving it an extra attractiveness to visitors. At Northampton, for instance (see Chapter Three), the space of the battlefield has been converted into the municipal golf course; at Quebec in Canada the site of the conflict of 1759 has been used as a place of recreation since the beginning of the twentieth century.

Accordingly, we also ask of all such sites: To what use(s) has the battlefield been put, and what is it used for today? From this we can ascertain the various uses over time to which the space has been put – other than, or at least as well as, for war-making – and from this gain some insight into the level of significance the place has acquired over time.

CHOOSING SITES FOR RESEARCH

The focus of the Bloody Meadows Project is upon the older and perhaps less well-known sites of violence in the past.

We deliberately stop short of the twentieth century since a wide variety of research is already being conducted into the warfare of our own age (Saunders, 2001, **76**, 101–8; Schofield, 2002) and modern battlefields tend to be both very large and very well promoted. In addition, twentieth-century warfare has disconcertingly extended from the surface of our globe into other realms: into the air; under the sea; into the most inhospitable regions of the world, such as mountain ranges, jungles, deserts, the Arctic and Antarctic; and even into outer space. It has also gone beyond the physical into more conceptual regions: into the relations of government to people; into the realm of science and technology; and, with the rise of the computer, into the so-called 'infosphere' and electronically generated cyberspace (Carman, 2002). The battles of our age can be said to have no limits or boundaries: they frequently cannot be seen or measured, nor physically controlled. Unlike the warfare of previous ages, they do not occupy a particular location but are at once nowhere and everywhere. Their understanding thus lies beyond the methodology of this particular project, and we leave them to others with more appropriate styles of approach.

Earlier in this chapter, the issue of 'decisiveness' appeared. In general, as outlined at that point in the discussion, the purpose of battle was held to be the achievement of some kind of decision. However, as Weigley (1991) has pointed out, the battles of the era from the seventeenth to nineteenth centuries were for the most part indecisive. What we tend to remember are those battles that can be held in some sense to have resulted in a clear decision: for instance, by forcing a change of strategy upon one side in a conflict; by closing off a military or political option during the course of a conflict; or by bringing about the final defeat of one nation by another and thus an end, however temporarily sometimes, to a conflict. But the majority of battles do not achieve such decisiveness: instead they lead to more violence elsewhere at a later time. These battles – more readily and more easily forgotten – represent the majority of battles fought and the more typical form of battle in any period of history. What their study has to tell us is less about the outcome of wars and the political and social changes they engender than what war was generally like in that period and how the people involved perceived and understood the role of war in their lives. By focusing on such less spectacular and less historically significant events we gain a different kind of insight into war in the past than from much military history.

CONCLUSION: STANDING IN EMPTY SPACES . . .

Historic battlefields are locations where events once took place. They are now places marked by those events and accordingly of interest to students of those events. To study them is to stand in a place today dreaming of an event of yesterday, an event that has passed and is gone. All one can do is stand and dream, and that, put simply and bluntly, is the methodology of the Bloody Meadows Project. But there is more to dreaming than inactivity, and to dream effectively one must also take note and respond to the images that present themselves. That too is part of the methodology of the Bloody Meadows Project.

Table 2.4 *Bloody Meadows Project: research questions*

Of Battle Sites as Historic Places

How clearly bounded is the battlefield space (does it have clear boundaries, such as impassable ground or a water obstacle)?

Is is located on high or low ground relative to the surrounding space?

What kind of use (other than for war) was the site put to, if any?

Is it near or distant from settlement?

Is it visible from settlement?

Does the ground contain particular types of landscape features – natural or built – which play a part in the battlefield action?

What features present in the landscape (if any) played no part in the battlefield action?

Of Battle Sites as Heritage

Was the battlefield subsequently marked by a monument or memorial in any way?

If 'yes'

Where is it in relation to the battle site?

What form does it take?

Who or what does it commemorate?

Who raised it?

When was it raised?

Is there any indication of the specific audience it is intended to address?

What does it say about the relations of commemorator or commemoratee to the battle site?

Are links made with other sites or to other events?

To what use(s) has the battlefield been put, and what is it used for today?

Appendix: the Bloody Meadows Approach to Visiting a Historic Battlefield

Choose your battlefield There are many such places known all over the world – approximately 3,000 at a conservative count (see for instance the information in Dupuy and Dupuy, 1970; Laffin, 1995; Perrett, 1992). For locating specific sites, a good source of advice is one of the many gazetteers or guidebooks available (e.g. for Britain: Guest and Guest, 1996; Smurthwaite, 1993; for Europe, Chandler, 1989).

Learn the story of the place Read up on your chosen battlefield. Guidebooks and gazetteers often contain a short description of the events of the battle and a map or plan, but also usually give a list of other sources. Read more than one of these additional sources – several if you can – in order to understand the sequence of events, how they relate to positions in the landscape, and especially any different versions of events.

Do not rush the experience Assume the visit will take at least half a day, probably the whole day. In some instances, more than one visit will be necessary to gain an impression of the place. Enjoy the chance to explore a place in detail and to get to know it really well.

Do not go alone The experience of visiting a site will be enhanced if you have someone (or several people) with you with whom you can talk about the place. More than one pair of eyes can be very useful to identify features and to seek them out. Other people are especially useful as 'measuring rods' to get a feeling for the size of a feature or area in relation to the human body (and many archaeologists have used human beings in just such a way).

Equipment Take with you a camera to record the visit, a map of the area to find your way, a plan of the battle to help you find your way around the space, and a compass for orientation in the landscape. You can also put together a checklist of features and places to look out for, and a notebook or pad may be useful for recording what you see and your impressions.

Walk the space Most pre-twentieth-century battlefields are relatively small – maybe only a few hundred metres wide by a kilometre or less deep. Be prepared to walk through the space as the soldiers did on the day, rather than drive or ride through it. If a battlefield walk or route is offered, take it as a preliminary guide but not as the whole experience: get to know the place on your own terms. Locate, for instance, the viewpoints of the two opposing commanders, then go to the ground on which their soldiers stood to get a different view. Walk the line of advance of one army or the other (and preferably both), asking yourself what it is like to be in that place: what you can see, what you cannot see, how easy it is to walk, how long does it take at a steady pace, what obstacles are in the way, how large is the space as you experience it. Ask yourself how the place feels: do you feel high up or low down, are you in an open space or is it claustrophobic and oppressive, what landscape features catch the eye. Think of the space in terms of your understanding of the progress of the battle: ask if you can recognise any landscape features, natural or built, that played a part in the action; ask what has changed, been added or seems to have been removed from the landscape.

Seek out memorials and commemoration Many battlefields are marked by a monument or memorial. Take note of its position in the space: does it occupy a central position, is it overlooking the battlefield, or is it some distance away? Take note of what it commemorates: the event itself; a particular person or unit involved in the action; or is it a monument to victory or defeat? Take note of other monuments in the battlefield space, to other events or other people, and of any part turned over to use as a cemetery: is reference made between the battle and other events (such as more recent warfare?), or does one overlie the other?

Contribute to the Bloody Meadows Project by compiling your own report in the style of those in Chapter Three and sending it to us. The source of all such reports will be fully acknowledged in publications and you will receive a copy of your report when it is published (please note: this may be a long time after you have sent it to us).

THREE

BATTLEFIELD REPORTS:

FIELDWORK FROM 1998 TO 2001 ON TWENTY-THREE SITES OF BATTLE IN WESTERN EUROPE

This chapter consists of standardised descriptions – arranged in alphabetical order by the name by which they are generally known – of sites of battles in Belgium, England, France, Portugal and Spain from AD 991 to 1813. All the sites were visited as part of the programme of preliminary research intended to establish and consolidate the methodology of the Bloody Meadows Project. The majority of those in England were visited in July and September 1998 and were the sites where the methodology was first established. Those in Portugal and Spain were visited in September 2000 and were sites where the methodology was first tested for its international applicability. Those in France and Belgium were visited in August 2001 to provide a further test of the methodology, and to provide a broader selection of battle sites to fill out the sample in terms of chronological range.

Each site description is based upon data collected at the site and from relevant standard literature consulted both prior to and after the visit. The summary table included with each description presents in a digested form the information contained in the longer site description; it coincides with the parameters for studying battlefields established prior to undertaking fieldwork, the development of which is described in Chapter Two. Site locations were fixed by reference to standard and readily accessible guides to battlefields in Britain and Europe, and other reference texts (e.g. Chandler, 1989; Dupuy and Dupuy, 1970; Fuller, 1970; Guest and Guest, 1996; Laffin, 1995; Seymour, 1975; Smurthwaite, 1993). Data concerning the events of the battle were gained from standard accounts of each battle as well as the guides consulted. Much of the literature of battlefield studies, and therefore that cited here, is secondary – or even tertiary – in nature, having been distilled from primary sources subject to considerable interpretation. Once an agreed interpretation is settled upon, however, authors (as in so many other fields of enquiry) tend to draw upon each other so that different published versions of the battle tend to agree on the central issues. Occasionally, battles come up for reassessment and this is where disputes arise. One such dispute is addressed here, in the case of Assandun, for which two alternative sites have been proposed and which are compared by us in landscape terms. Others featured here where some measure of reassessment has taken place include Naseby and Northampton: in these cases, reassessment comprised mainly the search for battlefield landscape features thought to be lost, but they also have an impact on locating the precise site of the battle.

The sites included here comprise:

In England
Assandun
Bosworth
Cropredy Bridge
Linton
Maldon
Naseby
Northampton
Roundway Down
Sedgemoor
St Albans I and II
Stamford Bridge
Stoke
Tewkesbury

In Belgium
Courtrai
Oudenaarde

In France
Bouvines
Fontenoy
The Dunes

In Portugal
Aljubarrota
Roliça

In Spain
Corunna
Sorauren I and II

The form and content of each site report is as follows:

THE NAME OF THE BATTLE   THE YEAR IN WHICH IT TOOK PLACE

Location – a note of how to reach the site.

Extent – its size in terms of width and depth.

Landscape Type – a short description of the kind of landscape in one or two sentences.

Description of Landscape and Current Use – a longer description of the landscape, its form and current uses.

Description of the Battle – a description of the events of the battle as agreed by military historians.

Battlefield Architecture – a description of the objects and landscape features present on the day of the battle, distinguishing between those used as part of the action on the day and those ignored.

Rules of War – a description of those aspects of the battle action giving an insight to the ideology of war and the norms of warfare practice in the period of the battle.

Functional Aspects – a discussion of those aspects of battle practice that meet expectations of rational actors.

Dysfunctional Aspects – a discussion of those aspects of battle practice that do not meet the expectations of rational actors.

Marking of Battlefield and Interpretation – a description of whether the battlefield was marked as the site of an event of significance at the time or subsequently, and of the form of any kind of monument or memorialisation.

Summary table – a summary of the information contained in the site report (see Table 2.2).

ALJUBARROTA, AD 1385

Location

Some 9km from Aljubarrota itself, in the village of San Jorge, approximately 2km south of Batalha, Leiria, Portugal.

Extent

Approximately 500m × 500m.

Landscape Type

Wooded hilltop.

Description of Landscape and Current Use

Access to the site is good by main road (Route 8) from Batalha (2km) or Aljubarrota (9km).

Fought at the top of an incline flanked by very steep slopes, the battlefield consists of agricultural fields and orchards contained between woods (Plate 1). In front of the Anglo-Portuguese position at the top of the slope was a natural *fosse* or ditch containing water, subsequently filled and now partially revealed by excavation in 1960. The first position of the attacking Franco-Spanish forces lay at the foot of the slope, which itself is steep in places. The line of the modern side road from the battlefield into the valley below provides convenient access and the fields either side give a good impression of the lie of the land on the day of battle, although high walls either side of the road impede more general views. The battlefield contains a late fourteenth-century church built after the event. In general, views of the battlefield landscape from the site are poor, being masked by a large concrete monument, buildings and trees, although this may give a good impression of the experience on the day, since the trees, assisted in masking the disposition of the Anglo-Portuguese army.

The land continues to be used mainly for arable agriculture and some modern housing. The site of the Anglo-Portuguese position contains a modern (1960) monument to the battle and a museum (also 1960) dedicated to the Portuguese military: the museum was closed for refurbishment on the day visited, and we suspect it is now permanently closed.

Description of the Battle

Aljubarrota is one of several battles fought outside metropolitan France but nevertheless forming part of the so-called Hundred Years War between France and England. In these actions, England generally supported Portuguese claims to independence, while France supported Spanish claims to sovereignty throughout Iberia.

Adopting a position very similar to that taken years earlier by the English at Poitiers (1356) and again at Navarrete (1367), the Anglo-Portuguese force stood at the top of the slope, their front covered by the *fosse* and to either side by fallen trees acting as a barrier. In the centre stood men-at-arms, while the flanks – partially contained behind the fallen trees and also within and hidden by woods – were composed of archers and crossbowmen. The larger Franco-Spanish army consisted of mounted men-at-arms and crossbowmen.

The French and Spanish advanced in three waves – of dismounted men-at-arms, of cavalry and finally crossbowmen. The forward wave arrived at the battlefield in late afternoon, the remainder still being some kilometres to the rear: attacking without support, they were virtually annihilated after a tough half-hour's fighting. The remainder of the Franco-Spanish army arrived later and launched a general attack all along the Anglo-Portuguese line with an attempt to outflank the two wings. The centre attack resulted in fierce fighting, the advantage going to the Anglo-Portuguese through flanking fire from their archers. On the wings, confusion among the French and Spanish as they tried to find their way through enclosed fields and orchards while avoiding ravines led to a failure to successfully outflank the defenders' strong position. At dusk, the Franco-Spanish army retreated having suffered severe losses: those killed included virtually the entire first wave, and all the mounted knights who crossed the *fosse*, since they were unable to return (Oman, 1898, 648–53).

Battlefield Architecture

The slope to the front of the Anglo-Portuguese position and the steep ravines either side – together with the *fosse* to the front and the fallen and cut timbers to either side – provided difficult terrain for the approaching Franco-Spanish forces to manoeuvre through and over. Similarly, the woods on the flank of the position served to obscure from view the men-at-arms and archers concealed there.

Standing at the top of the slope, however, and leaving a gap between the woods either side clearly indicated the position to the approaching enemy. The latter, however, took little notice of the terrain before them and attacked as opportunity presented itself.

Both sides formed infantry in regular 'battles' – closely ordered formations, up to twenty soldiers deep. Cavalry attacked in lines. Archers would have been in more open formations, with perhaps five or ten to a file.

Rules of War

The choice of position adopted by the Anglo-Portuguese forces clearly indicates a decision to give battle. The Franco-Spanish response confirms that battle was the subject of agreement by both sides, rather than the result of being forced upon one or the other. In turn, this indicates that each saw the other as a legitimate enemy to be engaged in formal battle.

The high level of violence – especially as inflicted upon the Franco-Spanish attackers – is a product of the use of professional soldiers and the circumstances of the fight, which lies at the emergence of a sense of 'national' identity among European populations.

Functional Aspects

There was good use of the terrain made by the smaller Anglo-Portuguese army, who positioned themselves in a place inviting direct frontal assault, difficult to outflank, and with concealment and cover for archers and other more lightly armed troops. Both sides showed courage and determination.

Dysfunctional Aspects

There was clearly no alternative considered by either side but battle. The Anglo-Portuguese positioned themselves to offer this, despite representing the much smaller force. The Franco-Spanish forces rushed headlong into combat without preparation, failing to use missile weapons for an initial exchange, failing to provide mutual support and without any effort to reconnoitre the ground. The latter is particularly interesting given the previous experience of French forces in meeting English armies in very similar circumstances, and the development in France of effective countermeasures.

Marking of Battlefield and Interpretation

The battlefield itself was marked by a small chapel built in the years shortly after the battle (Plate 1). At 2km distance and only three years after, however, the victorious king of Portugal began construction of the great monastery Santa Maria da Vitória (also known as Batalha, the name of the modern town where it stands) (Plate 46). Inside the great church in a side chapel lies King John I, victor of Aljubarrota, and at the entrance the tomb of the knight who saved his life on the day, guarding him in death as he did in life. Elsewhere in the monastery stands the Portuguese Tomb of the Unknown Soldier, guarded night and day (Plate 45). Outside the monastery in the Praça de João I stands the equestrian monument to Commander Nuno Alvares Pereira, commander of the Anglo-Portuguese army during the battle, constructed in 1968.

The battle site is now commemorated by a plinth showing a map of the remade ground and a concrete monument to all the early battles of Portugal's history (Plate 39). The fourteenth-century chapel contains a notice of the archaeological excavations carried out by the army in 1960 (Cunha and Silva, 1997, 595–9; do Paço, 1962, 115–63), which located the *fosse* and the positions of sharpened stakes covering the flanking archers. The site is dominated by the modern brutalist Military Museum, now closed.

Table 3.1:   *Aljubarrota*

Rules of War	Battlefield Architecture
Agreement to fight: Y	Features present:
	Hillslope
	Fosse
	Woods
	Individual trees

Mutual recognition as 'legitimate' enemies: Y

Level of violence: High

Marking of battle site:
Construction of chapel on site. Now contains information on 1960 excavation.
Subsequent construction of monastery of Santa Maria da Vitória some 2km distant (now Batalha). Monuments to battle and Portuguese commander inside and outside monastery, together with Portuguese Tomb of the Unknown Soldier.
1960: Excavation of site by Portuguese army, raising of concrete monument to this battle and others, and opening of Military Museum of Portugal (now closed).

Participants:
Soldiers of England, France, Portugal and Spain.

Type of feature used:
 Hillslope
 Fosse
 Woods
 Individual trees
Type of feature not used:
 None
Use of terrain:
 as cover: Y
 to impede visibility: Y
 to impede movement: Y
Structured formations: Y

Functional Aspects

Good use of position and weapons made by Anglo-Portuguese. Courage and determination shown by both sides.

Dysfunctional Aspects

No consideration of any alternative but battle by either side, and offered by Anglo-Portuguese even though the smaller force. Franco-Spanish rushed headlong into combat without reconnaissance, without ensuring support, and without use of all available (especially missile) weapons, despite knowledge of previous experience of such forces on such ground in the past.

ASSANDUN, AD 1016

Location

Disputed, between:
1. English National Grid reference TL 579420
   On the slope between Church End, Ashdon, Essex and the River Bourne.
2. English National Grid reference TO 875955
   On the Crouch river flats between Ashingdon and Canewdon, Essex.

Extent

500m × 500m.

Landscape type

1. Chalk hillslope.
2. River floodplain.

Description of Landscape and Current Use

1. Ashdon is a linear village on the road between Saffron Walden (6km south-west) and Bartlow (3km north). It stands beside the River Bourne, whose steep valley sides would have been the location for the battle (Plate 2).

   Church End, at the southern end of the village, contains the current fourteenth-century church (at TL 581415) around which the road bends eastwards. To the north lies the high ground between the main river and a tributary running parallel before joining it from the west. The north-facing slope between the road and this tributary is known as 'Old Church' which suggests the existence of a church previous to the current one: Rodwell (1993) suggests this is the site of Cnut's memorial church built to celebrate his victory and therefore the site of the battle. The land is steep and now lightly wooded, divided into fields for arable farming. Access is by way of footpaths across the space.

2. Ashingdon occupies a hilltop 2km south of the River Crouch. The church at the wooded summit of the hill – providing excellent views of the land east and north – may be a descendant of the church built by Cnut to celebrate his victory. Alternatively, that on Beacon Hill at Canewdon (TL 895945) some 4km to the east, may be the descendant of Cnut's church. The battle site is generally located between the two villages, in the low-lying ground adjacent to the river (Plate 3). It is cut now by small water channels and used for arable agriculture. Access is by way of the road between Ashingdon and Canewdon and footpaths across adjacent fields.

Description of the Battle

Cnut of Norway was raiding the east coast of England when overtaken by an army of levies from Wessex, East Anglia and Mercia led by Edmund Ironside. Cnut occupied high ground that lay between the English and the Norse ships. Edmund led a fierce attack against Cnut's force, but it became disorganised allowing the more experienced Norse to close in on his flank. After fierce fighting, with many English casualties, Edmund escaped with the remainder of his army.

Cnut's decisive victory led to the partition of England into a portion ruled by Edmund and the remainder by Cnut. After Edmund's death, Cnut acceded to the throne of the entire country (Rodwell, 1993, 127–58; Savage, 1982, 164–5).

Battlefield Architecture

The ground at both possible sites is open and uncluttered.

1. At Ashdon the ground slopes steeply to the river which may make manoeuvre and deployment difficult, but which would hinder an attacking force. The high ground is near to the river itself, making for easy and relatively quick access to the ships.

2. At Ashingdon, the ground is generally low-lying apart from the Ashingdon and Canewdon hills, making manoeuvre relatively easy but providing little major obstacle to an uphill attack. Access to the river is easy across flat ground, but the distance is more than a kilometre, making movement to the ships slower.

No use was made of existing landscape features to provide cover or to impede visibility.

Rules of War

Both sides appear to have allowed the other to form before fighting, indicating a mutual agreement to fight. In turn, this suggests that they saw each other as legitimate enemies. The level of violence was kept relatively low, since Edmund was able to disengage and escape with part of his force intact.

Formations present appear to have been relatively structured and well ordered, although a more disorganised 'swarming' of the enemy by both sides is also possible.

Functional Aspects

The Norse army made good use of available high ground to ensure a dominating position from which they could also protect their ships. Rather than launch an attack, they held their position and waited for the English to do so. The English attack ensured that the Norse could not avoid a fight and wait to escape with their booty under cover of dark. There was a relatively low level of violence as indicated by Edmund's ability to eventually break off the action and retire.

Dysfunctional Aspects

The Norse were dependent upon the safety of their ships and were weighed down with captured booty from raids. The English levies lacked experience of fighting and allowed their formations to become disorganised and vulnerable to a flanking movement.

Marking of Battlefield and Interpretation

After his victory and conquest of part of England, Cnut raised a church (now lost) to commemorate the event.

1. No marking of Ashdon as the possible site is evident. The part of the modern village called 'Old Church' contains no visible structures.
2. The Ashingdon village sign displays a Saxon and Norse warrior, indicating their claim to be the site of the action.

No interpretation is offered of the battle.

The most likely site may be that at Ashingdon (site 2) since it corresponds to a more likely landform for fighting at this period than Ashdon (site 1). Ashingdon (site 2) is also that most often accepted as the site.

Table 3.2   *Assandun*

Rules of War

Agreement to fight: Y

Mutual recognition as 'legitimate' enemies: Y

Level of violence: Medium

Marking of battle site:
Construction of commemorative church on site by Cnut.

Participants:
Levies from Wessex, East Anglia and Mercia. Experienced troops and raiders from Norway and Denmark.

Battlefield Architecture

Features present:
    High ground
    River estuary
Type of feature used:
    High ground
    River estuary
Type of feature not used:
    None
Use of terrain:
    as cover:
    to impede visibility:
    to impede movement: Y
Structured formations: Y?

Functional Aspects

Use of high ground by Norse to dominate position and protect access to ships. Attack by English to prevent Norse escape.

Dysfunctional Aspects

Reliance of Norse upon water transport and need to protect ships. English inexperience leading to disorganisation and ultimate defeat.

BOSWORTH, AD 1485

Location

English National Grid reference: SK 001398
At Ambion Hill Farm, 3km south of Market Bosworth, Leicestershire.

Extent

1km × 500m.

Landscape Type

Open pasture: rolling hills. Low marsh.

Description of Landscape and Current Use

The battlefield at Bosworth is the only one in England with a dedicated visitor centre. Access is good by road and there is a local railway station. There are marked waypaths around the battle site with explanatory plinths, and flags on tall poles mark the positions of the main protagonists. Although the shape of the land itself remains similar, more recent features and drainage of the marsh west of Ambion Hill have changed it appreciably.

Ambion Hill rises gently from the surrounding countryside (Plate 4). The Ashby de la Zouch Canal runs through the space of the battle along the southern side of Ambion Hill, then turns northwards around its western side. A railway line – used for leisure trips – runs almost due north along the western side of the hill, crossing the canal at several points, and the Battlefield station stands approximately where Henry Tudor's household stood during the battle. In the low ground to the west of the hill, between the railway and the canal, lies a small field (formerly marsh, now drained) where the mounted skirmish in which Richard III was killed took place. It contains a stone monument to 'The last Plantagenet King of England' (Plate 35).

The buildings of Ambion Farm, to the east of the hill, house the visitor centre and amenity site. A diorama of the battle together with extracts of Laurence Olivier's film of Shakespeare's *Richard III* illustrate the event. A museum, a shop and a restaurant complete the complex.

Description of the Battle

Bosworth is remembered incorrectly as the last battle of the Wars of the Roses. Lancastrian Henry Tudor invaded England from Wales to challenge Yorkist Richard III's claim to the throne.

Richard formed his army on Ambion Hill facing west, his infantry under Norfolk in a single battle to his front, he with his bodyguard of cavalry to the rear at the top of the hill. Henry Tudor formed on the low ground to the front,

45

his infantry under Oxford also in a single battle, his bodyguard cavalry to the right. Some distance away, Stanley with his mixed force watched from Tudor's right. With the infantry engaged in a balanced fight on the hillslope, Richard rode to challenge Stanley and was intercepted by Tudor's cavalry: in the skirmish that ensued, Richard was killed (Bennett, 1985; Brooke, 1854, 157–76; Gairdner, 1975; Hutton, 1999; Kendall, 1972a, 491–2; Walton, 1998).

Battlefield Architecture

The top of Ambion Hill was used by the Yorkists only as a place to form and to provide visibility around the area of the battlefield. No effort was made to fortify the position or to impede the Lancastrian advance or attack. No troops were placed under cover of nearby woodland, nor was advantage taken of the marshy ground below: indeed, in the closing stages of the battle three contending parties led troops into the marshy area, suggesting a general lack of aversion to such terrain.

Rules of War

There was a clear mutual agreement to fight, and this implies mutual recognition as legitimate warriors. The level of violence was high, as in most later battles of the Wars of the Roses, perhaps indicating the degree of mutual hostility that had developed between contending forces, composed by this time predominately of professional soldiers.

Functional Aspects

Use of the Ambion Hill top to form indicates an appreciation of the usefulness of good visibility. All involved showed skill, determination and courage in the fighting.

Dysfunctional Aspects

The level of violence was very high. No advantage was made by any of those involved of terrain features such as high ground, wooded cover, or streams or marshy areas to impede movement. There was in general a lack of good command and control: individual nobles operated independently of overall commanders and loyalty was a large factor, the final result being achieved more by treason than by victorious arms. The battle was finally decided by a small skirmish away from the main fighting: this may reflect ideas about 'honour' and the status of the warrior current at the time.

Marking of Battlefield and Interpretation

The battlefield was not marked immediately, although Dadlington chapel (2km distant southwards) was built to commemorate the event, and the first stone marking the traditional place where Richard III was killed pre-dates the twentieth century by some time. Sutton Cheney church (2km distant to the east) contains a memorial to Richard III, who prayed there the night before the battle. The visitor centre at Ambion Hill Farm provides tourist amenities and a focus for a visit. Marked walkways around Ambion Hill indicate the events of the fight and point out local landmarks, and flags on tall poles mark the supposed positions of the combatants on the day.

Table 3.3   *Bosworth*

Rules of War
Agreement to fight: Y

Mutual recognition as 'legitimate' enemies: Y

Level of violence: High

Marking of battle site:
Nothing on day.
Subsequent memorials to Richard III and battle; now a visitor centre/tourist site.

Participants:
Professional soldiers raised by competing nobles in support of rivals for the Crown.

Battlefield Architecture
Features present:
   Hillslope
   Marshy ground/stream
   Woodland (cover)
Type of feature used:
   Hilltop for forming
Type of feature not used:
   Adjacent woods
   Marshy ground/stream
Use of terrain:
   as cover: N
   to impede visibility: N
   to impede movement: N
Structured formations: Y

Functional Aspects
Use of hillslope to form: good visibility; potential to impede enemy approach.

Dysfunctional Aspects
Failure to exploit high ground. High level of violence. Poor command and control: individual units deployed in accordance with wishes of commanding nobles rather than overall commanders; some uncertainty as to loyalty of forces (represented by intervention of Stanley on side of non-incumbent); perceived need for overall commanders to meet/engage Stanley forces (especially in the case of Richard III whose forces were gaining upper hand).

BOUVINES, AD 1214

Location

Michelin map 51, 6 SE. Lat. 50°35'N, Long. 3°11'E
To the north-east of Bouvines village, approximately 8km south-east of Lille.

Extent

500m × 250m.

Landscape Type

Open hilltop.

Description of Landscape and Current Use

Access to the battlefield is good by road and track (the latter following the line of the Roman road under the modern railway line). Bouvines can be reached by train and bus from Lille.

The modern village of Bouvines occupies the steep rise of ground on the eastern side of the River Marque: the modern bridge does not stand on the same spot as that of its medieval predecessor. To the north and east of the village is an extensive area of flat high ground used for arable agriculture (Plate 5). The southern side is marked by the line of the curving modern road to Cysoing, lying some 2km distant to the south-east. To the north, also some 2km distant, lies the village of Gruson.

Running directly between Bouvines and Cysoing is the line of the Roman road that crossed the battlefield, now used as a footpath and farm track. Beside the track just beyond the north-eastern edge of the modern village lie the earthworks marking the site of the medieval settlement and monastery. At right angles to the track and crossing the Roman road approximately 1km from Bouvines is the railway line from Cysoing to Lille.

Description of the Battle

While King John of England attacked southern France to win back Angevin lands, his ally the Emperor invaded northern France with the support of several disaffected French nobles and Burgundian allies. The French and Imperial armies met on the eastern side of the River Marque, where the French had hoped to cross to block the way to Paris. Turning about, the French formed on the high ground beside the Roman road in three lines of crossbowmen, cavalry and infantry, arrayed roughly south–north. The Imperial army formed opposite, a line of pikemen supported by cavalry.

French cavalry on the southern flank engaged in a confused fight with Imperialist pikes and cavalry. In the centre the Imperial infantry was able to advance against the French, and repeated French cavalry attacks supported by archery finally halted but did not break the Imperialist attack. On the northern flank the French cavalry defeated the Imperialists who fell back behind their own cavalry. The battle line thus swung gradually south-west–north-east. The battle in the centre continued with French reinforcements arriving from the north-eastern flank, and increasing numbers of Imperialists fled the field. On the south-western flank, fierce fighting continued with the Burgundians eventually forming a circle of pikes around their exhausted cavalry, but this was finally defeated by the weight of French numbers (Duby, 1973; Hadengue, 1935; Oman, 1898, 457–77).

Battlefield Architecture

The ground chosen presents no features other than those of height and openness. No use was made of any available cover nor difficult terrain. It was very suitable ground on which to deploy: flanks seem to have been left open, but no attempt to outflank was made by either side. The Roman road was the line of advance and retreat for both sides, but otherwise served no function in the battle. Both sides formed in a conventional manner appropriate for the forces available.

Rules of War

While the French sought to place themselves between the enemy and Paris before offering battle, the Imperialists actively sought it: both sides were therefore in agreement as to fighting and neither sought any alternative to battle. This indicates each thought the other a suitable opponent to engage in battle. The level of violence was high, as demonstrated by the determination of the French throughout and that of the Burgundians towards the end. Partly this may have been due to the employment by both sides of professionals and mercenaries, and recognition of the high stakes for winners and losers (loss of throne, for instance); but particular enmities (French versus German and Burgundian, for instance) may also have played a part.

Functional Aspects

Both sides used their forces in an effective manner. Courage and determination was shown by the fighters on both sides, but especially by the French and the Burgundians towards the end. The French king made effective use of the victory.

Dysfunctional Aspects

The French were unable to avoid battle, which was actively desired by the Imperialists. There was a high level of violence, combined – especially on the part of the Burgundians – with an unwillingness to accept the inevitability of defeat.

Marking of Battlefield and Interpretation

The battle of Bouvines is recognised as an important date in the history of France, carrying some of the status accorded in England to Hastings or in the USA to Yorktown.

The 1914–1918 war memorial in Bouvines (Plate 44) carries the legend: 'Bouvines 1214–1914' making a clear association between the medieval conflict and the First World War (also fought between France and Germany). Bouvines lay upon the route of march of defeated French troops withdrawing to the line of the Marne in 1914: on the right-hand panel of the Bouvines memorial are the words of a French general of the First World War, *'La bataille de la Marne était la bataille de Bouvines renouvelée'* (the battle of the Marne [1914] was the battle of Bouvines renewed).

Near to the war memorial stands a nineteenth-century memorial to the 1214 battle in the form of an obelisk.

The church of Bouvines (rebuilt in 1878) contains twenty-one stained-glass windows (completed in 1906) depicting the events of the battle. A leaflet available in the church explains the images and tells the story. Also in the church, an information board locates the battle on a map of the locality and also tells the story.

Table 3.4   *Bouvines*

Rules of War	Battlefield Architecture
Agreement to fight: Y	Features present:
	High ground
	River and bridge
	Roman road
	Monastery and village

Mutual recognition as 'legitimate' enemies: Y

Level of violence: High

Marking of battle site:
None on day.
Modern church in Bouvines (1878) contains stained-glass.
windows (1906) celebrating events of battle.
Monument in village.
1914–1918 war memorial in Bouvines also makes specific
reference to 1214 battle.

Participants:
Professional and mercenary soldiers of France, Empire,
England and Burgundy.

Type of feature used:
  High ground
  Roman road
Type of feature not used:
  River and bridge
  Monastery and village
Use of terrain:
  as cover: N
  to impede visibility: N
  to impede movement: N
Structured formations: Y

Functional Aspects

Effective use of forces by both sides. Courage and determination shown by all. Effective use of victory made by French.

Dysfunctional Aspects

Inability of French to avoid battle, which was actively desired by the Imperialists. High level of violence and unwillingness of Burgundians to accept the inevitability of defeat.

ELVIÑA/CORUNNA, AD 1809

Named locally for the village that saw much of the fighting (now a suburb of the city) and in English for the port-city itself.

Location

In the hills above the village of Elviña, 6km south of the city of A Coruña/La Coruña, Galicia, Spain.

Extent

3km × 1km.

Landscape Type

Mountainous.

Description of Landscape and Current Use

Access to the battlefield is good, by road and farm track.

Elviña is now the name of the wooded suburb occupying the space of the battle. The separate villages have been incorporated into the built-up space so that Elviña today comprises the former settlements of Elviña, Eiris and Piedrolonga.

The western extreme of the battlefield is marked by the village of San Cristobal, lying in the valley bottom, now including the La Coruña municipal sports complex and industrial buildings. A kilometre to the south-east, Elviña hugs the steep northern slope of the wooded hills, and most of the village lies at the foot of the slope above the stream running along the valley bottom. On the north-facing slope above and south-west of Elviña, and directly facing San Cristobal, stand the long white buildings of the new University of La Coruña, visible from high points in and beyond the city itself (Plate 6).

The original core of Elviña stays much as it was in 1809: a few farmhouses and other structures of local stone connected by narrow and steep alleys and roads. The floor of the valley is flat and extends for a kilometre north from Elviña and its stream before rising again into the hills that separate Elviña from the city of A Coruña/La Coruña. Across the valley, 1km away from Elviña, on the southern-facing slopes of a gentler hill, the original core of Eiris now includes the church for Elviña, providing good views towards Elviña and the university. The core of Piedrolonga – comprising housing and the occasional hotel – lies on the top of the slope 1km south-east of Elviña: on lower ground close by to the east runs the main highway from La Coruña south to the airport and the city of Santiago de Compostela (approximately 50km distant). Beyond the road, the estuary of the River Mero marks the eastern extreme of the battlefield space.

Where not built upon, the area – and indeed much of the valley – is used for arable agriculture, giving a good impression of the look of the space in 1809. The hillslopes are steep, but well provided with paths and roads. From the university to Elviña a path and then a road follow the hillslope east–west below the crest. The tops of the hills are generally flat. In the valley, roads – many of them on the line of those present in 1809 – lead ultimately towards La Coruña. About 500m below Elviña is a major junction of these roads: although accounts of the battle talk of the forces standing upon opposed high ground, it is clear from the ground itself that the British must have occupied the villages and the low ground beyond, the major features of note being the roads towards the city.

Description of the Battle

During the earliest phase of the Peninsular War, a British army fleeing from superior French forces aimed to take ship from La Coruña harbour. Caught by the French before the fleet arrived, the British turned to fight on the hills about 6km south of the city. The city walls were defended by some British and Spanish forces, and the La Coruña city militia.

The French occupied the tops of the hills above San Cristobal and Elviña while the British held the valley and the hills 1km opposite. The French launched powerful attacks particularly in the centre around Elviña, which changed hands several times during the fighting. Their attacks making little headway and with British control of the action disordered by the loss of the commander, battle reduced into desultory artillery exchanges followed by British withdrawal to the city and the fleet (Hibbert, 1961; Oman, 1902a, 583–95; Parkinson, 1973, 68–75; Weller, 1962, 66–9).

Battlefield Architecture

The flat tops to the hills above Elviña provided a good position on which the French could form in the standard columns and lines of troops typical for the day, while the opposing hills and the valley below provided similarly good ground for the British on which to form in their standard linear manner. The stone-built villages provided good defensive strong points for the defending British and clear objectives for the attacking French. No particular use appears to have been made of streams as obstacles, nor field boundaries as cover or obstacles. While the roads leading towards La Coruña may have been the real French objectives, and thus the object of British defence, accounts of the battle do not emphasise this.

Rules of War

It is clear from the deliberate manner in which both armies formed that they intended battle, and no other alternative was considered. The intent to fight indicates that each saw the other as a 'legitimate' enemy. Although the fighting was stiff at times, casualties were relatively light for the forces engaged and battle ended as a series of exchanges by artillery units, each distant from its enemy. Accordingly, the level of violence may be considered 'medium' rather than high, possibly due to the early stage of the war when clear animosities had not yet formed.

Functional Aspects

The British made good use of their position and the villages to resist French attacks, while the French position on the top of the hills in some measure provided protection from British counter-attacks. Troops of both sides fought with skill and determination.

Dysfunctional Aspects

Neither side considered any alternative to fighting, and some of the fighting was violent. Despite this, neither side pressed home attacks sufficiently to break the other, and the French were left in possession of the battlefield while the British made good their escape by sea. A French concern with the British-held villages may have distracted them from their true objectives, most likely the roads to the city which conjoined below Elviña.

Marking of Battlefield and Interpretation

A monument to the British commander (although not seen) marks the spot where he was killed above the village of Elviña.

The new University of La Coruña occupies the ground comprising much of the battlefield (Plate 6): local recognition of the association between the siting and the battle is widespread, and it is clear the association is a deliberate one. The name Elviña is now applied to all the ground of the battlefield, including the new university, and the church formerly at Eiris is now that of Elviña.

Monuments to the men of English regiments who fought at Elviña were mounted on the exterior of the church, adjacent to the door, in 1999 (Plate 48).

A monument to the battle stands at the entrance to the city of La Coruña, at the point where the road entered from the south: the walls and the original gate are now missing.

The battle is well covered in the Coruña Museum of Archaeology and History, housed in the fortress of San Anton at the northern edge of the harbour. An entire room is devoted to the battle and the role of the Coruña militia in guarding the city and providing a rearguard for the British evacuation after the battle.

Table 3.5   *Elviña/Corunna*

Rules of War	**Battlefield Architecture**
Agreement to fight: Y	Features present:
	Hills
	Streams
	Villages
	Roads
	Fields

Mutual recognition as 'legitimate' enemies: Y

Level of violence: Medium

Marking of battle site:
None immediately afterwards.
Memorial to British commander on site (unseen).
Memorial on site of city walls.
Memorials placed on Elviña church in 1999.
Display in Coruña Archaeological and Historical Museum.
New university constructed on site of battle.

Type of feature used:
  Hills
  Villages
Type of feature not used:
  Streams
  Roads?
  Fields
Use of terrain:
  as cover: Y
  to impede visibility: N
  to impede movement: Y
Structured formations: Y

Participants:
Professional soldiers of the British and French armies.

Functional Aspects

Good use made of terrain and defensive strength of villages by both sides. Troops of both sides fought with skill and determination.

Dysfunctional Aspects

No consideration by either side of alternatives to battle. Some violence in fighting. Attacks insufficiently pressed to achieve a decision. Possible misidentification by French of the villages as key objectives rather than the roads beyond.

COURTRAI/BATTLE OF THE SPURS, AD 1302

Location

Michelin map 51, 6 SE. Lat. 50°50′N, Long. 3°18′E
On the eastern side of the centre of Kortrijk, Flanders, Belgium, immediately outside the Groeningenpoort.

Extent

500m × 500m.

Landscape Type

Urban.

Description of Landscape and Current Use

The site of the battle is now built over, lying just beyond the Groeningen gate to the city, on its eastern side (Plate 7).

    The Groeningen gate of Kortrijk is an impressive stone structure, the city walls (now gone) extending from it to north and south. The ground is flat and low-lying; the former Groeningen stream is now built over, its approximate line marked by the street called Groeningelaan. The only sign of the battle is the large monument topped by a gilded bronze figure of Victory holding up a spear in the small park within which the gate stands.

Description of the Battle

During an uprising by the people of Flanders against French rule, the Fleming army of infantry armed mostly with pikes stood with its back to the gate of the French-held city of Courtrai. The Flemings' front was protected by the Groeningen stream and the marshy ground either side of the stream. A rearguard stood to prevent French troops emerging from the city. On the opposite side of the stream the French army was composed mostly of mounted men-at-arms with some crossbowmen and infantry.

After an initial volley of crossbows, the French cavalry attacked across the stream and were thrown into disorder by the marshy ground and the presence of their own infantry. A fierce push-of-pikes by the Flemings forced the French back with heavy losses. Fresh French forces refusing to advance against the pikes, the French withdrew (Montgomery, 1968, 194; Oman, 1953, 64–5; Tuchman, 1978, 76–7; Verbrüggen, 2002).

Battlefield Architecture

The presence of the city wall would have prevented an effective retreat by the Flemings. This was, however, offset by the fact that the stream and its marshy banks provided difficult ground for cavalry. Both sides were in standard formations of cavalry and close-formed infantry: while this played to the advantage of the Flemings, their own infantry proved a complicating factor for the French cavalry.

Rules of War

The Flemings, caught with their backs to a hostile city, clearly had no option but battle, while the French sought it; but the Flemings, too, may have preferred battle. Although the Flemings were rebels against established authority, and the French professional military, the French nevertheless treated them as 'legitimate' enemies against whom a battle could be fought. (Compare with today: the definitions of legitimacy may not have been so tightly drawn.) The level of violence was high, probably on the Fleming side because of the likely consequences of defeat.

Functional Aspects

The Flemings showed a good appreciation of the strength of their position and were able to apply their forces accordingly.

Dysfunctional Aspects

It is not clear why the Flemings chose to take up position with their backs to a hostile fortress. Neither side appears to have considered any alternative to battle: the French were determined upon it, and the Flemings may have been forced to it. The level of violence was high, probably due to the likely consequences (at least for the rebels) of defeat. The French mis-handled their advance against the Fleming infantry, and misread the state of the ground, leading to confusion which could be exploited by the Flemings. The latter, however, having achieved a significant victory failed to follow it up.

Marking of Battlefield and Interpretation

The site of the battle is now marked by the presence of the medieval gate outside which it was fought, and the monument to the battle immediately outside it (Plate 7). It is on the main tourist route around the city, but does not attract large numbers of visitors at any one time.

The nearby Groeningeabdij Museum contains a model of medieval Courtrai with the possible positions of the French and Flemish marked upon it, although the extent of the battlefield seems exaggerated.

The battle is referred to in guidebooks to the city but not described in detail.

Table 3.6   *Courtrai/Battle of the Spurs*

Rules of War	Battlefield Architecture
Agreement to fight: Y	Features present:
	Flat ground
	Stream
Mutual recognition as 'legitimate' enemies: Y	City gate and wall
	Type of feature used:
	Flat ground
Level of violence: High	Stream

Marking of battle site:
None on day
Monument to battle outside Groeningen gate.
Interpretation in Groeningeabdij Museum.

Participants:
Flemish insurgents and French men-at-arms.

Type of feature not used:
  City gate and wall
Use of terrain:
  as cover: N
  to impede visibility: N
  to impede movement: Y
Structured formations: Y

Functional Aspects

Effective use of terrain and forces by Flemish insurgents.

Dysfunctional Aspects

Retreating rebels take up position outside the only French-held city in Flanders. No alternative to battle sought by either side, although the Flemings had been retreating and it can be considered to have been forced upon them. Level of violence high. Confusion among French due to mishandling of forces and misreading of terrain. No effective follow-up by Flemings after victory.

CROPREDY BRIDGE, AD 1644

Location

English National Grid reference SP 475465

Immediately to the east of the village of Cropredy, approximately 4.5km north of Banbury, Oxfordshire.

Extent

3km × 2km.

Landscape Type

River floodplain.

Description of Landscape and Current Use

Access is good by a combination of road, bridleways and footpaths. The line of the Oxford Canal from Peewit Farm to Cropredy comprises part of the marked Oxford Canal Walk.

The River Cherwell – a stretch of which forms part of the Oxford Canal – runs approximately due north–south between Peewit Farm (SP 473450) and Cropredy village, where it turns north-east away from the canal towards Edgcote, crossed by the main north–south A361 road at Hays Bridge (SP 489476). Eastwards from the river, the land rises steadily towards the main

A361 road and Wardington, standing 2km east of Cropredy on the line of the A361. To the west of the river at Cropredy, the ground is flat for 1km then rises sharply. From the high ground to east and west, a good view can be had of the river valley and the higher ground beyond (Plate 8).

The villages of Cropredy and Wardington and the hamlet at Williamscot are all small communities. The land between – especially that in the river floodplain where the fighting took place – is used for arable agriculture and pasture.

Description of the Battle

A Parliamentarian army was shadowing the movements of a Royalist army led by the King. Each was moving north, on opposite sides of the River Cherwell, which could be crossed by various bridges in the vicinity of Cropredy. The Parliamentarians, seeing the King's forces in extended line of march to their east on the line of what is now the A361 road to Daventry and apparently at a disadvantage, moved down into the river valley to catch them in flank. The King, having seen the Parliamentarians apparently at a similar disadvantage from across the valley, also decided to engage. Both sides moved down into the valley bottom where the forces engaged and where fighting ended in a stalemate, although more casualties were suffered by Parliamentarian forces.

Focusing on crossing points and the bridges at Peewit Farm, Cropredy and Hays Bridge, both sides divided their forces and were extended through the entire 3km length of the battlefield. Neither side gained a significant advantage at any point, although Royalist forces were able to effectively prevent Parliamentarian forces from crossing at Hays Bridge, and to prevent a junction of Parliamentarian forces from Slat Mill Ford (at the modern Peewit Farm) with those at Cropredy itself. The battle was relatively mobile and, rare for its period, more of an 'encounter' battle than was normal, which explains the relatively large area covered by the fighting. Although not defeated, the Parliamentarian army suffered severe loss of morale after the battle and dispersed (Toynbee and Young, 1970; Wedgwood, 1966, 308–11; Woolrych, 1966, 59).

Battlefield Architecture

The river and its crossings represent the main battlefield architecture. Little use was made of built-up areas for defence or as strong points, and fighting took place in the open with no available features on which to fix the extended flanks of individual units. Roads were in use before the battle as the main routes for movement, but until a decision to fight was made, neither side attempted to make use of the river or to secure the crossings. Rising ground to east and west was used for visibility but not occupied for defensive or other purpose: fighting took place on the low ground by the river. Both sides maintained good order throughout, fighting in the rigid formations of the time: a degree of mutual support was denied both sides by the division of forces to cover the full length of the battlespace.

Rules of War

There was clear mutual agreement to fight since both armies – experienced by now in confronting one another – moved simultaneously, implying a clear recognition of each other as an appropriate enemy. The level of violence was relatively low.

Functional Aspects

Both sides sought to spring a surprise assault on the other, which they saw to be at a disadvantage. The importance of securing the river crossings was evident to both armies. The presence of high ground allowed a clear view of the opening situation. There was relatively better coordination, command and control by the Royalists.

Dysfunctional Aspects

There was no use made by either side of features to provide advantage: both moved from high ground to low, failed to secure the bridges as lines of retreat, and did not use the river as an obstacle to enemy advance. The battle was fought on open low ground where neither could gain much advantage. Both sides divided their forces rather than concentrating them.

Marking of Battlefield and Interpretation

The battle is commemorated by a plaque on the modern bridge at Cropredy (Plate 36). Cropredy church contains replica armour from the period, the original having been subject to theft some years ago. An annual re-enactment takes place: regiments involved lay wreaths on the bridge to their seventeenth-century originals.

The battlefield is included in the *Register of Historic Battlefields*. Part falls within the Cropredy, Williamscot and Wardington Conservation Areas.

Table 3.7   *Cropredy Bridge*

Rules of War

Agreement to fight: Y

Mutual recognition as 'legitimate' enemies: Y

Level of violence: Medium

Marking of battle site:
Monument recording the battle on Cropredy Bridge.
Replica armour in Cropredy church.
Annual re-enactment.

Participants:
Volunteer soldiers raised by Parliament and King.
Some professionals present: otherwise experienced but
unprofessional soldiers.

Battlefield Architecture

Features present:
    Rising ground both sides of
    river
    River
    Bridges
    Roads
    Cropredy village (buildings)
Type of feature used:
    Bridges
    Roads
Type of feature not used:
    Rising ground
    River (obstacle)
    Village (obstacle, cover)
Use of terrain:
    as cover: N
    to impede visibility: N
    to impede movement: N
Structured formations: Y

Functional Aspects

Advantage taken by both sides of unreadiness of the other to fight: an 'encounter' battle. Use of high ground to provide visibility. Better use of available forces and faster movement by Royalists.

Dysfunctional Aspects

No use of features to provide advantage: both move from high ground to low, fail to secure bridges as lines of retreat, do not use river as an obstacle, etc. Battle fought in open low ground where neither can gain much advantage. Both sides divide their forces rather than concentrating them.

FONTENOY, AD 1745

Location

Michelin map 51, 7 SW. Lat. 50°34′N, Long. 3°25′E
Approximately 6km south-east of Tournai/Doornik, Belgium, along the road east and then north from Antoing through Fontenoy to Gaurain-Ramecroix.

Extent

3km × 1km.

Landscape Type

Open plain.

Description of Landscape and Current Use

Access to the area of the battle is good by road. Antoing can be reached by train from Tournai.

Antoing is a small town set on high ground overlooking the steep-sided valley of the River Scheldt/Escaut: its chateau (open to the public one afternoon a week) is contained within high walls. A minor road runs 2km eastward to the village of Fontenoy, which is set on a slight rise with higher ground to the west and a shallow plain to the east. The minor roads from Fontenoy run east to Vezon (1km) and north to Gaurain-Ramecroix (2km). North of the eastward (Vezon) road are the trees of the Bois du Barry, now much reduced in size. One kilometre west of Fontenoy – possibly marking the approximate position of the furthest advance of the British centre during the battle – lies the main N52 road linking the N507 from Valenciennes with the E42 to Mons.

The landscape is largely rural and used for arable agriculture, especially the growing of corn (Plate 10). Views of the steep-sided river valley and the landscape eastward are good from Antoing. Some buildings in Fontenoy – especially the barn behind the modern monument to the battle – would have been present on the day; modern rendering on the external walls may disguise loopholes and bullet holes from the battle. From Fontenoy, views across the shallow eastward plain are also good, although ultimately blocked by the modern railway embankment, as are those northwards along the road to Gaurain-Ramecroix by the gradual rise of ground. At approximately 1km along the Gaurain-Ramecroix road stands a small walled cemetery from which a good impression of the shallow fall of ground eastward can be gained and there are good views all around. The cemetery wall includes a monument to the Irish fallen of Fontenoy and the fallen of twentieth-century wars.

Description of the Battle

During the War of the Austrian Succession, the French army was besieging the town of Tournai/Doornik in the Austrian Netherlands when challenged by an Anglo-Dutch force. In order to protect the French king from capture, the French left the siege and took up a fortified position centred on the village of Fontenoy. One flank was extended north along the top of the shallow rise to Gaurain-Ramecroix, the other bent west towards Antoing where it was anchored on the chateau and river. In the Bois du Barry the French located batteries of guns in earth redoubts supported by infantry sharpshooters armed with muskets.

Fontenoy village itself was fortified and its buildings occupied as strong points. The Anglo-Dutch took up positions in the open country opposite the French. While a Dutch force threatened Antoing from the south, the remainder formed opposite Fontenoy and the road to Gaurain-Ramecroix.

Advancing in the centre, the mostly British force attempted to storm Fontenoy. Fired upon from the north flank by the forces in the Bois du Barry and facing disciplined musketry from in front, they penetrated at least as far as the interior of the village, and possibly beyond, but failed to break the French line. The Dutch forces to the south failed to make headway against the French, and the British found themselves virtually encircled by shaken but not beaten French forces, both infantry and cavalry. Unable to advance further, the British withdrew in orderly fashion and the allied army retreated from the field during the night (Bois, 1992, 339–57; Green, 1976, 44–51; Weigley, 1991, 203–7).

Battlefield Architecture

The chateau of Antoing and its village, together with the buildings in the village of Fontenoy itself, made strong fortified positions on relatively high ground. Antoing was also effectively protected by the line of the river to the south. The placement of artillery and infantry in the Bois du Barry provided a secure location from which to fire upon the flank of advancing British troops. The slight rise below Fontenoy provided a minor obstacle for advancing British troops but not enough to prevent penetration of the village and possibly beyond. The open ground to the east provided a good place for the Anglo-Dutch army to form prior to the attack. Both sides formed in regular lines in accordance with then standard military practice.

Rules of War

The adoption by the French of a fortified position indicates their willingness to fight, and it would seem no other option was considered by the Anglo-Dutch. This in turn indicates that they each thought the other legitimate opponents for a battle. The level of violence was relatively high, due in part to the use by both sides of experienced professionals and also of ongoing antagonism between British Irish and French Irish regiments.

Functional Aspects

There was excellent use of the terrain by the French to create a strongly defensive position. The Anglo-Dutch were able to appreciate the strength of the position at

Antoing and did not assault it directly. Both sides fought with skill and courage, and the ability of the British to withdraw in good order indicates a high level of discipline.

Dysfunctional Aspects

Alternatives to battle were not considered by either side. The Anglo-Dutch failed to recognise the full strength of the French position centred on Fontenoy and to reconnoitre the Bois du Barry for hidden enemies. The French failed to follow up the withdrawal of British troops from Fontenoy and the subsequent retreat of the Anglo-Dutch army, but made good use of the victory over succeeding months to consolidate their position in the Austrian Netherlands.

Marking of Battlefield and Interpretation

The battlefield was marked by nothing on the day or shortly after.

In the centre of Fontenoy – in a 'village green' adjacent to the church – stands a monument in the form of a Celtic cross raised in 1874 by the Irish Military Historical Society, commemorating the battle and especially the role of Irish troops in the service of the French (Plate 28). Two further smaller monuments upon the wall of the cemetery on the road to Gaurain-Ramecroix commemorate them also.

The battle is described on plinths outside the entrance to Antoing chateau in the centre of that village.

In Cysoing, some 16km westward, stands a further monument to the battle, commemorating the stay of Louis XV in the convent there on the night preceding the battle. The monument is little regarded and now vandalised (Plate 47).

Table 3.8   *Fontenoy*

Rules of War	Battlefield Architecture

Agreement to fight: Y	Features present:
	    Open fields
	    Rise of ground
	    River
	    Fortified villages
	    Woods

Mutual recognition as 'legitimate' enemies: Y	Type of feature used:
	    Open fields
	    Rise of ground

Level of violence: High

Marking of battle site: None on day. Monument to Irish troops at Fontenoy. Monument to French king at Cysoing.

Participants:
Professional soldiers of France, Britain and the Dutch Republic.

River
Fortified villages
Woods
Type of feature not used: None
Use of terrain:
    as cover: Y
    to impede visibility: Y
    to impede movement: Y
Structured formations: Y

Functional Aspects
Good use of terrain by French. Both sides fought with discipline and courage.

Dysfunctional Aspects
Failure by either side to consider alternatives to battle. Failure of the Anglo-Dutch to recognise the strength of the French position or to reconnoitre the Bois du Barry on their flank where French troops were hidden. Failure of the French to follow up immediately the Anglo-Dutch withdrawal.

LINTON, AD 1648

Location
Two locations:
1. English National Grid reference TL 563468
   In the streets of the village of Linton, Cambridgeshire, England, located (a) some 9km north-east of Saffron Walden, Essex along the secondary B1052 road; and (b) some 16km from Cambridge, Cambridgeshire south-east along the main A603 road.
2. English National Grid reference TL 560455
   On the slopes of Haw's Hill, 1.5km south of Linton.

Extent

2km × 2km.

Landscape Types

Open hillslope and urban.

Description of Landscape and Current Use

Access to the space of the fight is good by road and footpath.

Haw's Hill is a rolling hill rising to 83m, approximately 1.5km immediately south of Linton, overlooking the village. Its western slope dominates the line of the B1052 from Saffron Walden through Hadstock (approximately 2km south of Linton). It is open arable farming land, crossed by an easily walkable footpath north–south. Views from its summit to Linton and to the road to the west are good.

The village of Linton lies on the lower southern slopes of Rivey Hill (112m), some 1.5km south of the line of the Roman road between Cambridge and Colchester and in the valley of the River Granta. It is a sizeable village, chiefly consisting of a single street following the line of the B1052. Entering from the south (Plate 11), the street curves eastward to pass north of the church, to which a south-leading lane provides access. Buildings such as the church, the Griffin Inn (now a private house) and others were present on the day. In general, although altered by some modern building, the street plan is identical to that on the day.

Description of the Battle

Technically, this was not a battle but a 'skirmish' or 'uprising'. Its extent reflects the degree of movement involved rather than the size of the forces engaged; a battle would have been a more static event.

Local gentry raised support for the King against parliamentary rule. Falling back upon Linton in the face of the despatch of troops by Parliament from Colchester, the rebels placed a blocking force on the slope of Haw's Hill and across the road leading from Saffron Walden. Suffering casualties, the rebels were forced back into Linton where the main road into the village had been blocked by further barricades. The Parliamentary troops maintained their advance, however, and – some rebels fleeing towards the Roman road on the crest above – forced the rebels back towards the church, where they made a strong resistance but were ultimately overcome (Sutton, 2000, entry 54).

Battlefield Architecture

The road from Saffron Walden (now the B1052) provided good access for the attacking force, while the slopes of Haw's Hill made a convenient location for a force covering and attempting to block the road access to Linton. The streets and lanes of Linton provided convenient sites for barricades, but also restricted the movement of the rebels who were forced back along such routes with few alternatives available to them. The main alternative was to flee northwards up-slope towards the Roman road, a route taken by some. Walls and buildings were available to be used for cover, and the churchyard especially provided a strong defensive position. The River Granta at Linton proved no obstacle to the attacking force.

Rules of War

Both sides were clearly ready for a violent encounter, although the rebels may have been forced to it earlier than they were prepared for. The use of troops to put down the rebellion and their use in a clearly military way suggests that both sides did indeed see themselves as legitimate enemies. (Compare with today: the definitions of legitimacy may not have been so tightly drawn.) The level of violence was not especially high, although some casualties were suffered by the rebels: there may have been some unwillingness on the part of the rebels to inflict serious harm to representatives of the ruling authority and both sides may have been unwilling to inflict heavy casualties on their fellow English.

Functional Aspects

Courage and determination were shown by the Parliamentary troops in their attacks on rebel positions, while rebel attempts to block road access to Linton demonstrate a good grasp of the disadvantages of Parliamentary focus on road access. A relatively low level of violence was employed by both sides.

Dysfunctional Aspects

Neither side sought to find an alternative to a violent encounter, including occupation of the countryside by troops to keep the rebels in one place or dispersal by the rebels across a largely friendly countryside. The concentration of the Parliamentary forces on road access to Linton – rather than using open country for manoeuvre – made them vulnerable to attempts to block the roads. The decision of the rebels to fight in the streets of Linton restricted them to those streets, rather than allowing movement (including, if necessary, retreat) across wider spaces.

Marking of Battlefield and Interpretation

None.

Table 3.9   *Linton*

Rules of War	Battlefield Architecture

Agreement to fight: Y	Features present:
	    Hillslope
	    River
	    Road
	    Village and buildings
	    Church

Mutual recognition as 'legitimate' enemies: Y	Type of feature used:
	    Hillslope
	    Road
	    Village and buildings
	    Church

Level of violence: Medium	Type of feature not used: River

Marking of battle site: None	Use of terrain:
	    as cover: Y
	    to impede visibility: N
	    to impede movement: N

Participants: Experienced soldiers of the Parliamentary army; armed yeomen of Cambridgeshire and Essex with some prior military experience.	Structured formations: Y

Functional Aspects

Courage and determination on the part of the Parliamentary troops. Attempts at blocking access by the rebels. Relatively low level of violence by both sides.

Dysfunctional Aspects

No attempt to resolve issues by any means except violence. Concentration by Parliamentary troops on road access rather than using open country to advantage. Decision by rebels to restrict themselves to an urban space rather than seeking to operate in the countryside where movement (and especially retreat in the face of greater force) would have been easier.

MALDON, AD 991

Location

English National Grid reference TL 870057

Approximately 1km south-east of Maldon, Essex, England, on the shore of the estuary of the River Blackwater opposite Northey Island, 500m east-north-east of South House Farm.

Extent

Approximately 250m wide × 100m deep, depending upon the precise size and disposition of forces.

Landscape Type

Coastal.

Description of Landscape and Current Use

The site of the battle was finally identified in 1925 and is easily accessible by road and footpath along the shoreline. The shore itself is now an area of low-lying salt marsh cut by small runnels (Plate 12). Inland it is flat, dry and featureless. The causeway to Northey Island is flooded at high tide. Access is either by road running through South House Farm to Northey Island via the causeway or by the footpath from the town of Maldon along the top of the flood defence bank on the south side of the river. The small extent of the battlefield and the open nature of the terrain make visibility very easy.

The landscape has changed significantly since the date of the battle (Petty and Petty, 1993, 159–69). In particular, the sea level has risen by up to 2m: what is now salt marsh would then have been solid dry ground, Northey Island would have been higher and larger and the channel only half as wide. Features added since the tenth century include gravel roads, South House Farm and its buildings, modern field boundaries marked by fences, the flood defence bank along the riverside (dated 1822) and ponds for farm animal use.

The land today is used for agriculture, nature preservation and tourism. Northey Island is a National Trust bird sanctuary and the National Trust also controls the land on which the battle was fought. The battlefield is included in the English Heritage *Register of Historic Battlefields* and it is included in the Coastal Protection Belt. Northey Island is a Special Landscape Area and, together with the salt marshes, a Site of Special Scientific Interest.

Description of the Battle

The Battle of Maldon (AD 991) is the earliest event in English history to which the term 'battle' can be applied and of which the location is securely known. We know of the battle from a large fragment of Anglo-Saxon poetry that has survived, along with entries in various contemporary and near-contemporary chronicles.

The story of the event is simple: a band of Vikings landed on the Essex coast, and were met by armed men drawn from the surrounding region. The Saxons drew up on the shoreline before the Vikings crossed from Northey Island where their ships lay. After an exchange of bravado speeches (conveniently recorded for posterity), there was a tough fight in which the heroic leader of the Anglo-Saxons was killed. The Vikings were victorious but, due to heavy losses, unable to exploit their victory beyond the demand of payment, after receiving which they went home. The site of this action as described in the various literary references was finally identified in 1925 and is generally regarded as the correct spot (Cooper, 1993; Swagg, 1981).

Today's wet and marshy landscape has led writers to include in accounts of the battle a withdrawal by the Saxon army to dry ground to allow the Vikings to form in battle array (Guest and Guest, 1996, 8–11; Smurthwaite, 1993, 43–5). Since the sea level has risen significantly since the tenth century and the ground at that time would have been firm and dry (Petty and Petty, 1993, 159–69), it follows there would have been no need to withdraw to dryer ground, and it is possible that the battle was no more than a bloody brawl fought right at the water's edge.

Battlefield Architecture

The battlefield itself is featureless, the land surface flat. The sea is clearly nearby and is in itself a significant feature since the incoming tide covers the causeway to Northey Island, which lies approximately 250m from the mainland shoreline. These were the features exploited by the battlefield action: an unencumbered flat surface on which to array armies, and a protected landfall – in the lee of the island – to harbour ships. The causeway appears to have played no part, since its restricted width would have hampered deployment.

No use was made of existing landscape features to provide cover, to impede visibility or to impede enemy movement, unless fighting took place right at the water's edge, which is (as indicated above) a possibility.

Formations present appear to have been relatively structured and well ordered, although a more disorganised 'swarming' of the enemy by both sides is also possible.

Rules of War

There appears to have been a ritualised form for ascertaining a mutual agreement to fight: if in fact not, the Danes could have stayed on their ships and attempted a landing elsewhere, or the English withdrawn to allow the Danes to land. Since neither of these happened, both sides must have been ready for a battle.

If battle was mutually agreed by formal procedures, then it follows they each saw the other as a legitimate opponent worthy of battle.

The level of violence applied appears to have been relatively high on both sides, indicating either marked mutual hostility or a 'warrior' code.

Participants were Danish and Anglo-Saxon warriors only: although only the local *fyrd* was called out, these would have been trained, if not very experienced, fighters rather than a group of armed civilians.

Functional Aspects

The use by both sides of open ground on which to deploy will have aided their style of fighting. The choice by the Anglo-Saxons to fight on the beach rather than inland may have saved much destruction. The Danes chose a good place to beach their ships, allowing a successful withdrawal to the sea after the battle.

Dysfunctional Aspects

There was use of extreme violence on both sides. Neither side used landscape features to gain advantage. Battle was essentially a deadly slugging match.

Marking of Battlefield and Interpretation

There was no attempt to mark the site of the battle at the time it was fought: but the poem concerning it marks it as an event seen as significant.

A plaque on the farm gate adjacent to the National Trust car park marks the site itself. It comprises part of the Maldon Millennium Walk and is celebrated in the Maeldune millennium tapestry in the Heritage Centre in the town. In addition, various leaflets from the Heritage Centre, museum and tourist information office provide information on the battle. The battlefield is included in the English Heritage *Register of Historic Battlefields*.

Table 3.10 *Maldon*

Rules of War	Battlefield Architecture
Agreement to fight: Y	Features present:
	Sea
	Island and causeway
Mutual recognition as 'legitimate' enemies: Y	Dry flat land
	Type of feature used:
	Flat land to fight
Level of violence: High	Island/sea for ships and landing
	Type of feature not used:
Marking of battle site:	Causeway (impede deployment)
Nothing on day.	Use of terrain:
Anglo-Saxon poem records the event, although inaccurately.	as cover: N

Now marked by plaque, and guide to visitors.

Participants:
Anglo-Saxon and Danish warriors.

to impede visibility: N
to impede movement: N
Structured formations: Y

Functional Aspects

The use by both sides of open ground on which to deploy will have aided their style of fighting. The choice by the Anglo-Saxons to fight on the beach rather than inland may have saved much destruction. The Danes chose a good place to beach their ships, allowing a successful withdrawal to the sea after the battle.

Dysfunctional Aspects

Extreme violence on both sides. No use of features to gain advantage. Essentially a deadly slugging match.

NASEBY, AD 1645

Location

English National Grid reference SP 685804

2km north of Naseby village, Northamptonshire, centred on Broadmoor Farm (SP 679804).

Extent

2km × 1km.

Landscape Type

Rolling hills.

Description of Landscape and Current Use

The modern main A14 road cuts east–west through the space of the battle-field approximately 500m north of Naseby village, where the Parliament-arian baggage train was located. The road from Naseby to Sibbertoft (SP 680825) runs south–north through the battlefield space, providing good access to the centre of the space: no other access is possible by public right of way.

The battlefield lies in the shallow valley between Fenny Hill to the south and Dust Hill to the north. It is open arable land, comprising several fields enclosed by hedges and fences (Plate 13). A small stream runs west–east through the centre. Visibility across the valley from the slope of Fenny Hill is good, giving a fine impression of the landscape. An old hedgerow boundary at approximately SP 685804 may be the location of the 'Selby Hedges' along which Parlia-mentarian dragoons were aligned to fire upon Royalist cavalry.

A monument and descriptive plinth stand off the Naseby–Sibbertoft road (at SP 685799), marking the front of the Parliamentarian position, with another celebrating Cromwell's victory north-east of Naseby village (at SP 694784).

Description of the Battle

The main Parliamentarian and Royalist armies confronted each other on opposite sides of the shallow valley, the Parliamentarians to the south, the Royalists to the north. The Royalists opened the battle with a cavalry attack on the Parliamentarian left (western) flank. Although Parliamentarian musketeers had been hidden behind the hedge on the western side of the battlefield – and were thus able to fire into the flank of the attacking cavalry – the attack was successful, the Parliamentarian cavalry broke and ran, and the Royalists were able to attack the Parliamentarian baggage train near Naseby village. The infantry of both sides then engaged in the centre, where the well-trained Parliamentarian forces gained the upper hand. On returning to the battle, the Royalist cavalry found their army at a serious disadvantage and withdrew, leaving the infantry to their fate.

This battle was the first to test the 'New Model' army raised by Cromwell and settled the Civil War (Burton *et al.*, 2002; Foard, 1995; Wedgwood, 1966, 422–8; Woolrych, 1966, 112–38).

Battlefield Architecture

Rising ground to either side of the valley was used to form troops and position artillery prior to the engagement, and as a point from which to view the initial position of the enemy. The stream appears not to have provided an obstacle to either infantry or cavalry. The Naseby–Sibbertoft road seems to have played no part in the battle itself, except as the means by which forces were brought to the location. The few hedgerows then existing were used by the Parliamentarians to position troops behind, but otherwise units formed in an open landscape with few features.

Rules of War

There was clear mutual agreement to fight since both armies were fully formed prior to engagement, and this, together with the history of the Civil War to that point, indicates that each side recognised the other as a valid opponent. The level of violence on both sides was quite high, possibly a product of growing professionalism among the experienced troops, or growing animosity as the conflict continued, or both. Both sides formed in the tightly structured formations typical of the period.

Functional Aspects

The use of the hedge as a place to position Parliamentarian troops on the flank of an attacking enemy indicates an innovative approach to battlefield planning. The highly trained 'New Model' army, in particular, had adopted new techniques and organisational structures that had proved highly successful in wars on the European continent.

Dysfunctional Aspects

High ground was used by both sides only to form and as a site from which to view the enemy: neither side used slopes, any buildings or other features as defensive positions or to impede enemy movement.

Marking of Battlefield and Interpretation

There was no marking of the battlefield on the day.

Nineteenth-century monuments and modern descriptive plinths stand on the battlefield (at SP 685799) and nearer Naseby (at SP 694784).

Table 3.11   *Naseby*

Rules of War	Battlefield Architecture

Agreement to fight: Y	Features present:
	    Rising ground
	    Stream
	    Hedges (DMV)*
	    Road

Mutual recognition as 'legitimate' enemies: Y	Type of feature used:
	    Rising ground (visibility)
	    Hedges (concealment of forces)
	    Roads (movement)

Level of violence: High	Type of feature not used:
	    Rising ground (impede
	    movement)
	    Stream

74

Marking of battle site:
None on day.
Later monuments to battle.

Participants: .
Volunteer soldiers raised by Parliament and King
Some professionals present: otherwise experienced but
unprofessional soldiers.

Use of terrain:
    as cover: N
    to impede visibility: N
    to impede movement: N
Structured formations: Y

Functional Aspects

Use of hedges (actually deserted village site) by one side only to conceal musketeers able to fire on flank of advancing enemy cavalry.

Dysfunctional Aspects

Use of high ground only to see prospective battle site. No large-scale advantage taken of available cover or obstacles. Both sides abandon positions on high ground to engage enemy.

* DMV – Deserted Medieval Village.

NORTHAMPTON, AD 1460

Location

English National Grid reference SP 764592
Immediately south of the River Nene at Northampton, adjacent to the buildings of Delapre House on the municipal Delapre Golf Centre.

Extent

1km × 500m.

Landscape Type

River floodplain.

Description of Landscape and Current Use

Access to the battlefield is good by footpath from the centre of Northampton.

The battlefield stands in a rough triangle of land contained within the lines of the river running west–east along the northern side, the main A508 on the western side and the main A45 road to the east and south. Most of this area is in use as the Delapre Golf Centre, owned by Northampton City Council (Plate 14).

In the approximate centre of the triangle (at SP 760593) is the house and garden of the former Delapre Abbey (Plate 30). Due south of this, running north–south, is the linear wood known as The Rookery, and at the extreme southern edge of the triangle, providing a visual barrier from the A45 and its junction with the A508, is the high wooded ground of Delapre Wood. The northern extent immediately south of the river – and at one time thought to be the battlefield itself – is marked by the line of a disused railway and a derelict area of industrial development containing ruined factory buildings.

The landscape is flat and low lying, containing relatively little except for features associated with the golf course and the riding course immediately north of it. The medieval core of the convent at Delapre Abbey is now disguised by later additions. Work by Glenn Foard of Northamptonshire County Council has revealed the presence of remains of the 'Battel Dike' as a below-ground feature. Delapre Wood (at SP 754582) contains an Eleanor Cross from which one of the participants was able to watch the battle. West of The Rookery the parkland of Delapre House is preserved, together with ridge and furrow to the east of Delapre House (at SP 762591).

Description of the Battle

During one of the cycles of armed dispute making up the so-called Wars of the Roses in fifteenth-century England, King Henry VI encamped his army on the southern side of Northampton by the River Nene behind prepared entrenchments. On the hills to the south lay the rebel army of the Earl of Warwick.

Negotiations during the heavy rain overnight led to nothing and in the morning Warwick's troops advanced down the hill towards the earthworks. Because of the rain, the entrenchments built in the floodplain were inundated as the river overran its banks and the gunpowder for the cannon became too wet to use. In addition, one of the lords notionally on the King's side had in fact gone over to the rebels. As Warwick's men were helped over the parapet, the King's loyal troops fled towards the town. Behind them lay the swollen river with a single bridge. Thousands were drowned as they tried to cross (Brooke, 1854, 39–52; Kendall, 1972b, 54–65).

Battlefield Architecture

The high ground of Delapre Wood provided a good space for Warwick's army to camp and form prior to the attack. The river floodplain provided low ground on which entrenchments could be constructed, although the liability to flooding (as events showed) was high. Both sides adopted the standard fighting formations of the time. Although the river was adjacent no attempt was made to use it or the city defences as obstacles to an enemy. Similarly, although battlefield casualties were tended by the nuns of Delapre Abbey after the event, no attempt was made to use the buildings as part of a defensive strategy.

Rules of War

Although negotiations were in train, there was clearly also an intent to fight, as indicated by the construction of earthwork defences and the advance to the attack. This in turn clearly indicates that each side – composed of hired soldiers – saw the other as a 'legitimate' enemy, in possible contrast to a more modern and more tightly drawn distinction between categories of combatants. The level of violence was low, due to the result being achieved by treason rather than by force of arms, although many died in attempts to ford the swollen river.

Functional Aspects

In the absence of using city defences, the construction of an earthwork entrenchment provided valuable defensive strength. Both sides saw negotiation as a viable alternative to actual battle; and when this failed, treason on one side delivered a clear result without high levels of violence.

Dysfunctional Aspects

The Royalist engineers failed to take into account the problems of construction in a floodplain: flooding rendered both the earthworks and the cannon useless. Neither side made any use of higher ground available nearby except for visibility, and neither side sought to use the river or the city as a source of defence. Negotiations were undone by a premature assault. There was no attempt by the Royalists to secure the river crossings or to provide alternative lines of retreat, resulting in heavy losses to the river.

Marking of Battlefield and Interpretation

The 'Battel Dike' remained a feature of note until enclosure. The battlefield is included in the English Heritage *Register of Historic Battlefields*.

Table 3.12   *Northampton*

Rules of War	Battlefield Architecture
Agreement to fight: Y	Features present:
	City of Northampton
	River
	Built defences
	Rising ground
	Floodplain
	Nunnery
Mutual recognition as 'legitimate' enemies: Y	Type of feature used:
	Built defences
	(Nunnery for casualties)
Level of violence: Low	
But heavy casualties caused in panicked retreat into swollen river.	Type of feature not used:
	Nunnery (defence)
	River (obstacle)
	Rising ground
	City (defence, support)
Marking of battle site:	Use of terrain:
'Battel Dike' a local landmark until eighteenth century.	as cover: N
	to impede visibility: N
	to impede movement: N
Participants:	Structured formations: Y
Professional soldiers raised by competing nobles.	

Functional Aspects

Built defences for Royalist army. Preparedness to negotiate and treason within Royalist camp result in low level of violence.

Dysfunctional Aspects

No concern with state of ground: rising water floods defences, renders artillery useless. No use by either side of higher ground except for visibility. No use of city as a source of support or for defence. Negotiation undone by premature (treasonous?) attack: possible assistance from within defences. No attempt by Royalists to secure bridges as retreat: no attempt to provide lines of retreat avoiding swollen river, leading to high casualties.

OUDENAARDE, AD 1708

Location

Michelin map 51, 7SE. Lat. 50°60′N, Long. 3°37′E
Approximately 2km north-west of the town of Oudenaarde, Belgium, to the east of the main N459 road.

Extent

3km × 1km.

Landscape Type

Shallow valley.

Description of Landscape and Current Use

Access to the battlefield is good by the main N459 road north-west from Oudenaarde and side roads at Breween Farm.

The site is an open, shallow valley running roughly east–west rising to ridges to north and south and approximately 1km across (Plate 15). The southern ridge is low and gentle: along its foot runs the narrow and shallow Diepenbeek brook. Beyond, approximately 2km distant, is the town of Oudenaarde: the spire of its church can be seen from the valley. The ridge to the north is higher and slightly steeper but presents no difficulty.

A minor road runs along the floor of the valley with parallel roads below the crests of the northern and southern ridges: other roads run between them, providing good access to all parts of the valley which is dotted with small settlements and arable farms. On the northern ridge stands Royegem Farm and its apple orchard, dating from the late seventeenth or early eighteenth century: it was most likely present during the fighting. Beside the N459 on the southern side at Breween Farm stands a low earth mound, square in plan, marking the site of a former castle used by the British commander as his headquarters (Plate 29).

Description of the Battle

During the War of the Spanish Succession, Anglo-Dutch and Imperial forces sought to drive the French out of the fortresses of the Spanish Netherlands. In a campaign of manoeuvre, advance units of the Anglo-Dutch-Imperial army encountered forward units of the French main army north of the River Scheldt at Oudenaarde. Attacking so as to pin the French in position, and employing other forces to secure the crossing of the Scheldt to their rear, the allies sought to bring their scattered units into action in order to bring on a full-scale battle and destroy the French as an effective fighting force.

Hurrying their scattered forces to the site, both sides brought units into action as they arrived, each attempting to outflank the other to the east and being blocked by the arrival of new units. The French formed along the slope of the northern ridge, occupying the farm at Royegem. The allies took up position along the east–west Diepenbeek brook. Tough fighting during the afternoon and into the evening brought the allies some but not overwhelming advantage, even though the axis of the fighting shifted from east–west to almost north–south as the French right wing wheeled eastwards during the course of the day. Finally, a long flank march through Oudenaarde by units of the Anglo-Dutch-Imperial army caught the French in flank and rear, causing them to retreat. Although many of the French were able to escape through gaps in the surrounding army, the victory was sufficient to cause a large number of key fortresses to fall into Anglo-Dutch-Imperial hands (Barnett, 1974, 203–12; Churchill, 1967b, 333–56; Trevelyan, 1965, 376–89; Weigley, 1991, 92–6).

Battlefield Architecture

The open and featureless space of the battlefield provided clear ground upon which to deploy infantry of both sides in the long thin lines flanked by cavalry conventional for the time. The Diepenbeek brook was a convenient line for the allies along which to do so, although it presented very little in the way of an obstacle to an attacker. The ridge along which the French formed provided convenient high ground for observation – especially at Royegem, which was roughly in the centre of the line – but was insufficiently steep to provide an obstacle to advance or a particularly strong defensive position. Similarly, the castle mound at Breween provided a convenient observation post for the allied commander but not a defensible strong point. Farms were occupied but not fortified: untypically for the period, this was throughout a battle of manoeuvre rather than of fixed positions.

Rules of War

The allies deliberately sought to bring the French to battle, and once contact was made the French complied, clearly indicating they saw each other as 'legitimate' enemies. The level of violence was high due to the employment on both sides of professional soldiers who had been fighting each other for a considerable time.

Functional Aspects

The allies were able to pin the French in position and force battle, and there was an appropriate use of forces by both sides. The choice of ground allowed conventional deployment by both sides. The allied decision to secure the river crossings allowed the final flank march to achieve victory, and good strategic use was made of the victory once achieved.

Dysfunctional Aspects

Neither side considered any alternative to battle: manoeuvre alone may have placed the French in the same disadvantage, and the French could have withheld forces from the fighting once it had started. Neither side showed any particular imagination in its deployment, although the manner in which troops were brought into action was especially skilful upon the allied side. The level of violence was high for a battle fought over unfortified ground. The allied failure to prevent the escape of French forces and to follow up their retreat ensured these troops were available in future actions.

Marking of Battlefield and Interpretation

The battlefield is not marked or commemorated in any way.

Table 3.13   *Oudenaarde*

Rules of War

Agreement to fight: Y

Mutual recognition as 'legitimate' enemies: Y

Level of violence: High

Marking of battle site:
None.

Participants:
Experienced professional soldiers of the British, Dutch, Imperial and French armies.

Battlefield Architecture

Features present:
    Rise of ground
    Diepenbeek brook
    Farmsteads
    Castle mound
Type of feature used:
    Rise of ground
    Diepenbeek brook
    Farmsteads
    Castle mound
Type of feature not used: None
Use of terrain:
    as cover: N
    to impede visibility: N
    to impede movement: Y
Structured formations: Y

Functional Aspects
An appropriate use of available forces by both sides. Decision of the allies to secure the river crossings allowed final flank march. Choice of terrain allowed deployment in the conventional manner. Good use by allies of victory.

Dysfunctional Aspects
No attempt by either side to find an alternative to battle. Conventional deployment and use of forces. High level of violence. Failure to prevent French escape or to follow up French retreat.

ROLIÇA, AD 1808

Location

On the heights above Roliça and Columbeira villages, 6km south of Obidos, Leiria, Portugal.

Extent

1km × 3km.

Landscape Type

Mountainous.

Description of Landscape and Current Use

Access to the hilltop battle site is good by road and footpath from Roliça, which in turn can be reached easily by road from Obidos. Obidos is easily accessible by train from Lisbon.

The medieval walled town of Obidos stands at the northern end of a natural bowl surrounded by high hills on the east, west and southern sides. From the southern end of Obidos is a good view of the line of hills 6km away where the battle was fought: the villages of Roliça in the centre of the bowl and Columbeira (Plate 38) at the foot of the hills can also be seen. The ground between Obidos and the hills is broken with high rock outcrops (not un-like those on Dartmoor) in a number of places. The land is used for arable agriculture but modern development is also taking up space, and modern housing now occupies large areas. Maroons fired from Obidos can be clearly heard from the hills above Columbeira, indicating the acoustic quality of the area: the sounds of battle would have been clearly audible from the town.

The hills on the southern edge are very steep and high with flat summits (Plate 16). Their slopes are rocky and overgrown, and access is difficult, although there are a few footpaths (mostly used by tourists interested in the flora and fauna of the area). A modern road from Roliça through Columbeira and thence up a narrow gorge via the back of the hills also provides access to the main area of the battlefield and the monuments. The monuments to the battle and Lake's tomb are signposted, with access by dirt road. Work is at present being undertaken at the highest point to construct a reservoir to provide water to the local population, and also a caravan, camping and car park for nature tourists. This is part of a wider plan to turn the entire site over to a Nature Park.

Description of the Battle

In the earliest stages of the Peninsular War the French made an effort to drive the British army out of Portugal by landing on the coast and marching inland, taking up a position in the broken country just north of Roliça. Threatened with being outflanked by a superior British force and by British occupation of the high ground to the east and west, the French retreated south and took up a new position on the tops of the hills above Columbeira.

While a British force attacked their front, seeking to find a way up the steep slopes against heavy French fire, other forces sought to move to outflank and attack the French from the rear. Drawn into a narrow gorge in the belief that they were penetrating the French positions – the same gorge the road now takes from Columbeira to the summit – part of the British army led by Colonel Lake found itself below and behind French positions and cut off from support. Fighting hard, they climbed to the top of the hill but took heavy losses, including that of their commander. In response, a general British attack was launched against the whole French line. Ultimately outnumbered and with British units finding access routes to the summit, the French withdrew in good order. Due to the nearby presence of a superior French force threatening British positions, the outcome of the battle was indecisive (Oman, 1902b, 236–41; Parkinson, 1973, 30–2; Weller, 1962, 34–41).

Battlefield Architecture

The broken nature of the valley floor provided ground for the French on which to form and impeded access by the advancing British. However, by not occupying the high ground to east and west the French opened themselves to the possibility of an outflanking movement. Withdrawal to the high ground above Columbeira provided a site of good visibility and a strong defensive position. No attempt was made by either side to fortify the villages as strong points nor to attempt to block access by road. The battle was throughout one of manoeuvre in the standard formations of column and line.

Rules of War

Clearly both sides intended to fight and this strongly suggests they saw each other as 'legitimate' enemies. Although the professional and experienced soldiers of both sides fought with determination, the level of violence remained medium rather than high: the animosity that would grow over the period of the war was not yet evident.

Functional Aspects

The French made good use of the broken terrain of the valley and the summits of the hills to impede access by the superior British. Both sides fought with courage and determination.

Dysfunctional Aspects

Both sides failed adequately to reconnoitre the positions taken up, the French thus leaving themselves open to the threat of a flanking movement by the superior British force, and the British to being led into traps in the hills above Columbeira. Neither side fortified or even occupied the stone-built villages which would have made suitable strong points. The British were unable to make any strategic use of the victory nor could they pursue the retreating French effectively.

Marking of Battlefield and Interpretation

A ceramic monument depicting the battle stands in the centre of Roliça village at a point from where the hills marking the second French position can be clearly seen. The street names of both Roliça and Columbeira villages (e.g. 'Rue des Anglais') recall the event.

The site of the death and burial of Colonel Lake is marked by a stone monument on the top of the hill his men attacked. The monument was raised in the late nineteenth century by the British regiments involved in that part of the action (Plate 49).

The top of the highest hill is now used as a viewpoint for the surrounding area. Plans to turn the region into a Nature Park will de-emphasise its history in favour of its natural beauty, although it is likely that the fact that a historically significant battle was fought there has contributed to its appeal. (The battle did not involve Portuguese troops and therefore may be less significant to the local population than to British visitors. Compare with other battlefields of Iberia: Aljubarrota, Elviña/Corunna, Sorauren.)

Table 3.14   *Roliça*

Rules of War	**Battlefield Architecture**
Agreement to fight: Y	Features present:
	Hills
	Valley floor
Mutual recognition as 'legitimate' enemies: Y	Villages and buildings
	Type of feature used:
	Hills
Level of violence: Medium	Valley floor
	Type of feature not used:
Marking of battle site:	Villages and buildings
Monument to Colonel Lake. Ceramic monument in Roliça.	Use of terrain:
Hill-top development.	as cover: Y
	to impede visibility: N
Participants:	to impede movement: Y
Professional soldiers of the British and French armies.	Structured formations: Y

Functional Aspects

Good use made by French of broken valley terrain and hills to impede British advance. Both sides fought with determination.

Dysfunctional Aspects

Failure by both sides to reconnoitre positions. No fortification of villages or blocking of access routes to French positions. British failure to follow up victory.

ROUNDWAY DOWN, AD 1643

Location

English National Grid reference ST 029649

From the foot of the north-eastern scarp face of Roundway Hill (at ST 029649) 4.5km north-east of Devizes, Wiltshire, England, up and over the scarp, along the crest of the hill and down the scarp below Oliver's Castle (at ST 001645). The battlefield is bounded 1km to the east by the main A361 road between Devizes and Avebury and 1km to the north by the old main Bath road, now reduced to a side road and footpath.

Extent

500m × 3km.

Landscape Type

Chalk downland.

Description of Landscape and Current Use

Access to the battlefield is good by road and footpath north from Devizes.

The valley of the battlefield is bounded by hills: to the west and south, Roundway Hill; to the north King's Play Hill 1.5km away; and to the north-east some 2km away, Morgan's Hill. Although fought at some 180m OD, the battlefield appears to be low lying because of the rise of the hills around to heights above 230m (Plate 17).

Roundway Hill (242m) offers a steep southern slope above the village of Roundway, 2km north of Devizes. The slope to the north, down towards the old Bath road which runs at the foot of King's Play Hill, is much shallower. The gentle east-facing upward slope of the top of the hill is truncated sharply by the escarpment immediately above where the two armies formed and fought. The top of the hill appears flat when upon it, but the incline is clearly visible from along the old Bath road. The steep southern slope turns northward immediately above Roundway village, where it is now covered in trees. Oliver's Castle (198m) is a well-preserved Iron Age promontory fort on a south-west-facing spur providing excellent views west and south. The steep slope continues north from here to Beacon Hill (198m), continues along the north side of that hill and forms the steeper northern slope of King's Play Hill (232m). Becoming shallower, it continues further to become the northern slope of Morgan's Hill (260m). The battlefield itself, therefore, lies in a shallow bowl of relatively high ground, surrounded by higher ground in all directions.

The area is one rich in archaeological features: these include Oliver's Castle, barrows upon the summits and slopes of Roundway Hill, King's Play Hill and Morgan's Hill, and the Wansdyke, which runs across the main A361 below Morgan's Hill to rise over the crest of that hill.

The scarp slope below Oliver's Castle where the Parliamentary cavalry crashed to disaster (known as 'Bloody Ditch') is extremely steep and presents itself suddenly even to walkers (Plate 31). The ground before it along the crest of Roundway Hill is relatively flat and easy to traverse. There are many rights of way across Roundway Hill and towards King's Play and Morgan's Hills, together with the A361 and old Bath roads to east and north respectively of the battlefield, but no access to the site of the battle itself. The highest point of Roundway Hill – immediately above the point where the two armies clashed – is closed to access, but good views of the battlefield can be had from the line of the old Bath road below King's Play Hill, and from along the A361. Oliver's Castle is accessible, from which the steepness of the Bloody Ditch (Plate 31) can be well appreciated.

The land is predominately used for arable agriculture with some sheep and cattle grazing. An area of preserved downland under a conservation management scheme lies on the south-eastern slope of Roundway Hill, giving an impression of the type of land use on the day of the battle.

Description of the Battle

During the English Civil War, a mixed-force Parliamentarian army had forced a Royalist army composed of infantry only, to retreat into the town of Devizes where they were besieged. Royalist cavalry supported by artillery rushed to the aid of Devizes' defenders but the superior Parliamentarian force came out to meet them.

The Royalist commanders sent messages to Devizes to warn the besieged infantry of their coming and to arrange with them a signal for an infantry attack from the town. When the infantry heard a single gun fire, they were to leave Devizes and attack the western end of Roundway Hill. The cavalry would attack simultaneously at the eastern end, and between them the Parliamentarian force would be defeated. Unfortunately, both messengers sent were captured. Accordingly, the soldiers inside the town did not hear of the plan and their allies outside had no reason to believe that the message had not got through. The cavalry launched their attack, preceding it with the fire of a single cannon. Inside Devizes the Royalist infantry pondered what it meant: not knowing for sure, they called a meeting to discuss what to do.

Meanwhile, the Royalist cavalry – unsupported except by a few small guns – had completely overwhelmed the larger force. So great was the catastrophe that the defeated cavalry fled in terror directly away from the Royalists, falling ultimately into the Bloody Ditch below Oliver's Castle hillfort. By this time the infantry in Devizes had at last come out and together with the victorious cavalry they closed in on the enemy infantry. Overwhelmed by a united force of all arms, the Parliamentary infantry fled or were captured or killed (Colman and Coupe, n.d.; Wedgwood, 1966, 214–16; Woolrych, 1966, 43).

Battlefield Architecture

The landscape of the battle features both high and low ground, the earthworks of Oliver's Castle, the earthen barrow mounds on the high ground, and roads that cross-cut the terrain. Apart from roads, however, none of these features was used by either side except by accident. The Parliamentarians formed at the foot of the slope of Roundway Hill, and traversed the top of it only in retreat. No use was made of other features for observation, defence or as obstacles. Both sides formed in standard lines of cavalry and infantry with supporting artillery.

Rules of War

Both sides showed a clear determination to fight, which strongly implies that they each saw the other as a 'legitimate' enemy. The level of violence was high, partly due to the presence of experienced troops on both sides and the experience such troops had of earlier campaigns and battles against each other.

Functional Aspects

Effective use of the forces available was made by both sides. The attempt by the Royalists to combine attacks from within and without the town, although thwarted, shows a good understanding of the military situation.

Dysfunctional Aspects

Neither side sought any alternative to battle, and fighting when it came was fierce. There was no attempt by either side to use terrain to advantage, by occupying high ground or fortifying already strong positions such as Oliver's Castle. Instead, battle was sought on open ground at the foot of slopes.

Marking of Battlefield and Interpretation

The entire battlefield lies within the North Wessex Downs area of Outstanding Natural Beauty and the preserved downland is an area of High Ecological Value. The whole area is one of High Archaeological Potential, and both King's Play Hill and Roundway Down are Sites of Special Scientific Interest. The battlefield is included in the English Heritage *Register of Historic Battlefields*.

Table 3.15   *Roundway Down*

Rules of War	Battlefield Architecture
Agreement to fight: Y	Features present:
	Barrows
	Hillfort
	High ground
	Roads

Mutual recognition as 'legitimate' enemies: Y

Level of violence: High

Marking of battle site:
None.

Participants:
Volunteer soldiers raised by Parliament and King.
Some professionals present; otherwise experienced but
unprofessional soldiers.

Type of feature used: Roads
Type of feature not used:
    Barrows
    Hillfort
    High ground
Use of terrain:
    as cover: N
    to impede visibility: N
    to impede movement: N
Structured formations: Y

Functional Aspects

Effective use of arms by both sides. Good appreciation of military situation by Royalists, leading to
development of a plan to envelop the Parliamentary forces.

Dysfunctional Aspects

No attempt to find an alternative to battle. High level of violence. Battle fought on open ground with few
features. Failure to exploit either high ground or the defensible position and possible suitability for artillery of
Oliver's Castle hillfort.

SEDGEMOOR, AD 1685

Location

English National Grid reference ST 352357
Immediately north of the village of Westonzoyland, Somerset, England, which
lies in the Somerset Levels 5km south-east of Bridgwater along the main A372
road.

Extent

1km × 2km.

Landscape Type

Flat wetland.

Description of Landscape and Current Use

Access to the battlefield is good by footpath from either Westonzoyland or
Chedzoy.

   The ground is flat and relatively featureless (Plate 20), except for built
watercourses and settlements. To the north-east, the line of the Polden Hills
(3km distant) dominates the landscape. Entirely used for arable farming, there

is a good impression of the shape of the ground on the day, although the Bussex Rhine is no longer present, having been replaced in the eighteenth century by a straighter drain. The villages of Westonzoyland and Chedzoy are both small and contain few buildings present in the seventeenth century, but both retain their medieval churches, in which the battle is marked and commemorated.

Description of the Battle

Officially at least, Sedgemoor is the last battle on English soil and the decisive moment of Monmouth's rebellion against his uncle King James II in 1685. Monmouth landed near Bridgwater and raised troops in the West Country of England, especially from Cornwall and the Bridgwater area. In response, an army was sent from London to capture and detain him.

The royal force of professional soldiers camped immediately south of the drain called the Bussex Rhine in the Somerset Levels, outside the village of Westonzoyland. The rebels conceived the daring plan to launch a night attack which would catch the professional soldiers at a disadvantage. Overnight, they crept through the low-lying landscape aiming for one of two crossing places, called 'plungeons', across the Rhine. They lost their way and missed both. Instead, they approached the deepest part of the drain, where they were spotted by a Royalist sentry and fired upon. In panic, instead of retiring into the dark and trying again, they engaged in musket volleys across the water. Against trained and experienced professionals in linear formations they stood little chance. Eventually, they broke and ran, heading into the Moor Drove, another waterway that cuts across the landscape of the Levels, 2km north of Westonzoyland and 1km south of Chedzoy, in the area of Fowler's Plot Farm (ST 338365). Caught by Royalist cavalry, they fought and died or were taken as prisoners. Later, they would be hanged or transported to distant places as slave labourers (Chandler, 1995; Churchill, 1967a, 182–91).

Battlefield Architecture

The only features used in the battle were the waterways and drainage ditches of the area. The rebels chose to ignore the dangers of all obstacles in seeking to cross the Bussex Rhine, while the Royalists used the Bussex Rhine as cover for their front. The featureless nature of the landscape, especially at night, contributed to the rebels' loss of their route: many of them stumbled into the

Moor Drove. Neither side sought to exploit the defensive capacities of buildings or villages, nor to occupy the higher ground to the north-east.

Rules of War

By occupying a position behind the Bussex Rhine, the Royalists indicated their willingness to fight, even though the assault itself caught them unawares. The rebels, in their turn, deliberately sought battle. Accordingly, each saw the other as a 'legitimate' enemy. The level of violence was not particularly high: as possibly at Linton, there may have been some unwillingness on the part of the rebels to inflict really serious harm to representatives of the ruling authority and both sides may have been unwilling to inflict heavy casualties on their fellow English.

Functional Aspects

The planned use of a night attack by the rebels indicates a good appreciation of the relative merits of volunteers versus professionals. The Royalist choice of a position behind the Bussex Rhine demonstrated an appreciation of the effectiveness of water obstacles to attackers, and throughout, the Royalists demonstrated effective command and control.

Dysfunctional Aspects

There was a marked failure by both sides to reconnoitre the ground: the Royalists were unaware of rebel presence in the area, while the rebels lost their way during the night attack. The rebel systems of command and control were inadequate to the task of a night assault, while the Royalists were unprepared for the threat of a night attack. Neither side prepared lines of retreat nor ensured knowledge of the dangers in the terrain of the battlefield (especially the presence of watercourses and ditches).

Marking of Battlefield and Interpretation

The site of the battlefield is marked by a descriptive plinth located immediately over the line of the Bussex Rhine. Beyond is a small field devoted to memorials to the dead of Sedgemoor and the local dead of later wars, especially those of locally raised regiments in the British army (Plate 50).

Chedzoy is the start of the 'Pitchfork Rebellion Trail' celebrating the events of 1685. Westonzoyland church contains a replica of the contemporary letter describing the battle, together with maps and plans of the action.

The ground between the battlefield and Chedzoy is recognised as an Area of High Archaeological Potential, and part of the battlefield lies within a Special Landscape Area. The battlefield is included in the English Heritage *Register of Historic Battlefields*.

Table 3.16   *Sedgemoor*

Rules of War

Agreement to fight: Y

Mutual recognition as 'legitimate' enemies: Y

Level of violence: Medium

Marking of battle site:
Monuments to the dead of the battle and later wars on the battlefield.
Descriptive plinth.
Memorials to the rebel dead in local churches.
Inn sign in Westonzoyland.

Participants:
Volunteer rebels from locality; professional English soldiers of Crown.

Battlefield Architecture

Features present:
  Droves
  Rhines
  Villages (buildings)
  High ground
  Roads
Type of feature used: Bussex Rhine as obstacle
Type of feature not used:
  Droves, rhines as obstacles by rebels
  High ground for movement/defence
  Roads for movement
  Villages/buildings for defence
Use of terrain:
  as cover: N
  to impede visibility: N
  to impede movement: Y – by Royalists
Structured formations: Y for Royalists
                       N (?) for rebels

Functional Aspects

Planned surprise night attack by rebels. Use of Bussex Rhine as defensive feature by Royalists. Effective use of arms, good command and control by Royalists.

Dysfunctional Aspects

Failure of both sides to reconnoitre before deployment. Failure of rebels to ensure systems of command and control effective during night assault. Unpreparedness of Royalists for night attack: non-presence of commander. Failure of either side to secure lines of retreat, or to ensure awareness among troops of presence of dangerous terrain.

SORAUREN I AND II, AD 1813

Location

Approximately 6km north of the city of Pampeluna/Iruña, Navarra, Spain. The narrow valley that comprises the main part of the battlefield runs east–west between the rivers Arga and Ulzama, on which stand (respectively) the villages of Zabaldica and Sorauren. Zabaldica lies beside Route 135 and Sorauren beside Route 121 to San Sebastián/Donostia and Bayonne. The *camiño de santiago* (which runs through the Pyrenees towards Pamplona and on to Santiago de Compostela) passes through Zabaldica and then through the hills to the south of the battlefield.

Extent

Approximately 3km × 1km.

Landscape Type

Mountain valley.

Description of Landscape and Current Use

Access to the battlefield is good by road north from Pampeluna to Sorauren or Zabaldica, and then by farm track into the valley of the battle.

The two main roads run north–south along the rivers Arga and Ulzama, which mark respectively the eastern and western extent of the battlefield. The villages of Sorauren and Zabaldica are both small and are composed of stone houses and other structures closely hugging the steep hillslopes to their back. Sorauren to the west is the larger and contains an imposing church: its tall stone walls flank a maze of small alleys (Plate 33). It is contained entirely on the eastern side of the main road north, which lies between it and the river. Zabaldica comprises a scatter of small farmhouses and associated buildings on both sides of the main road north. Both villages have bridges that cross the adjacent river.

Sorauren village marks the junction of the main Ulzama valley with a smaller valley at right angles, over which the battles were fought. This valley is deep, with a fast-flowing stream at the foot of steep slopes to the enclosing ridges to north and south (Plate 21). The ridges are narrow and flat at the top, making them easy to manoeuvre along; the slopes are overgrown and generally rocky, making them difficult to climb. At the eastern end of the valley, immediately above Zabaldica which lies beyond, is a narrow saddle joining the north and south ridges (Plate 26). To the south of the southern terminal of this saddle lies a conical hill on which a regiment of Spanish troops took up position.

From Sorauren, footpaths, roads and tracks run through and over the ground in the valley, making access along the valley to the top of the linking saddle and to the crest on the southern side relatively easy; access to the heavily wooded northern crest is more difficult. Zabaldica is easy to reach by road; access to the battlefield – although possible by footpath across worked fields – is more difficult because of the problem of identifying the route.

The land is currently used – as it was on the dates of battle – for agriculture, especially the growing of corn and the grazing of sheep and goats. It is also now part of a leisure route comprising the *Camiño de Santiago* and routes for walkers through the Pyrenees.

Description of the Battle

The two battles of Sorauren in northern Spain are the two main actions of the series of fights called collectively 'The Battles of the Pyrenees', fought by an Anglo-Portuguese-Spanish army to force their way into metropolitan France at the close of the Napoleonic wars (Chandler, 1989, 327–8; Oman, 1902c, 654–79, 681–706; Weller, 1962, 270–302). Bypassing Pampeluna, which was held by the French, the allies sought a route northwards through the Pyrenees towards San Sebastián. Their movement north was halted by the arrival of a large French army, which had marched south along the main Pampeluna–San Sebastián road (now Route 121). Allied troops occupied a number of positions between the French and Pampeluna, including that at Sorauren.

The main French attacks took the form of solid columns of infantry supported by artillery and cavalry on the relatively flat ground along the riverside, through the villages and across the saddle linking the two main ridges. The allied army responded with musket fire from within buildings and from thin lines of infantry occupying positions between the high ground and the river or on the ridges, also supported by artillery and cavalry. The Spanish regiment on top of the conical hill to the south-east of the battlefield was also attacked strongly. Light infantry of both sides – operating in small groups and firing from cover – moved over the rocky and overgrown slopes of the main ridges and the saddle linking them in an effort to disrupt enemy main formations and artillery batteries. In both battles, fighting was contained between the eastern shore of the Ulzama and the western shore of the Arga, these rivers thus acting as the edges of the battlespace.

The first battle was indecisive, and two days later fighting took place at exactly the same place: this time, the allies were able to send the French troops back in retreat across the border into France (Oman, 1902c, 656–79, 682–700; Parkinson, 1973, 187–9; Weller, 1962, 290–302).

Battlefield Architecture

A classic 'featured' battlespace, the most visible features are the steep slopes of the ridges north and south of the valley which comprise most of the battlefield space. The tops of the ridges provided good places on which to form for offence or defence and on which to position artillery. The steep slopes and the stream at the foot provided considerable obstacles to movement for an attacking force. The stone buildings of the villages provided good protection for troops and difficult obstacles to attackers. The flat ground beside the rivers Ulzama and Arga provided a good space for forming an attack and for forward movement, especially of cavalry.

One of the paths from the top of the southern ridge to Sorauren village is most likely a part of the *camiño des inglés* (Plate 27), constructed to allow passage of the Pyrenees by the allied army without having to pass through major road junctions, which were held by the French.

The two bridges at Sorauren and Zabaldica were not used for any purpose during the battles, although the bridge at Sorauren was the point from which French movement against allied positions was first noticed.

The 'pilgrim chapel' on the lower slopes of the ally-held southern ridge, which was used as the allied headquarters, is no longer evident. A small fountain, however, can be found here and it is more likely this was a small wayside shrine rather than anything larger. Excavation on the spot might ascertain this more clearly.

The French would have formed in columns of infantry – a relatively deep formation with up to ten or fifteen solders in a file, but relatively narrow of front. The British, Spanish and Portuguese formed infantry in longer lines only three deep. Before both such formations would have been infantry skirmishers fighting in loosely organised groups of two or three. Cavalry would have formed in lines up to three deep.

Rules of War

The time taken by both sides to form appropriately meant that battle was mutually agreed even though no other formal exchanges took place. This, in turn, meant that both sides saw the other as a 'legitimate' enemy. The level of violence was high – partly as a result of the use of firearms but also because the war had been a long and hard one, and both sides saw the end approaching swiftly as the allies pressed on into France. Participation was limited to regular soldiers of the British, Portuguese, Spanish and French armies.

Functional Aspects

There was good use made of high ground by both sides to establish dominating positions. The French, in particular, made excellent use of the linking saddle between the ridges and of roads through the villages and beside the rivers as lines of attack, facilitating movement. The construction by the allies of the *camiño des inglés* – an alternative route bypassing French control of roads – reduced French control of the countryside. There were effective systems of command and control on both sides, and effective use of appropriate tactical systems.

Dysfunctional Aspects

There was no attempt by the French to outflank British positions by passing on the other side of the rivers Ulzama and Arga, and no manoeuvres by the British to avoid engagement: fierce battle was strongly desired by both sides, even though other means may have been found to achieve tactical and strategic objectives. There was by both sides a willing return to battle after a first indecisive result. The fierceness of fighting effectively denied any chance of strong pursuit by the victorious allies after the second battle.

Marking of Battlefield and Interpretation

The battlefield is not marked as such in any way. Local memory does not make reference to the events of the battles, although a strong local historical consciousness is evidenced by knowledge of the *Camiño de Santiago* and other things. Local museums do not make reference to the battles nor is there any monument to the dead or other remembrance.

Sorauren lies in the Basque area of modern Spain while Pampeluna is the former capital of the medieval kingdom of Navarra. Recent attempts to promote a regional identity as distinct from that of Spain – evidenced in particular by monuments to ETA activists and use of the local (Navarrese or Basque rather than Spanish) languages in Pampeluna and the surrounding area – have overwritten other aspects of the region's history. The Spanish Civil War and its legacy are of much more importance to the local communities than the more distant war against Napoleon.

Table 3.17   *Sorauren*

Rules of War	Battlefield Architecture
Agreement to fight: Y	Features present:
	Hillslopes
	Valley
	Rivers
	Villages
	Roads
	camiño des inglés
Mutual recognition as 'legitimate' enemies: Y	Type of feature used:
	Hillslopes
	Valley
	Rivers
	Villages
	Roads
Level of violence: High	*camiño des inglés*
	Type of feature not used: None
Marking of battle site:	Use of terrain:
None.	as cover: Y
	to impede visibility: Y
	to impede movement: Y
Participants:	Structured formations: Y
Professional soldiers of the British, Portuguese, Spanish and French armies.	

Functional Aspects

Use of high ground by both sides to dominate position. Use by French of linking ridge and roads through villages as lines of attack, facilitating movement. Construction by allies of *camiño des inglés* – an alternative route bypassing French control of roads. Effective systems of command and control on both sides, and effective use of appropriate tactical systems.

Dysfunctional Aspects

No attempt by French to outflank British position and no manoeuvres by British to avoid engagement: fierce battle was strongly desired by both sides, even though other means may have been found to achieve tactical and strategic objectives. A return to battle after an indecisive result. Fierceness of fighting effectively denied any chance of strong pursuit by victorious British after second battle.

St Albans I, ad 1455

Location

English National Grid reference TL 150071
In the centre of St Albans, Hertfordshire, north-east of the Abbey, along St Peter's Street and the A1081 and A1057 roads that join it from east and south-east.

Extent

500m × 1km.

Landscape Type

Urban.

Description of Landscape and Current Use

The medieval and modern town of St Albans sits on a ridge about 30m high running south-west–north-east immediately above the River Ver. Across the river on low ground lie the remains of the Roman city of Verulamium, much of which underlies Verulam Park, a local amenity. On the hill above the park to the north-east, the Abbey is clearly visible.

The streets of the modern town lie on roughly the same lines as those in the fifteenth century (Plate 18). The A1081 and A1057 entering from the east and south-east – the route to London – climb the shallow eastern side of the ridge to St Peter's Street, the wide main street and market place of St Albans. Although most buildings postdate the fifteenth-century conflict, there are some survivals, especially at the corner of Sopwell Lane and Hopewell Street (TL 150071). The new shopping, area on the east of St Peter's Street occupies the site of the gardens used by York's attacking forces: the maze of small lanes and passages here give some impression of the ground on the day.

Description of the Battle

The first Battle of St Albans was the first violent encounter of the so-called Wars of the Roses. The authority of the King and his chosen ministers was challenged by other members of the aristocracy. Armies were raised by the King and by his cousin the Duke of York. They came together at St Albans. The King gathered his forces in the centre of the town, where the wide market place was suitable for the mustering of an army. The Duke of York sent emissaries to negotiate with the King, and the King stood his army down while he talked. The King's soldiers took off their armour and went into bars and inns to drink and eat. After waiting for a response that did not come, York launched an attack up the narrow streets towards the centre of town and through gardens at the rear of buildings fronting the market place. Barricades along the line of the old town ditch were thrown down and the defenders retreated towards the town centre. York's soldiers followed and suddenly the attackers entered the centre of town, finding themselves among the King's soldiers, who were not ready to fight. A confused half-hour of slaughter followed, but by then the King was a prisoner, his chief minister was dead, and other great nobles dead, wounded or prisoners. The rest of the royal army had fled. Negotiations led to the King's release and pardons for York and his followers (Kendall, 1972b, 26–8).

Battlefield Architecture

The town itself was fortified by the placing of troops along the line of the city boundary ditch and the construction of barricades at road junctions. Access was achieved by the attacking force by use of existing roads and lanes: where this was blocked, access was gained by using undefended garden spaces at the rear of buildings. No particular use was made of buildings as strong points or of high structures as lookout or defensive posts.

Rules of War

While mutual recognition as legitimate enemies is implied by the negotiations undertaken before and after fighting, a mutual agreement to fight is less clear since this took the form of a surprise assault against unprepared and (sometimes) unarmed troops. Structured formations would have been normal for the time, but it is unclear whether these were evident here: passing over broken ground may have disarrayed attackers, while defenders were stood down.

Functional Aspects

There was a clear willingness on both sides to negotiate. The Lancastrian forces took up a good defensive position in the town, especially using barricades along the line of the city ditch to impede the enemy approach. The use of alternative access by the Yorkists allowed them nevertheless to enter the town.

Dysfunctional Aspects

Battle appears to have started before negotiations were complete. It is unclear whether this was the result of accident, poor command and control, deliberate treason or a combination of any of these. The Lancastrians were clearly unprepared for the attack, as indicated by the removal of armour and the putting-by of weapons. There was a relatively high level of violence by the Yorkists even though the Lancastrians were clearly unable to respond effectively. Final negotiations led to a reassertion of the status quo by the defeated side.

Marking of Battlefield and Interpretation

The battlefield is marked by a plaque commemorating the death of the Duke of Somerset at the junction of St Peter's Street and Victoria Street, previously Shropshire Lane (at TL 150071) (Plate 40). A local historian conducts guided walks through the battlefield for tourists.

Table 3.18 *St Albans I*

Rules of War	Battlefield Architecture
Agreement to fight: N	Features present:
	Town (buildings)
	Cathedral
	Roads/streets
	Back gardens/yards
	High ground
	City boundary ditch
Mutual recognition as 'legitimate' enemies: Y	Type of feature used:
	Roads/streets
	Back gardens/yards
	High ground
	City boundary ditch
Level of violence: High	Type of feature not used:
	Cathedral
	Town buildings
Marking of battle site:	Use of terrain:
Plaque indicating site of death of a main protagonist.	as cover: N
	to impede visibility: N
Participants:	to impede movement: Y
Professional soldiers raised by competing nobles.	Structured formations: Not known

Functional Aspects

Willingness of both sides to negotiate. Occupation of town by Lancastrians: good defensive position. Use of barricades along line of city ditch to impede enemy approach. Use of alternative access by Yorkists to enter town.

Dysfunctional Aspects

Battle appears to have started before negotiations complete: accident? Poor command and control by Yorkists? Deliberate treason? Unpreparedness for attack by Lancastrians: removal of armour, putting-by of weapons. High level of violence by Yorkists when Lancastrians clearly unable to respond effectively. Reassertion of status quo by defeated side.

ST ALBANS II, AD 1461

Location

English National Grid references:
Phase I: TL 149071, in the centre of St Albans at the junction of St Peter's Street and George Street.

Phase II: TL 155083, at Barnard's Heath, approximately 1km north from the site of Phase I, along the B651 road to Sandridge (Plate 19).

Phase III: TL 165105, on the high ground of Nomansland Common, north-west of the village of Sandridge (Plate 25).

Extent

500m × 3km.

Landscape Type

Urban. Rolling hills.

Description of Landscape and Current Use

Phase I: The medieval and modern town of St Albans sits on a ridge approximately 30 metres high running south-west–north-east immediately above the River Ver. Across the river on low ground lie the remains of the Roman city of Verulamium, much of which underlies Verulam Park, a local amenity. It was here that Queen Margaret's army mustered for the initial attack up Fishpool Street and George Street, and the subsequent attack up Folly Lane and Catherine Street. The Abbey stands a few metres off this line of march, to the right as you pass up George Street. These streets of the modern town lie on the same lines as those in the fifteenth century and give a good impression of what it was like on the day.

Phase II: Barnard's Heath (Plate 19) is part of the expansion of St Albans and is now largely built up, much of it with nineteenth-century houses. At the centre lies a small green space: it stands opposite the line of nineteenth-century houses called Battle Row. The streets running to the north-west fall steeply down the slope of the ridge, giving a good impression of the relative height of this position. The ground at the top of this slope – on which the second phase of the battle was fought in a snowstorm – is flat and unencumbered with features, although the naming of Boundary Road, which enters from the south-east, may indicate the existence of some earlier barrier. At the foot of the north-eastern slope (at TL 155085) lie the earthworks of the Beech Bottom Ditch, invisible now but valuable as a defensive line for the defeated Yorkists to retreat to.

Phase III: The open high ground above Sandridge village is empty of features and used for arable agriculture (Plate 25).

Description of the Battle

Queen Margaret's Lancastrian army marched towards London after having defeated the Yorkists at Wakefield. The Earl of Warwick, leading a Yorkist army, advanced to meet her at St Albans. Occupying the town, especially St Peter's Street, he placed additional strong forces at Barnard's Heath 1km north and at Sandridge a further 2km northwards.

Phase I: Queen Margaret mustered her army at the foot of the steep southern slope of the ridge on which the town stands, on the site of Roman Verulamium. From there, she advanced up Fishpool and George Streets towards the town centre. The Yorkist archers positioned in St Peter's Street were able to repulse the attack with heavy losses, causing the Lancastrians to retreat. Reforming and moving a little north, they advanced up Folly Lane and Catherine Street to take the Yorkists in the flank and rear, causing them to retreat and abandon the town.

Phase II: The Yorkists occupied a strong position at Barnard's Heath, on flat high ground with slopes on either side and barricades to their front. Fierce fighting took place here, with heavy losses to both sides, in a snowstorm. The tendency of Yorkist artillery pieces to explode and the defection of part of the Yorkist army, however, led to defeat and a hurried retreat first to the bottom of the eastern slope, where the Beech Bottom Ditch provided a line of defence, and then to Sandridge where reinforcements stood.

Phase III: The Yorkists re-formed on the high ground above Sandridge village. The Lancastrian pursuit halted and did not attempt to attack as night fell, and the remaining Yorkist forces were able to slip away at night in good order (Kendall, 1972b, 82–4).

Battlefield Architecture

The Yorkists showed an intent to defend the town against attack, reversing their role at St Albans I, but once again made no particular use of individual buildings or tall structures. Roads, however, were effectively barricaded and at first good use was made of the narrow approach that was the only route available to the Lancastrians. Not all access routes were covered, however, leading to Yorkist defeat in Phase I.

At Barnard's Heath, high ground was occupied, providing cover for the flanks, and the front barricaded, but the position was in essence an open one with few features. The position at Sandridge was on open high ground.

Rules of War

There was a clear mutual agreement to fight, and this implies mutual recognition as legitimate foes. The level of violence was quite high on both sides, which may indicate growing animosity as the conflict of which this battle was a part increased in intensity. Both sides drew up in the close-order formations conventional for the time.

Functional Aspects

The Lancastrians made good use of surprise in their first assault into the town, also making good use of the cover provided by streets for the attack. Both sides used weapons effectively, although the failure of Yorkist artillery may have contributed to defeat at Barnard's Heath. The Yorkists made good use of existing boundaries – of the town and more ancient (at Beech Bottom) – in defence. The fierceness of Lancastrian assaults was appropriate to break these defensive lines.

Dysfunctional Aspects

The Yorkist occupation of the centre of the town was not sufficiently connected with proper defensive preparations and the defenders failed to cover all access points. Similarly, in Phase I, the Lancastrian attackers failed to reconnoitre for uncovered access. There was slowness on the part of the Lancastrians in preparation for attack in Phase II, making the assault at Barnard's Heath more difficult. Treason was a powerful factor in the Yorkist defeat. The Lancastrians were unprepared to follow through their success quickly, leading to the escape of large numbers of defeated troops.

Marking of Battlefield and Interpretation

The battlefield is not formally marked, although the names of some streets – Battle Row, Archers Fields – at Barnard's Heath clearly indicates an awareness of the history of the location.

Table 3.19   *St Albans II*

Rules of War
Agreement to fight: Y

Battlefield Architecture
Features present:
    Town (buildings)
    Abbey
    Roads/streets

Mutual recognition as 'legitimate' enemies: Y

Level of violence: High

Marking of battle site:
Local names for site of Barnard's Heath encounter:
Archer's Fields, Battle Row.

Participants:
Professional soldiers raised by competing nobles.

High ground
City boundary ditch
Type of feature used:
Roads/streets
High ground
City boundary ditch
Type of feature not used:
Town (buildings)
Abbey
Use of terrain:
as cover: Y
to impede visibility: N
to impede movement: Y
Structured formations: Y

Functional Aspects

Surprise in assault. Use of street as covered routes for attack. Effective use of weapons at street junction to repulse assault. Use of boundary ditch as defensive line. Fierceness of attack (Lancastrians) to break defences.

Dysfunctional Aspects

Occupation of town not connected with proper defensive preparations. Failure by attackers to reconnoitre for uncovered access. Failure by defenders to defend all access points. Slowness in preparation for attack. Unpreparedness to follow through success quickly leading to escape of large numbers of defeated troops. Treason a factor in Yorkist defeat.

STAMFORD BRIDGE, AD 1066

Location

English National Grid reference SE 715565
On the high ground east of the River Derwent at Stamford Bridge, N. Yorks, under the King's Manor housing estate.

Extent

500m × 1km.

Landscape Type

River crossing, open hilltop, partly urban.

Description of Landscape and Current Use

The site of the battle is now built over (Plate 22). Access is good by road from the centre of Stamford Bridge.

The original bridge over the Derwent is now lost, and stood approximately 500m downstream from where the modern roadbridge is located. Beyond, the ground rises steeply to the 'Battle Flats', an area of open flat high ground, suitable for the deployment of both infantry and mounted troops. The new housing estate of King's Manor (including streets named for the battle) now occupies the actual site of the main action.

The land beyond is used for arable agriculture, easily accessible by road and footpath. The line of a modern railway (now disused) marks the south-western extent of the battlefield. The main A166 road to Driffield (following the line of a Roman road) marks the northern extent. Central to the battlefield is an area of ridge and furrow.

Description of the Battle

Harald Hardrada of Norway assisted by Tostig, brother to the English king Harold Godwinson, and taking advantage of the latter's concern for an invasion of the south by William of Normandy, invaded the north-east of England with the intention of re-establishing Norse rule in England. On hearing of the defeat of the northern earls, Harold hurriedly marched north and caught the Norse by surprise at their camp at Stamford Bridge.

Hardrada and Tostig deployed a unit on the western side of the bridge to delay the English while they formed their main army on the flat ground above the eastern side of the river. The English attacked immediately, ultimately killing the bridge defending force and advancing over the river on to the high ground. In fierce fighting, Hardrada and Tostig were killed and late-arriving Norse reinforcements were unable to affect the result. The remaining Norse (perhaps as few as 12 per cent of the original force) were allowed to sail home (Brooks, 1956; DeVries, 1999; McLynn, 1999; Savage, 1983, 194).

Battlefield Architecture

The river and its bridge provided an effective block to a full English advance against the Norse positions, buying valuable time for Norse deployment. The buildings of the settlement appear to have been ignored as possible obstacles to enemy advance.

The open high ground above the river was used for deployment by both sides but not to provide any kind of tactical advantage by either.

Rules of War

The Norse were not expecting an English attack and were caught awaiting emissaries from the conquered region. On apprehending the English approach, however, they deployed to fight. The English were clearly determined to force a battle: they did not wait to attack even after a long forced march and pressed home with determination after seizing the river crossing. This indicates an agreement to fight by both sides, and thus their mutual recognition as legitimate enemies.

Both sides deployed experienced and trained fighters.

The level of violence was high, as indicated by the casualty rates among the Norse; casualties among the English (caused not only by battle but by the attrition of forced marches of several hundred kilometres in a few days) would have consequences at the Battle of Hastings between Harold and William of Normandy. Harold's determination to fight and the fierceness of the violence can be explained by his concern about an invasion of the south, as well as by the effects of Tostig's treason.

Functional Aspects

The Norse displayed an appreciation of the value of terrain features by stationing troops on the bridge to delay or perhaps even prevent an attack on their main force. The English displayed an appropriate fierceness and determination in overcoming the bridge defence, which would allow them to close with the main enemy force.

Dysfunctional Aspects

The Norse employed too few troops on the bridge to defend it effectively, resulting in the loss of them all. High ground was occupied but too far back from the bridge to prevent the establishment of a bridgehead by the English. Fighting may have been a matter of 'honour' for both sides, even at the risk of abandoning significant tactical and strategic advantage. The level of violence was exceptionally high.

Marking of Battlefield and Interpretation

The battle was not marked in any way at the time, although reports tell of the dead being left on the site for some days afterwards: the normal practice would have been to clear the battlefield almost immediately.

A modern monument to the battle stands in the town square, near to the site of the original bridge (Plate 51). There is no interpretation other than text on the town tourist map. The naming of the housing estate built on the battle site – King's Manor – refers to the battle, as do individual street names in that area.

The battlefield is included in the English Heritage *Register of Historic Battlefields*, but this did not prevent its being built over.

Table 3.20   *Stamford Bridge*

Rules of War	Battlefield Architecture
Agreement to fight: Y	Features present: 　　Settlement (buildings) 　　River 　　Bridge 　　High ground
Mutual recognition as 'legitimate' enemies: Y	Type of feature used: 　　Bridge 　　High ground
Level of violence: High	River (obstacle) Type of feature not used: Settlement (buildings)
Marking of battle site: None (but remains of dead reported still on site some days later).	Use of terrain: 　　as cover: N 　　to impede visibility: N 　　to impede movement: Y
Participants: *Fyrd* and levies of Anglo-Saxon king; soldiers of Norwegian king.	Structured formations: Y

Functional Aspects

Stationing troops on bridge to prevent/delay attack on main force. Fierceness and determination of attack to overcome bridge defence.

Dysfunctional Aspects

Too few troops on bridge to defend effectively: loss of all. High ground occupied but too far back from bridge to prevent establishment of bridgehead. Fighting a matter of 'honour' for both sides even at the risk of abandoning significant tactical and strategic advantage.

STOKE, AD 1487

Location

English National Grid reference SK 751495
On high ground to the west of the main A46 road between Nottingham and Newark, immediately south-west of East Stoke village, Nottinghamshire.

Extent

500m × 500m.

Landscape Type

Open hilltop.

Description of Landscape and Current Use

Access on to the battlefield is good by footpaths and to the river crossing by road, both from East Stoke. The landscape gives a good impression of the site as it was on the day (Plate 23).

East Stoke itself is a small linear village, running east–west at approximately right angles to the line of the main A46 road between Nottingham and Newark. At the extreme eastern end, enclosed within the bounds of the manorial estate, stands the fifteenth-century church of St Oswald, otherwise known as the 'Battle Church' (Plate 52). A small stone monument – replacing a much earlier one – stands beside the church wall on the southern side (Plate 42). South-west of the church – on either side of the sunken lane that runs through the village, connecting the A46 with the River Trent to the east – lie the earthworks marking the site of the medieval settlement of East Stoke. At the junction of this sunken lane with the A46 was found a burial pit from the battle.

The battle itself took place on the flat high ground south of the village and west of the river (Plate 23). Now used for growing crops, it is accessed by footpaths running south-west from opposite the gate to the manor of Syerston Hall and farm tracks through the woods to the west. The ground slopes steeply down to the main road on the east, and has a sharp scarp on the western side facing the river; there is a more gentle slope to the south. From the crest of the hill it is possible to see, to the north, Newark (6.5km distant) and, from the western scarp, Nottingham to the south-west (14km distant). The steep western scarp (now heavily wooded), which provided the escape route for defeated troops, is cut by the 'Red Gully', possibly named for the slaughter that accompanied the battle but more likely because of the colour of the soil.

Approximately 1km north-west of the battlefield, and overlooked by the western scarp, is Fiskerton, the site of the ferry crossing over the River Trent by which retreating soldiers sought to escape.

Description of the Battle

Stoke is the last battle of the Wars of the Roses.

A Yorkist army largely composed of Irish and German mercenaries invaded England from Ireland, marched through Yorkshire and crossed into Nottinghamshire at Newark. The army of King Henry intercepted them on the line of the Roman road (now the A46) at Stoke. After finding the road south blocked to them, the Yorkists attacked but were repulsed with heavy losses.

Retreating towards the river the Irish were cut down in the narrow Red Gully and by the riverside, where the ferry at Fiskerton was not operating. The German forces stood their ground until they too were overwhelmed, with large numbers killed (Bennett, 1987; Brooke, 1854, 177–97).

Battlefield Architecture

The high ground was occupied by both sides rather than either seeking to take advantage of a dominating position. The road was used by both as a means of access. No use was made of any woods or buildings to provide cover for troops or to prevent enemy observation.

Rules of War

Both sides appear to have been formed in a structured and organised manner, despite the Lancastrian need to force battle.

The blocking of the road by the Lancastrian army effectively forced the Yorkists to fight, which they were clearly prepared to do. In this sense, battle was mutually agreed, and indicates a preparedness on both sides to treat the other as a legitimate opponent. The level of violence was especially high: this may be due to the King's determination to put an end to threats to the throne, or to hostility on the part of English soldiers towards the presence of foreign mercenaries, or both.

Functional Aspects

The blocking of the road prevented any further Yorkist advance and ensured that they would either have to fight or retreat. Determination and courage were shown by troops on both sides, especially the German mercenaries, who chose to stay on the battlefield rather than retreat.

Dysfunctional Aspects

Neither side made any attempt to gain advantage from the terrain: the presence of high ground was not used to impede enemy advance, nor were troops stationed within available buildings and woods. The Yorkists, in particular, failed to secure lines of retreat through the settlement or across the river, leading to heavy casualties as they scattered. There was a very high level of violence.

Marking of Battlefield and Interpretation

A monument in the churchyard commemorates especially the German mercenaries killed in the battle (Plate 42). The village earthworks are a Scheduled Monument and the battlefield falls within the East Stoke Conservation Area. The battlefield is included in the English Heritage *Register of Historic Battlefields*.

Table 3.21 *Stoke*

Rules of War

Agreement to fight: Y

Mutual recognition as 'legitimate' enemies: Y

Level of violence: High

Marking of battle site:
Monument at church shortly after.
Church popularly known locally as 'Battle Church'.
Places named 'Red Gully' and 'Stoke Field' supposed to be related to memory of battle.

Participants:
Professional soldiers and foreign mercenaries raised by nobles in support of rivals for the Crown.

Functional Aspects

Blocking of road to prevent enemy advance: forcing of battle.

Dysfunctional Aspects

No effective use made of terrain. High ground not used to impede movement. No cover sought. Yorkist failure to secure lines of retreat through settlement or via access routes to river. High level of violence.

Battlefield Architecture

Features present:
  High ground
  Settlement (buildings)
  Road
  Trees
Type of feature used:
  Road
  High ground
Type of feature not used:
  Settlement (buildings)
  Trees
Use of terrain:
  as cover: N
  to impede visibility: N
  to impede movement: N
Structured formations: Y

TEWKESBURY, AD 1471

Location

English National Grid reference SO 890315
Immediately south of Tewkesbury, Gloucestershire.

Extent

750m × 500m.

Landscape Type

River terraces Low hills.

Description of Landscape and Current Use

Access is good via footpaths and roads, with a marked battlefield way over part of the area.

The northern and western extent of the battlefield is marked by the Mill Avon stream, connecting two reaches of the River Severn. The eastern extent of the battlefield is now built up as the Prior's Park housing estate. Prior's Park surrounds on three sides the area called The Vineyards (at SO 895322), which provides a good view towards Tewkesbury Abbey, lying to the north-west (Plate 24). The impression of the ground is that it is generally flat, although it rises slightly between the Abbey and The Vineyards, and more obviously from the Abbey to the land above the Bloody Meadow. South of the Bloody Meadow it rises again towards Tewkesbury Park.

The Vineyards – now used as an amenity for the local population – contains a small nineteenth-century monument to the battle at its highest point, providing a good view over the area closest to the Abbey (Plate 43). At the southernmost edge of Prior's Park (at SO 896314) stands the medieval moated site called 'Margaret's Camp' (a reference to Queen Margaret, who commanded the Lancastrian forces, but the moated site itself may have played no part in the battle). From here, it is possible to gain an impression of the rise and fall of ground to the west, although house roofs, trees and field boundaries interrupt the view.

The area to the west of Prior's Park remains rural, used for pasturing animals, with some arable crops. The southernmost area is occupied by Tewkesbury Park Country Club and its golf course, where the rising ground offers a view north across the battlefield towards the Abbey and town just over a kilometre away.

In the centre of the battlefield, Lincoln Green (at SO 888318) preserves the layout of the field system present in the fifteenth century. The adjacent Bloody Meadow (at SO 886319) marks the spot where retreating Lancastrian forces were slaughtered by victorious Yorkists; here also is a descriptive plinth commemorating the battle. The ground here is low lying between steep rises to north and south, and was originally marshy.

Description of the Battle

The main Lancastrian and Yorkist armies confronted each other on the low hills south of Tewkesbury, the Lancastrians with their rear to the town, the Yorkists facing north on a line running roughly between the 'Margaret's Camp' earthwork and the modern Tewkesbury Park. An opening artillery bombardment and exchange of arrows was followed by a Lancastrian attack, which was repulsed with the assistance of a body of Yorkist spearmen hidden in trees to the rear of the Yorkist line. As the Lancastrians retreated, large numbers were trapped in the low ground of the Bloody Meadow and slaughtered. Others sought sanctuary in the Abbey to the north but were sought out and killed (Brooke, 1854, 131–55; Kendall, 1972a, 100–4; Oman, 1953, 147–8; Pereira, 1983).

Battlefield Architecture

The rising ground away from the River Severn and south of Tewkesbury Abbey provided a good base on which to form and fight, while the Mill Avon stream provided a clear north-western boundary to the battlespace but was not used to impede movements of troops. Available woodland to one side and behind the Yorkist line provided a place for the concealment of troops, but otherwise available landscape features – the 'Margaret's Camp' earthwork and the buildings and streets of Tewkesbury itself – do not appear to have played any part in the actual battle. High ground was not used for defensive purposes. The low-lying ground of the Bloody Meadow was a place in which fleeing troops became trapped, and the apparent security of the Abbey to fleeing soldiers was violated by Yorkist pursuers.

Rules of War

There was a clear and unanimous agreement to fight and this implies mutual recognition as legitimate enemies. Formations were well ordered on both sides, and the soldiers were by now experienced, with a history of antagonism going back over fifteen years. This may have contributed to the high level of violence, especially in the killing of defeated troops instead of accepting surrender. The hanging of the defeated side's banners in the Abbey after the battle indicates its recognition as a significant event at the time, securing as it did the throne for the Yorkist contender.

Functional Aspects

The concealment of troops in a wooded area was relatively rare for the time and indicates an understanding of the value of cover. The attempted use of the Abbey as a sanctuary suggests that some soldiers at least understood the importance of a secure place of retreat.

Dysfunctional Aspects

The mutual movement from occupied high ground to attacks on lower ground – rather than using high ground as a strong defensive position – appears to defy military common sense. The high level of violence employed after victory was achieved may represent an unnecessary slaughter of fleeing troops. There was a failure by the Lancastrians to secure lines of retreat across the Mill Avon stream, through the area of low-lying wetland to their flank and rear, or through the town. The Lancastrians demonstrated relatively poor command and control during the fighting, and the Yorkists also, once the fighting itself was over, leading to atrocities.

Marking of Battlefield and Interpretation

The banners of the defeated side were hung in the Abbey immediately after the battle.

The modern town of Tewkesbury trades upon its medieval associations, and a monument raised in the nineteenth century stands at The Vineyards (Plate 43).

There is a waymarked route around the battlefield (Plate 32). At the Bloody Meadow is a plinth describing the events of the battle: the meadow itself is planted with shrubs that produce red flowers in summer to reflect its name.

The local museum devotes space to the event, including a diorama and descriptive panels.

Table 3.22   *Tewkesbury*

Rules of War
Agreement to fight: Y

Battlefield Architecture
Features present:
    High ground
    Mill Avon stream
    Low-lying wetland (Bloody Meadow)
    Woodland
    Abbey
    Town (buildings)

Mutual recognition as 'legitimate' enemies: Y

Level of violence: High

Marking of battle site:
Banners displayed in abbey after battle.
Names of places associated: Margaret's Camp
(actually earlier moated site) and Bloody Meadow.
Later monument and interpretive panels and waymarked route.
Museum display.

Participants:
Professional soldiers raised by competing nobles
in support of rivals for the Crown.

Type of feature used:
 High ground
 Woodland (for concealing troops)
 Abbey (place of retreat)
 Low-lying wetland (Bloody Meadow)
Type of feature not used:
 Stream
 Town (buildings)
Use of terrain:
 as cover: N
 to impede visibility: N
 to impede movement: N
 waymarked route.
Structured formations: Y

Functional Aspects

Concealment of troops in wooded area. Attempted use of abbey as sanctuary.

Dysfunctional Aspects

Movement from occupied high ground to attack on lower ground. High level of violence after victory achieved: unnecessary (?) slaughter of fleeing troops. Failure by Lancastrians to secure lines of retreat across stream, through low-lying wetland or through town. Poor command and control.

THE DUNES, AD 1658

Location

Michelin map 51, 4 NE. Lat. 51°30′N, Long. 2°25′E
The seaside dunes east of Dunkerque, France Nord, France. Possibly on the site of the modern Malo-les-Bains seaside resort (2km from Dunkerque), but more probably at Leffrinckoucke, some 6km east-north-east of Dunkerque, where it is memorialised over the entrance to the nineteenth-century fortress.

Extent

1.50–1.75km × 500m.

Landscape Type

Coastal dunes.

Description of Landscape and Current Use

Access to the battle site is good by road and along the seafront and beach from Malo-les-Bains.

1. Aljubarrota: general view of the battlefield, with the church in middle ground.

2. Assandun site 1: near Ashdon, N. Essex, England – general view with fall of ground towards river.

3. Assandun site 2: near Ashingdon, S. Essex, England – general view with Canewdon rising from the plain in the middle distance.

4. *Bosworth: general view of battlefield from Ambion Hill.*

5. *Bouvines: general view of battlefield, with roofs of Bouvines village evident below the crest of the hill.*

6. *Corunna/Elviña: general view of the battlefield with University buildings.*

7. *Courtrai: general view of the urban location of the battlefield with monument.*

8. *Cropredy Bridge: general view of the battlefield with hills rising to the south.*

9. *The Dunes: general view of the site today.*

10. *Fontenoy: general view across the battlefield from Antoing, remnants of Bois du Barry in the distance.*

11. *Linton: today, from the point of view of attackers, with the surrounding hills visible in the distance.*

12. *Maldon: the site today, with Northey Island and the causeway in the distance.*

13. Naseby: general view of the battlefield from the site of the monument.

14. Northampton: general view of the battlefield from the south with Northampton visible in the background and the modern bridge across the Nene in the middle distance.

15. Oudenaarde: general view across the battlefield.

16. *Roliça: general view of the battlefield; French second position on the hills in the background.*

17. *Roundway Down: general view of the battlefield from the preserved downland on Roundway Hill.*

18. *St Albans I: Holywell Street today, where attackers entered the town.*

19. St Albans II: Barnard's Heath today, the second position of battle.

20. Sedgemoor: general view of the battlefield today with surrounding higher ground in the middle distance.

21. Sorauren: general view of the battlefield.

22. Stamford Bridge: site of the battlefield today marked by a street sign.

23. Stoke: general view of the battlefield.

24. Tewkesbury: general view of the battlefield with Tewkesbury Abbey in the middle distance.

The landscape is in two parts. To the south and east, flat arable land runs to the edge of the canal between Dunkerque and Veurne (22km). To the north and west lie the seaside sand dunes behind the beaches of Dunkerque. These are orientated roughly north–south and stand up to 15m high, no more than 50m apart and frequently less, covered in marram grass (Plate 9). Visibility from the top of a dune is good from beach to canal: between the dunes it is possible to see only the dunes themselves. Although the landscape today gives a good impression of the experience in 1658, the positions of the dunes themselves will have changed considerably and the use of the land by the canal is not that on the day of battle; in particular, new building will affect how the terrain is understood.

In 1940 these dunes housed large numbers of French, Belgian and British troops awaiting removal by sea to Britain. By 1944 the dunes formed part of *Festung Europa*, the Atlantic Wall built to prevent an invasion force from landing. The landscape is littered with the debris of modern war. Inland at Leffrinckoucke stands a fortress built in the nineteenth century and now used for training French army personnel. On the beach itself is a destroyed German-built fortress and gun emplacement constructed between 1940 and 1944. Between lie areas of barbed wire and other obstacles, with warning notices concerning the dangers of unexploded shells and bombs.

The arable land by the canal is used for agriculture and contains some industrial buildings. Beside the forts at Leffrinckoucke stands a small military cemetery for French soldiers killed in the Second World War. The dunes and the beach are mostly used for leisure purposes, and are designated as a 'Parc Naturel'. The forts at Leffrinckoucke and the dunes are part of the circuit memorialising the 1940 battle and evacuation.

Description of the Battle

During the Franco-Spanish war of 1653–9, Dunkerque (then part of the Spanish Netherlands) was besieged by a French force commanded by Marshal Turenne and containing a large contingent of allied Commonwealth English soldiers. In the relieving Spanish army approaching from the east served not only exiled Royalist English soldiers but also the (ageing) Great Condé, rival of Turenne as the greatest French soldier of the seventeenth century.

With the English fleet operating off the coast and thus threatening their flank on the sea, the Spanish formed a line that ran from the canal to the beach, positioning the English infantry in the dunes and on the beach, with cavalry on

115

the canal flank and in reserve on the beach. The French formed similarly, with their strongest force – including their English troops – among the dunes, but with their beach flank consisting mostly of cavalry. The Commonwealth English troops bore much of the fighting against both the Spanish and their own countrymen; in particular, their use of unsupported musketeers in a fiercely offensive manner proved very effective. The Spanish and Royalist English infantry in the dunes was broken largely by the efforts of the Commonwealth English with the support of French cavalry attacking along the beach. The Spanish line ultimately gave way except for Condé's Spanish forces beside the canal, who provided a rearguard until they too retreated. Within days, Dunkerque fell to the French (Inglis-Jones, 1994, 1.3, 249–77; Pujo, 1995, 246–7).

Battlefield Architecture

The flat terrain of the seashore and the land beside the canal provided good ground for cavalry, conventionally placed on the flanks of an army. Both the sea and the canal provided considerable water obstacles, limiting the opportunity for either side to outflank the other, although the English fleet was a constant threat to the Spanish army. Inland, the tops of the dunes provided good visibility all round, and the dunes were difficult to manoeuvre through, since general visibility was limited at the foot of a dune (although the immediate area would be clear to view) and they were both steep and difficult to climb.

The Spanish troops would have fought in large blocks of pikemen supported by relatively few musketeers (*tercios*). The French fought in a more 'linear' formation, of musketeers supported by pikemen. The English on both sides used fewer pikemen to musketeers, but the Commonwealth infantry in particular advanced as unsupported musketeers to engage in a fierce firefight with the Spanish. Cavalry were in relatively deep but linear formations, advancing at the trot to shoot with pistols and then press home with the sword.

Rules of War

The formal disposition of both armies indicates a clear agreement on both sides to fight, which in turn implies that each saw the other as a legitimate enemy to engage in formal battle. The relatively high level of violence was the product of the employment by both sides of experienced professional soldiers and, especially, the animosity of English troops towards each other.

Functional Aspects

There was effective use of terrain, manpower and weaponry by both sides, with particularly effective use by Commonwealth English of close-range musketry in an offensive mode unhampered by pikemen. The use of only professional soldiers in formal battle prevented civilian casualties and limited damage to the surrounding country.

Dysfunctional Aspects

The adoption of the 'standard' disposition of forces by both sides indicates a possible lack of imagination among commanders. Offering battle seems to have been the only option considered by either side, despite the possible availability of others (such as withdrawal behind defensive lines, or the use of sea power to attack or relieve Dunkerque). Both sides chose difficult terrain on which to deploy, rather than seeking more open ground which may have better suited the tactics and weapons of the time. There was a high level of violence, especially between the English forces employed by both sides.

Marking of Battlefield and Interpretation

The battlefield was not marked on the day nor shortly after, and no monument stands on the battlefield itself. The dunes are now remembered as the scene of the 1940 'Operation Dynamo' involving the rescue of French, Belgian and British forces after defeat by Germany.

The fort at Leffrinckoucke is named for 'Les Dunes' and the plaque over its entrance makes specific reference to the date of the battle. Outside the tourist information office at Leffrinckoucke there is an information board also making reference to the battle. The impression given is clear: that Leffrinckoucke is to be taken as the site of the engagement.

The Place de Turenne in Malo-les-Bains also lays a quieter claim: its shops display images of Marshal Turenne and of the battle, and several shops are named for 'Les Dunes'.

There are, however, no specific interpretations of the battle: no plinths with plans or other information, no leaflets or other materials available from local tourist information offices, no books on sale. In general, The Dunes has been overtaken by the events of 1940.

Table 3.23   *The Dunes*

Rules of War

Agreement to fight: Y

Mutual recognition as 'legitimate' enemies: Y

Level of violence: High

Marking of battle site:
None on day.
Plaque over entrance to Leffrinckoucke Fort refers to battle.
Place Turenne in Malo-les-Bains lays indirect claim with
pictures over doors of shops, etc.

Participants:
Professional and experienced French, Spanish and
Royalist and Commonwealth English soldiers.

Battlefield Architecture

Features present:
Beach
Dunes
Canal
Type of feature used:
Beach
Dunes
Canal
Type of feature not used: None
Use of terrain:
as cover: N
to impede visibility: N
to impede movement: Y
Structured formations: Y

Functional Aspects

Effective use of terrain, manpower and weaponry by both sides. Particularly effective use by
Commonwealth English of close-range musketry in an offensive mode unhampered by pikemen. Non-
involvement of civilians and limited damage to surrounding country.

Dysfunctional Aspects

Adoption of 'standard' disposition of forces by both sides. Decision to fight, when other options may have
been available. Choice by both sides of difficult terrain on which to deploy, rather than seeking more open
ground. High level of violence, especially between English forces employed by both sides.

FOUR

INTERPRETING BATTLEFIELDS

Chapter Three presented the battlefields we have visited in alphabetical order by name, with no regard for grouping by historical period, geographical location, or other factors. This is instead the job of this chapter, which will seek to identify those characteristics of battlefields that allow us to interpret their selection and the actions of those who fought there. Some implications for periodisation are immediately evident and these will be discussed further below, but other aspects also invite attention, such as changes of emphasis in the particular uses to which certain types of feature are put. Somewhat in defiance of our claims to adopting a 'phenomenological' approach set out in Chapter Two, here we adopt an explicitly analytical style, which is inevitably rather cold and clinical, towards our object of study. It is out of this analysis, however, that a more 'interpretive' approach to landscapes of battle can be built, which contributes to one of the aims we set out in Chapter One: that of contributing meaningfully to important issues of our time. A more interpretive stance towards the landscapes studied here will be taken in Chapter Five.

BATTLEFIELD LANDSCAPES AND FEATURES

The notion of 'terrain' discussed in Chapter Two is perhaps something different from the concept of 'landscape'. Battlefield terrain generally consists of those features considered relevant or important to military purposes. Landscape, by contrast, is all those features present regardless of their military usefulness. This includes the general shape of the area as it presents itself, and all those elements that help to define it, separate it from surrounding land, or bind it together as a more or less coherent space. The Bloody Meadows Project is concerned not with terrain but with landscape and so takes a view different from that of conventional military history. In broad terms, in addressing issues of landscape, we distinguish coastal or estuarine places from those further inland, and high places from lower. We also concern ourselves with the relation of the space to urban centres: battles may be fought through, just outside, within sight of or completely away from towns and cities. One of the things that is interesting is that, as Table 4.1 demonstrates, these different types of space cluster together as choices for battlefields in different periods of history.

Apart from the general shape of the land on which battles were fought, we are also interested in the specific features that may be scattered across the battlefield space; some of these are listed in Table 4.2 (see p. 127). There may be natural features – the products of geology such as ridges or depressions, or biological entities such as woods, forests or hedges – or man-made features, such as ancient burial mounds, earthen banks and ditches, or buildings. Some of these play a part in the battlefield action, many do not. Some may have been noticed on the day, and others not. The presence of some may have been one reason why the place was chosen for battle: that it was considered to be 'marked' in some way as significant to those who fought there.

Battlefield Landscapes

Table 4.1 presents the different kinds of landscapes in which were fought the battles we have visited for this first phase of our research. Not all possible types of landscape may be represented here: only those we identified in studying the twenty-three battlefields we are reporting on. By coastal we mean simply those places, beaches or strands, on the sea coast of the territory where the battle was fought. By estuarine we mean those places beside river estuaries – where they broaden out to allow their waters to flow to the sea: these may be close to or more distant from the actual sea itself. Maldon (Plate 12) was fought beside the River Blackwater, not too far from the sea but far enough inland to be called 'estuarine' rather than 'coastal'. The Dunes (Plate 9), by contrast, was fought on the beach and immediately inland: by the sea but not on a river. One of the sites for Assandun (the most commonly accepted) was by the estuary of the River Crouch but some 10km inland (Plate 3). Others involved the close presence of rivers and waterways – Stamford Bridge, Courtrai, Northampton, Cropredy Bridge, Sedgemoor – and in these cases the water obstacle played some important part in the action, but these were all well inland and so do not count as coastal or estuarine. Rivers are also present in the landscape of Sorauren but here provided the western and eastern boundaries to the battlefield space. In categorising the spaces of these latter fights we could have designated them as 'riverside' or 'riparian' actions but chose not to, since other, more important, factors would thereby have been excluded. A further decision-factor lies in recognising the role of water transport at Maldon and Assandun, and the role of naval forces lying offshore at The Dunes.

Table 4.1   *The shapes of some western European battlefields through time*

Battle	Date	Country	Battlefield Landscape Type							Period
			Coastal or Estuarine	High Ground[1]	Urban[2]	Visible from Urban Space	Defensive Structures	Low Ground[1]	Featured Ground[3]	
Maldon	991	UK	•					•		Early Medieval
Assandun[4]	1016	UK	•					•		
Stamford Bridge	1066	UK		•						Medieval
Bouvines	1214	France		•						
Courtrai	1302	Belgium				•		•		
Aljubarrota	1385	Portugal		•			•			
St Albans I	1455	UK		•	•		•			
Northampton	1460	UK				•	•	•		
St Albans II	1461	UK		•	•		•			
Tewkesbury	1471	UK		•		•				
Bosworth	1485	UK		•						
Stoke	1487	UK		•		•				
Roundway Down	1643	UK						•		Early Modern
Cropredy Bridge	1644	UK						•		
Naseby	1645	UK						•		
Linton[5]	1648	UK			•		•			
The Dunes	1658	France	•			?				
Sedgemoor	1685	UK						•		
Oudenaarde	1708	Belgium						•		
Fontenoy	1745	France					•	•		
Roliça	1808	Portugal				•			•	Modern
Corunna	1809	Spain				•			•	
Sorauren I and II	1813	Spain							•	

Notes
1. Relative to surrounding land.
2. i.e. fought within an existing urban space.
3. Containing recognisable landscape features which are used during the course of battlefield action.
4. The most likely, and generally accepted, site has been chosen for inclusion (see below).
5. Technically a skirmish or civil disorder, but nevertheless included here because it has sufficient 'battle-like' attributes.

In distinguishing high ground from low, we focus not upon objective height above sea level as might be expected, but upon height relative to surrounding land. The ground at Roundway Down (Plate 17), for instance, is relatively high when measured above sea level, but relatively low when compared to the chalk slopes rising in all directions from it. Although some fighting at Stamford Bridge was conducted at the riverside, which is on low ground relative to the surrounding heights, the majority took place on the flat ground above the river bank: it therefore can be considered high ground. At Bouvines (Plate 5), Aljubarrota (Plate 1), St Albans (Plates 18 and 19), Bosworth (Plate 4) and at Stoke (Plate 23), the ground chosen lies significantly above the surrounding land. Aljubarrota is distinctive in that the flat battle site looks over a relatively steep upward approach. The position of the battlefield at Stoke is on a broad flat hilltop with relatively shallow falls to the north and south and steeper falls to the east and west. The battles at St Albans were both fought, at least partly, through the streets of a town sitting on a hilltop. Others occupy relatively broad and open hilltops, with shallow slopes, good all-round visibility and few obstructions.

Coastal or estuarine landscapes are inevitably also low ground: they are near sea level and the land will tend to rise as one moves away from the water's edge. At both Courtrai (Plate 7) and Northampton (Plate 14), fighting on relatively low ground correlates to their proximity to urban space: this is despite what seems to be a general preference in the Middle Ages for fighting on ground relatively higher than surrounding land. No such correlation applies in the cases of Roundway Down, Cropredy Bridge, Naseby, Sedgemoor, Oudenaarde or Fontenoy despite the relative proximity sometimes of towns. Oudenaarde, for instance, is only a short walk from the town that gives the battle its name but separated from it by a river and rising ground. The town is also invisible from the battlefield and the battlefield from the town, except possibly from the summit of the town belfry (Plate 15). The battlefield itself lies in the shallow valley between two gentle rises, relatively high in objective terms but on lower ground than the surrounding land, from which one can look down into the battlefield space. Similarly, Roundway Down is separated from Devizes by the slope of Roundway Hill (Plate 17) and is overseen by a number of nearby heights but not from the town. The plain on which the most significant fight at Fontenoy took place (Plate 10) sits above the gorge through which the river passes at Antoing: the river gorge is invisible except from Antoing itself, and except as one climbs the steep streets of that town the ground feels low. In these cases, the space of the battlefield is a kind of 'hanging valley' – higher ground than the wider territory surrounding it, but immediately adjacent to even higher landscape features which make it a place that is experienced as low. Sedgemoor (Plate 20) was fought in the centre of the region known as the 'Somerset Levels' – an area of drained wetland at roughly sea level. The Purbeck Hills are highly visible as steeply rising land to the north and in other directions it is possible to see and sense the higher ground that surrounds the Levels. Sedgemoor is therefore low ground both objectively and subjectively. Cropredy Bridge (Plate 8) was fought in the valley between two lines of relatively steep and noticeably high escarpment along which the main roads parallel to the river also run: it, too, is experienced as low ground. The same is true of Naseby (Plate 13): lying in the valley between two parallel ridges the space is felt to be low. In all these cases, battle was joined away from urban populations and in a place that could be looked down into but not one that could be looked out from.

Three of the battles we have examined were fought through the streets of towns. The first battle of St Albans (Plate 18) was fought only in the streets, with the attacking force advancing up the side streets towards the central marketplace. The second battle began in this manner, moved along the hilltop to ground immediately outside the city boundary (Plate 19), and moved on again through a valley bottom to high ground completely outside the town (Plate 25). Linton (Plate 11) was fought almost entirely through the streets, culminating in a fierce firefight around the church. None of the battles of Courtrai (Plate 7), Northampton (Plate 14) or Tewkesbury (Plate 24) penetrated the towns where they were fought but the action would have been clearly visible from the nearby city walls, and Maldon was fought within sight of the much earlier hilltop enclosure that contains the settlement. Similarly, the battle at Stoke would have been visible from Newark to the north and Nottingham to the south-west, Roliça (Plates 16 and 38) was visible and audible from the walls of nearby Obidos, and the battle of Corunna (Plate 6) was visible from that city's walls and audible from its streets. The Dunes was fought sufficiently near to Dunkerque to have been visible from its walls assuming no intervening obstacle: the town is not visible from the site today and the site cannot be seen from either the edge of the town or the nearer Malo les Bains (the seaside suburb), but this may reflect the movement of the sand over the centuries (Plate 9). The battle of Sorauren (Plate 21) would not have been visible from Pampeluna but the sound of the action would have reverberated through the nearby hills to be heard in the streets.

Urban fights are particularly associated with the use of built defences, but not exclusively. At both battles at St Albans, moveable items (furniture, carts) were used to construct barriers across streets: in both cases they proved ineffective against the attack. The same applies at Linton, where a barrier was built to

25. St Albans II: Nomansland Common, the third position of battle.

prevent entry of the attacking force into the town: once it was overthrown, however, the fight became a mobile chase through the streets. The defences at Fontenoy not only involved moveable objects but also relied on the solidity of local stone buildings: these were more effective and played a significant part in slowing and then stopping the attack. A more permanent earthwork structure was built across the river from Northampton town: no longer extant as a visible feature, it nevertheless survives as a sub-surface trace identifiable by geophysics (G. Foard, personal comment, 1991). It proved of limited value in battle: instead, it provided a convenient dam for the rising river water, leading to flooding of the army camp, and was no defence against treachery. The *chevaux de frise* at Aljubarrota were designed to impede an attack by cavalry and provide some protection for lightly armoured archers: in this they were highly successful, as similar structures at Crécy, Poitiers and Navarrete had been and would be in the future at Agincourt. The use of built structures is current for a long period, but appears to wane with the adoption of a different approach to battlefield landscapes – one with which we are more familiar in its guise as 'terrain'.

The battlefields dating prior to 1800 are all relatively uncluttered in terms of features. The ground is mostly flat and open whether it is placed high or low, with few noticeable obstructions to view. Slopes are mostly shallow and obstacles generally minor: the streams at Courtrai, Tewkesbury, Naseby and

Oudenaarde are not wide and no water obstacles are evident on the battlefields at Maldon, Assandun, Bouvines, Aljubarrota, Bosworth, Stoke, Roundway Down or Linton. The river at Stamford Bridge plays a part in the battlefield action but the bulk of the fighting is on the high ground above the river, and at Northampton the fighting is on what should have been dry land away from the river. The river is a significant feature at Cropredy Bridge, but the bulk of the fighting is on the open ground of the dry valley floor. A river provides one boundary to the Fontenoy battlefield as it passes through the gorge at Antoing, and a canal marks the inland edge of the battlefield at The Dunes. Only at Sedgemoor (Plate 20) is the water obstacle integral to the battlefield action. The urban battlefields are much more featured spaces, simply because of the presence of buildings, but that is all that is present: at St Albans and at Linton fighting was limited to the spaces between the buildings rather than penetrating their walls.

Battlefields that we have visited dating after 1800 provide a much more varied collection of objects to consider. Both relatively high and relatively low ground are used in all three fights. Roliça (Plate 16) begins in the valley floor, and moves to the high ground further south. At Corunna (Plate 6) both armies occupy high ground for observation and to impede enemy movement, but fight on the lower slopes and in the valley bottom. At Sorauren (Plate 33) the ridges occupying the central ground of the battlefield are used both for observation and to impede enemy movement, while the scrub-overgrown and rocky slopes provide cover for detached infantry skirmishes (Plate 26), and beyond the central valley the low land of the main river and road routes provides the ground for massed infantry and cavalry assaults. The major rivers at Sorauren provide a convenient boundary to the battlefield space, but water obstacles – although also present at Corunna – otherwise play little part in these actions: bridges act as defensible positions to block attacks on the flanks of fighting units rather than as aids to manoeuvre. Built-up areas, however, are very significant at all three battles. The villages of Sorauren (Plate 33) and Zabaldica provide defensible positions at Sorauren, and also foci for assaults by massed infantry and artillery. The villages of the hills above Corunna (Plate 6) – especially Elviña, which hugs the slope closely – became fierce battlegrounds and provided both cover and objectives for both sides. At Roliça the village of Columbeira (Plate 38) especially provided access to the high ground above, a place to rally and organise assaults, and a convenient landscape feature for the orientation of attacking forces. The buildings of all these settlements were used to house, secrete and protect troops, taking the battle inside the walls as well as outside. The presence of roads was also of greater importance in these fights: they were more than a means of

26. *Sorauren: saddle across valley, showing the narrow access and steep flanks with the 'Spanish' hill on the extreme left.*

reaching the battlespace and were often integral to the action. At Sorauren, the roads along the main river valleys provided attackers with the main access to the defended villages. The road built by the allied army through the mountains to bypass French-held cities – the *camiño des inglés* (Plate 27) – provided also a means of positioning artillery and other forces during the battle itself. At Corunna, the roads provided lines on which to organise units, means of reaching key positions, routes of attack, and possibly – as will be discussed in Chapter Five – the reason for the battle. In all these battles, therefore, the ground was less open and uncluttered, and greater use was made of features present – water obstacles, roads, settlements and buildings, high and low ground.

Battlefield Features

Major landscape features – individual hills, ridges and depressions – form part of the general shape of the ground over which any particular battle was fought. At Sorauren, the hill positioned immediately above Zabaldica on the eastern side of the battlefield and slightly behind the British line was occupied by Spanish troops and became the focus of fierce fighting as the French attempted to break through (Plate 26). At Linton, free-standing Haw's Hill was occupied by the defenders in an attempt to block the attackers' advance down the sunken

Table 4.2   *Features present on battlefields*

Battle	Date	Country	Woods	Bridge	Monastic Site	Church/Chapel	Earthwork Monument	Mill	Castle/Chateau/Moated Site	Roads	Stone Monument	Period
Maldon	991	UK										Early Medieval
Assandun	1016	UK										
Stamford Bridge	1066	UK		•								
Bouvines	1214	France		•	•	•				•		
Courtrai	1302	Belgium			•							
Aljubarrota	1385	Portugal	•									Medieval
St Albans I	1455	UK	•		•	•				•		
Northampton	1460	UK		•	•					•	•	
St Albans II	1461	UK	•			•						
Tewkesbury	1471	UK	•			•			•			
Bosworth	1485	UK	•			•						
Stoke	1487	UK				•				•		
Roundway Down	1643	UK					•					
Cropredy Bridge	1644	UK		•								
Naseby	1645	UK					•					Early Modern
Linton	1648	UK				•						
The Dunes	1658	France										
Sedgemoor	1685	UK				•						
Oudenaarde	1708	Belgium						•				
Fontenoy	1745	France	•			•	•		•			
Roliça	1808	Portugal										Modern
Corunna	1809	Spain								•		
Sorauren I and II	1813	Spain				•				•		

127

road from Saffron Walden. Both sides occupied the tops of sand dunes at The Dunes (Plate 9) and also fought in the depressions between them. The ridges on the northern side of the battlefields of Oudenaarde and Fontenoy provided the line on which French troops chose to form and an objective for attack, and the lines of heights at Roliça (Plate 16), Corunna (Plate 6) and Sorauren (Plate 33) provided armies with places to stand and fight.

Woodland can offer a place to hide troops, may be an area to avoid or simply provide a source of raw material. At Aljubarrota and at Bosworth the woodland areas were avoided by troops and formed a boundary to the battlefield space. The trees themselves at Aljubarrota were a source for the material used to construct the *chevaux de frise* protecting the defenders' position, and their presence on steeply sloping ground served also to protect the flanks of the position. At Northampton the trees provided a boundary to the battlefield space along its southern edge but also gave a modicum of protection from the elements to troops encamped overnight. At Tewkesbury and at Fontenoy (Plate 10) the woods were used to hide the presence of troops from the enemy: spearmen at Tewkesbury were able to catch the Lancastrians by surprise; artillery at Fontenoy was able to enfilade the attacking troops. The specifics of particular circumstances seem to determine the role of woodland in battle: as an inconvenience or an asset, as a landscape feature or as merely a number of individual trees. The manner in which woodland is treated by soldiers in different periods may indicate how such features are perceived more generally in that period: these few examples may suggest that trees are more likely to be seen as woodland landscape features in more recent periods, and more as sources of material in earlier times. There may be scope for more research here.

Bridges and roadways offer routes of advance and retreat and can become military objectives in their own right. The bridge over the Derwent at Stamford Bridge served as an outpost for advance units of the Norse army and as a key initial objective for the Saxons, but once achieved, fighting shifted to the heights above where the main battle took place. The bridge at Cropredy (Plate 36) was also an objective, along with those either side of it, but the main fighting took place in the floodplain of the Cherwell. At Northampton, by contrast, the bridge in rear of the Lancastrian position (Plate 14) was never an objective of the fighting but was the only major escape route for the fleeing army: its choking with troops led others to seek escape in the flooded river itself, leading to the high level of casualties.

The presence of Roman roads gave access to several medieval battlefields, especially Bouvines, the battles at St Albans (where the remains of the Roman city also provided a convenient mustering-point in the second battle), and Stoke. More recent roadways were significant at Corunna and Sorauren. At the former, the roads leading to the city provided the means of escape for the retreating British army and needed to be kept secure from enemy threat: rather than defending high ground the army was more likely protecting its route to the sea (see Chapter Five for a justification of this). At Sorauren, the main routes through major cities were controlled by superior French forces: options were to force these forces to retreat or to bypass the roads; the latter course led to the construction of a new road through the mountains (the *camiño des inglés*, Plate 27) while the former resulted in battle. Elsewhere, such routes were not a reason for battle nor an objective during battle but only a means of bringing armies together to fight. The relative greater importance of bridges in earlier periods suggested here may be only apparent; but the greater significance of roads in nineteenth-century conflict may reflect reality with the increased reliance on artillery and wheeled supply trains.

Churches and chapels are a significant and common feature in any European landscape; accordingly their presence in the battlefield space may not be remarkable; however, as what is very often the largest stone structure in their area they may inevitably attract attention. The great churches at Tewkesbury (Plate 24) and St Albans dominate the space of and around those towns: battlefield action bypassed St Albans Abbey on both occasions, but at Tewkesbury may have penetrated the church itself and certainly reached as far as the doorway, where fleeing soldiers were caught and brutally killed. Fighting took place around Linton church and also the church at Fontenoy: in the former case it was sought as refuge for fleeing combatants, while the latter was central to the fortified village at the centre of the battlefield. Other church buildings are more ancillary to the battlefield action. Sutton Cheney church was the site of devotions prior to the battle of Bosworth and is visible from the battlefield, and the church at Westonzoyland is a few hundred metres only from the site of the action at Sedgemoor. Stoke church (Plate 52) stands off the battlefield across the road to the river: it is not visible today from the battlefield because of a stand of trees, but these may not have been present in 1487 and it may have been a dominant feature to combatants. By contrast, the chapel at Sorauren – not the village church, which may have been fortified, but a small hillside shrine no longer extant – provided a convenient location for scouting enemy dispositions, but no more.

Where churches are not evident, monastic establishments sometimes are. Monasteries stood just off the battlefield space at Bouvines and Courtrai, and a nunnery was immediately adjacent at Northampton (Plate 30). Battle avoided

27. *Sorauren: possible* camiño des inglés.

these places but they provided rescue for the wounded and medical aid once the fighting was over. At the time of the battles, both Tewkesbury and St Albans abbeys were centres of monastic activity and it is possible other battlefields may also have had monasteries or nunneries nearby. It may be significant therefore that eight out of our sample of nine medieval battlefields are known to be close to or involve churches and monasteries while only four out of eleven more modern sites do. Fighting penetrates only one such structure in the medieval period while three in the modern period are in the centre of the fighting. This suggests a change of attitude towards such places over time: while churches and church foundations are not to be fought in or over in the medieval period, their presence nearby is desired or expected; but in later times they form merely another part of the battlefield space and no longer command special respect.

Non-church buildings are relatively rare in the medieval battlefield landscape unless the battle takes place through urban space. The incorporation of settlements into battlefields in later periods – as at Linton (Plate 11), Fontenoy (Plate 28), Roliça (Plate 38), Corunna (Plate 6) and Sorauren (Plate 33) – increases the number of buildings present and such buildings are more likely to be used as part of the fighting. The moated site now called 'Margaret's Camp' at Tewkesbury is roughly contemporary with the battle and may by then have been abandoned, but appears nevertheless to have been ignored by combatants. By

28. Fontenoy: monument to Irish troops in Fontenoy village with a barn beyond.

contrast, the chateau at Antoing was particularly significant at Fontenoy, providing a strong point on which to hinge the defence of the position and an effective barrier to an attack on the southern flank: this in turn allowed the defenders to concentrate on the main attack from the east. The mill on the northern ridge at Oudenaarde provided a convenient command post for the French commander: although conventionally represented as a windmill, the actual structure is that of a small farm enclosure with a water-powered mill attached. Opposite in the valley floor stands the earth mound representing the remains of the castle of Breween (Plate 29), which was utilised by the allied commander as his command post: the low mound is all that remains today, although contemporary descriptions suggest the presence of stone ruins.

Other classes of ancient features are occasionally present on battlefields but rarely play a major part in the action. Field systems and other evidence of landscape use from earlier ages – some still in operation on the day of fighting – are evident at Northampton, Tewkesbury, Stoke and Roundway Down (Plate 17). They generally appear to fall outside the category of battlefield 'terrain' despite forming part of the background landscape: no particular use was made of them and no particular significance attaches apart from today as part of the historic environment of the battlefield space. Prehistoric burial mounds and earthwork features are evident particularly at Roundway Down where they litter the landscape: no use appears to have been made of these during the battle, either as positions for artillery nor for orientation, or even as places for command posts, despite their suitability for these functions. The nearby Iron Age hilltop enclosure of 'Oliver's Castle' (a name given after and in inaccurate memory of the battle at Roundway) may have been particularly suitable for use as a battery position and would have dominated the space of the battle, but it too was ignored. The similar hillfort at Maldon contained then as now the main settlement and overlooks the site of the battle: it was not, however, used for defensive or other purpose directly associated with the fight. The Eleanor Cross overlooking the battlefield at Northampton was used by the commander of the attacking army as a convenient location from which to observe enemy dispositions prior to the battle.

Boundedness and Usage

Chapter Two set out the specific questions we ask when visiting and investigating a battlefield site. Some of these – especially the height relative to surrounding ground, its proximity to or distance from towns, and the use put to particular kinds of landscape features – have been addressed here. Other issues were those of the 'boundedness' of the landscape as a whole and the use to which it was put at the time: these are summarised in Table 4.3.

Boundaries

The issue of boundaries is one that will reappear in Chapter Six, when we discuss the modern uses to which historic battlefields are put and their management as historic places. Here, we are concerned with how clearly physically bounded they may have been – or at least appeared – to those who fought there. Placing boundaries around a battlefield is surprisingly difficult: battles are, among other things, about movement through space and so placing limits on that space of

Table 4.3 *Boundedness and uses of battlefields*

Battle	Date	Country	Orientation	Bounded Y	Bounded Front (F)/Rear (R) and/or Laterally (L)	Bounded By (Features)	Use	Period
Maldon	991	UK	N–S				Beach	Early
Assandun	1016	UK	E–W				?	Medieval
Stamford Bridge	1066	UK	N–S				Pasture?	
Bouvines	1214	France	E–W	•	L	Slopes	Pasture	Medieval
Courtrai	1302	Belgium	E–W	•	R	Town walls	Agriculture	
Aljubarrota	1385	Portugal	E–W	•	L	Slope	Agriculture	
St Albans I	1455	UK	N–S				Urban	
Northampton	1460	UK	N–S				Agriculture	
St Albans II	1461	UK	E–W	•	L	Extent of town and slope	Urban and agriculture	
Tewkesbury	1471	UK	N–S				Pasture	
Bosworth	1485	UK	N–S				Pasture	
Stoke	1487	UK	N–S	•	L	Slope	Pasture	
Roundway Down	1643	UK	E–W				Pasture	Early Modern
Cropredy Bridge	1644	UK	N–S	•	FR	Hills	Pasture	
Naseby	1645	UK	N–S	•	FR	Hills	Agriculture	
Linton	1648	UK	N–S				Urban	
The Dunes	1658	France	E–W	•	L	Shore and canal	Shore and agriculture	
Sedgemoor	1685	UK	E–W				Pasture	
Oudenaarde	1708	Belgium	N–S	•	FR	Slope	Agriculture	Modern
Fontenoy	1745	France	E–W	•	L	Woods	Agriculture	
Rolica	1808	Portugal	N–S	•	F	Hills	Agriculture	
Corunna	1809	Spain	N–S	•	FR	Hills	Agriculture	Modern
Sorauren I and II	1813	Spain	N–S	•	FRL	Hills and rivers	Agriculture	

133

movement becomes troublesome. It raises questions about what is meant by the term 'battlefield': does it include any space through which relevant movement took place – such as marches prior to battle, bivouacs, baggage parks, or lines of retreat; or does it cover only that ground on which actual fighting took place? If the former, then how far should we extend our concern; if the latter, do we need to place outside the battlefield space those troops who stood in the battle line but who saw no actual combat? We take an unashamedly 'common sense' and pragmatic approach to these issues: so far as it can be identified, those places where troops concentrated with the intention of fighting are considered by us to be inside the battlefield space, and locations where no fighting either took place or was intended (so far as we can ascertain) lie outside. Where some kind of physical barrier or marker is evident at the junction between these two areas, and depending on other indicators as to whether it was 'seen' or not, it is taken by us to represent a boundary to the battlefield space.

This pragmatic approach requires us to establish the relationship of any boundary to the action taking place inside it. To grossly oversimplify, battlefields can be seen as spaces comprising four edges: a 'front' marking the edge of any overall movement in one direction; a 'rear' marking the edge of any overall movement in an opposite direction; and two 'sides' marking the edges of lateral movement (as in Fig 4.1). Inside this space lies the extent of the battlefield; outside is not part of the battlefield space. The size and precise shape of the bounded space depends on the action of the battle and its overall orientation, more north–south or more east–west. Some battlefields – as is evident from Table 4.3 – do not have physical boundaries: here, the space is still quadrangular and a front, rear and sides may be discerned, but these are determined by the perceptions of those involved. Other battlefields may have physical boundaries only to front and rear and not laterally, or vice versa. Distinguishing between spaces that are differentially bounded and these from entirely unbounded spaces may be able to tell us something about the perception of space in the past. Front and rear boundaries mark the limits of forward and rearward movement within the battlespace: they often mark the initial positions of bodies of troops, especially a victorious force. Physical features at these points will mark the limits of battlefield movement: as the point at which an army initially deployed for battle, or beyond which a defeated enemy was not pursued. Lateral boundaries mark the side edges of the battlespace: physical features may represent obstacles to movement, thus protecting one army or both from a flank assault, or simply a barrier to movement beyond it. Typically, any such boundary – to front, to rear or lateral – will take the form of a water obstacle, steep slopes, dense woodland, or a built-up area.

Figure 4.1 *Establishing boundaries to the battlefield space*

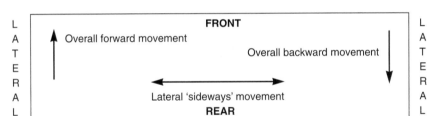

Notes to interpretation

1. In general, armies drawn up for battle occupy more space laterally than in depth.
2. In general, armies move towards each other to contact, rather than edging sideways, and retreat in the opposite direction.
3. Any turning movements in battle – whether of one army or of both – will tend to distort the overall shape of the battlespace, but the general lines of movement within the space will remain discernible.

The most clearly bounded sites examined by us – a factor that contributes to our designation of them as 'featured' (see Table 4.1 and Figure 4.2) – are those of the early nineteenth century in Iberia. At Sorauren, the two main rivers to east and west acted as lateral barriers to movement, restricting battlefield action to the area between them and denying the opportunity for flanking movements. The rising ground between these two rivers and enclosing the central valley comprised a further obstacle, containing the main action within the central valley. The two ridges marking this valley acted as the front and rear boundaries to the battlefield space, providing ground on which to form and stand: between them, in the valley itself, the actual fighting took place. At Roliça, no rear boundary is evident but the front edge comprises the line of hills on which the French army stood to fight and on the forward slopes of which the main action took place (Plate 16). The lateral boundary is comprised of the hills running perpendicular to the French position, enclosing the valley through which the British advanced (Plate 38). The Corunna battlefield is contained on one side by the waters of the River Mero and on the other by the heights above the village of San Cristobal. The front edge is marked by the line of hills held by the French army (Plate 6), and the rear by the opposite and lower hills occupied by the British.

By contrast, the least clearly bounded battlefields are those of the early medieval period. In part, this is due to the relatively small size of these spaces. At Maldon, the only clear boundary is the water's edge where the fighting most likely took place (Plate 12): the land beyond was relatively flat and featureless at

29. Oudenaarde: Breween farm and castle mound (centre); site of the allied commander's viewpoint.

the time, and there are no lateral features evident. The battlespace here was determined more by the area taken up by bodies of people than by physical land-marks. At Stamford Bridge the river edge and its bridge provides not a boundary but a point of initial contact for the two contending forces. The high ground above the river – where the main fight took place – is also unfeatured space where the limits are set by the human architecture of fighting formations. The most likely site for Assandun – on the river flats between Ashingdon and Canewdon (Plate 3) – is bounded laterally by the River Crouch and to front and rear by the hills on which stand the two villages. It is difficult to see these as true battlefield boundaries since they are all inevitably some distance – as much as a kilometre or more – from the actual place of fighting: they may, however, have provided convenient points of orientation for the two armies in choosing a place to fight.

Medieval battles fought on high ground are more likely to be bounded laterally, although boundedness may not be a particular feature of medieval battlefields. At Stoke, the north of the battlefield connects to the village and the southern slope is the more gentle, while to the east is a steep slope above the modern road and to the west lies the Red Gully and the scarp leading to the river: both of these provide reasonably clear lateral edges. At Bouvines, a similar lie of the land applies, although the western (rear) slope towards the village is as steep as the flanking inclines. At Aljubarrota, the lateral wooded slopes were included in the defensive plans of the Portuguese and their English allies: the steep slope to the front was a point of contact rather than a boundary. The edge of the hill upon which St Albans stands acted effectively as a lateral boundary for the main action of the second battle, but also provided a region of contact in the initial stages: the final stage above Sandridge was effectively unbounded. Courtrai was bounded to the rear by the walls of the city, but otherwise unbounded: the stream to the Flemish front acted as a point of contact; and the first battle of St Albans – although constrained by the extent of the town – was also not clearly bounded. Northampton was hemmed in by the river to the north, but fighting was not intended to reach so far, and in other circumstances it would have provided a means of escape for defeated troops. Similarly, at Tewkesbury, although constrained by the river to the west, the battlespace was determined more by the disposition of troops than the shape of the land. The main infantry fight at Bosworth was limited to the slope of Ambion Hill, but fighting extended also to the low ground beyond, unconstrained by physical barriers.

Those early modern battlefields that show boundaries tend, in contrast to the earlier periods, to be bounded to front and rear rather than laterally, although such boundedness is again not a constant feature. The clearest examples of front and rear boundaries are at Naseby (Plate 13), Cropredy Bridge (Plate 8) and at Oudenaarde, where the high ground marking the valleys in which the fights took place provided clear edges. The hills are steep and prominent at Cropredy, creating a deep basin where the armies could meet across the river. At Naseby and at Oudenaarde the rise of ground is shallower, at Oudenaarde significantly so, but sufficient to separate out the battlefield valley from surrounding space: in both cases, streams at the foot of the slope provide points of contact rather than barriers. Lateral boundedness is strongly evident at The Dunes, where the sea to the north and the canal to the south provide near-impassable obstacles, and is less evident but present at Fontenoy (Plate 10), where the woods were used as part of the battlefield action. By contrast to these, Roundway Down and Sedgemoor are unbounded, as is Linton except by the extent of the built-up area and the disposition of forces.

Land Use

The most common use for land chosen for battles in most periods seems to be that of pasturing animals, as at Stamford Bridge, Bouvines, Roundway Down, Cropredy Bridge and Sedgemoor. There is a clear utilitarian explanation for this, since grass provides good ground for footsoldiers and horses as well as fodder for the latter. At St Albans, especially in the first battle, use was made of gardens and enclosed orchards for access, and orchards and fields were a feature of the landscapes at Aljubarrota, Roliça, Corunna and Sorauren. The land at Northampton, Tewkesbury and Stoke shows evidence of medieval ploughing, and mixed agricultural use was made of the land at Fontenoy. At Maldon, the beach would have been just that and used in particular for landing from sea vessels. The Dunes was fought over sandhills but the region inland – reaching from the edge of the dunes themselves to the canal – was used for growing crops. The use put to the land at Assandun is unclear, although probably broadly agricultural, and the land outside the gate of Courtrai would have either been used for grazing animals or for crops, as would the field at Bosworth. The key factor in all cases prior to 1800 seems to have been relative openness and accessibility except where battle took place within an urban environment.

Characteristics of Battlefields: Results of Analysis

This section has looked at some length at the general shapes of the landscapes where the battles examined by us were fought. It has reviewed them in terms of their relative height to surrounding space, their proximity to and visibility from settlement, the features the landscape contained, the uses (if any) those features were put to in battle, the 'boundedness' of the space, and the use to which the land was put at the time of the battle. The discussion that follows will present an idea of what these things can tell us about war at various times in the past. Here, we will consider those elements that may be most relevant to gaining such an insight. Two aspects seem to be of immediate value in understanding the choice of battlefield in any particular period of history: whether it is situated on high or low ground relative to surrounding land, and how near or far it is from a major settlement. Individual features present are more varied, but some may be more typical than others in different historical contexts. Examining the use to which the land was put before and after conflict seems less significant, although our sample is sufficiently small that more complex patterns may not yet emerge. The same can perhaps be said in terms of looking for clear physical 'edges' to the battlefield space: some suggestions as to what to look for can perhaps be offered, but the sample size is too small to distinguish more than simple presence or absence, but not to indicate what this may mean in terms of the perception of space.

A factor that is interesting and perhaps indicative is that the general features of a battlefield for a particular period appear to be common, regardless of location: medieval and early-modern battlefields in England share the same general characteristics as those in Belgium, France, Spain and Portugal. It seems likely that those for the earlier and later periods (so far limited in our researches to only one or two countries) may also share characteristics. If so, then identifying the common features of battlefields for a particular period through researches in one country may assist with similar researches elsewhere. This is an aspect yet to be tested by us, and is part of the ongoing nature of the project, but adds, we feel, to its usefulness as a body of research. If we are right, then the 'discourses' of war we have unearthed are common at least across all of Europe

'DISCOURSES' OF WAR

Figure 4.2 (see p. 127) summarises chronologically the overall changes we have identified in battlefield landscapes. The small number of early-medieval battlefields we have looked at, all English, suggest a preference for low ground by the coast; but this may not be significant given the numbers of sites involved. On the other hand, Stamford Bridge shows some of the characteristics associated with battlefields from the later medieval period. From the eleventh to the fifteenth centuries there was a marked preference for two types of landscape: ground that is relatively higher than the land around it (irrespective of 'objectively measured' height above sea level; Plates 1, 4, 5, 23 and 25); and ground that is near to, or at least visible from, a population centre (Plates 14, 18, 19 and 24). In all cases, where one of these was not present, the other was; so it seems that a battle would either be fought on high ground, or near a town, or both. This applied even where it might be thought irrational to fight the battle at that site. At Courtrai, for instance (Plate 7), the battle was fought outside the gates of the French-held city at the instigation of the Flemish army, which had its back to the city walls. At Northampton, the battleground by the river outside the city walls was liable to severe flooding in heavy rain, which is indeed what happened. In the seventeenth and early eighteenth centuries the choice of ground shifted noticeably towards low ground away from population centres (Plates 8, 10, 13, 15, 17 and 20). There was also in this period a slight increase in the tendency of the ground to contain specific noticeable features, although these rarely took a direct role in the battlefield action. In general, however, and apart from a few examples, battles from the tenth to the eighteenth century were fought in empty spaces.

Use was made of built defensive features in both the medieval and early modern periods. This is most evident in the medieval period and especially where the battle was fought inside or very near to a town. But the trend continued into later periods as at Linton and again at Fontenoy, a battle deliberately mimicking that at Malplaquet thirty-five years earlier. By the early nineteenth century the use of built battlefield defences may diminish. The battles of the Peninsular War were fought in very highly featured landscapes, containing hills and low ground together with streams, walls, roadways, bridges and built-up areas (Plates 6, 16, 21, 38, 33, 26 and 27), all of which played a part in the story of the event that is the battle. In none of these were defensive structures built, but existing structures were used for cover or as obstacles to movement. Some battles of this period were visible from nearby urban centres, and in general battlefields of this period are much more like the kinds of place we would expect, whereas those of the earlier periods tend to be rather undistinguished. In contrast with the exciting mountain landscapes of Corunna, Roliça or Sorauren, for instance, the sites of Fontenoy and Oudenaarde are very flat and very empty.

There seem, therefore, to be clear differences in the kinds of places where battles were fought in western Europe over the last millennium. A preference for high ground near towns is replaced by a preference for low ground away from towns, and then by a preference for places that have a number of different types of features available for use. What we have not been able to identify from our research so far are particular military reasons for these changes. In particular, there seems to be no close association between the type of ground selected and available or applied technology and tactics: indeed, it is an axiom of war that tactics tend to be dictated by ground, rather than the other way around. In all periods, there is a mixture of missile weapons and both mounted and unmounted troops. Missile weapons from the fifteenth century to the early nineteenth century have approximately the same range and overall effectiveness; and although cannon technology improves significantly from the sixteenth century, artillery is relatively static from the fifteenth century until the eighteenth century. Some battles in the medieval period were fought in low areas, which seems to rule out any restriction on the appropriateness of weapons or tactics for that kind of terrain. Similarly, the technology available in the eighteenth century is not different from that in the early nineteenth, when battles involve both high and low ground. What we therefore suspect is that it is ideological factors that may be more important in determining the choice of particular kinds of ground.

For the medieval period we think the crucial factor is that of being seen, and one clue lies in the preference for visibility from population centres. The simultaneous preference for location near to a church or a monastic foundation (Plates 21, 30 and 52) may testify to a desire not only to be seen by the local population, but maybe also to be seen by God. The ideology of medieval warfare was to do with honour: battles were formal affairs, frequently arranged before-hand with much pomp and circumstance, the formal exchange of communications

30. *Northampton: Delapre Abbey gardens today.*

and hostages, with flags and banners very prominent, and highly regulated (Prestwich, 1996, 305–33). Later battles were equally formal, but these were fought out of sight except of the enemy army. We do not yet fully understand this change, but it may be related to the rise of the professional army: military display from the seventeenth century onwards may be only for other professionals, possibly as the result of a reaction against the aristocratic ideals of medieval knighthood among emerging citizen armies. By the nineteenth century this no longer applies and an ideology based upon functional utility may have become dominant.

These ideological changes represent the kind of changes in discourse introduced in Chapter Two: they represent not only decisions made on the basis of functional considerations but also in the ways that the landscape is perceived and understood. In certain periods, particular landscape features take on a wider significance than in others, while other features appear to be disregarded as if invisible to the eye.

LINKING LANDSCAPES TO ACTION

Tables 4.1 and 4.2 list battles by conventional and broadly drawn historic period: early medieval from an unspecified date to around 1100, medieval from 1100 to 1500, early modern to 1800, and finally fully modern to our own chosen cut-off

Figure 4.2   *Discourses of battle*

Date

| | 1000 | 1200 | 1400 | 1600 | 1800 |

Landscapes

Open
Maldon 991
Assandun 1016

Hilltop/Urban
Stamford Bridge 1066
Bouvines 1214
Courtrai 1302
Tewkesbury 1471
Bosworth 1485
Stoke 1487

Valley
Roundway Down 1643
Cropredy Bridge 1644
Naseby 1645
The Dunes 1658
Sedgemoor 1685
Oudenaarde 1708

Features
Roliça 1808
Corunna 1809
Sorauren 1813

Defensive Works
Aljubarrota 1385
St Albans I 1455
Northampton 1460
St Albans II 1461

Linton 1648
Fontenoy 1745

Desirable Features

Monastery/Church
Bouvines 1214
Courtrai 1302
St Albans I 1455
Northampton 1460
St Albans II 1461
Tewkesbury 1471
Bosworth 1485
Stoke 1487

Road
Bouvines 1214
St Albans I 1455
St Albans II 1461
Stoke 1487

Road
Corunna 1809
Sorauren 1813

date of 1900. Based on the data presented, these periods do seem to represent changes in battlefield preference as well as the wider historic changes they imply. What the tables do not offer is any explanation for these changes, and the most common reasons for any such changes that will be offered derive from the discourse of war applying in our own age: that they represent changes in landscape preference based upon functional and utilitarian need. We take the view that other factors are involved, especially ideological ones. This section will therefore examine the basis for a functionalist argument by looking at changes in warfare practice from the early medieval to modern periods. It will do so by considering the changes we identify in terms of models of 'revolutions' in evolving military thinking from the medieval to modern periods.

All the battles we have examined here predate the use of mechanised transport. Armies arrived mostly on foot, using wheeled vehicles pulled by animals, or on horseback. All relied upon close-order formations so as not to allow the enemy to penetrate and disrupt army organisation. Without radio or telephone, communication was by word of mouth brought by runner or rider, or more indirectly by trumpet call or by drumbeat. Information on the current state of an army or a unit was most often derived from direct observation. Preparation for battle took time and frequently took place in the plain view of the enemy; this means that battle sites were always a matter of choice, since there was ample opportunity to avoid engagement simply by retiring before the enemy was formed for battle. Nevertheless, battles were usually of relatively short duration: a matter of hours only in most cases. Distances were also short: the effective range of a missile fired by an individual was up to about 100m; or for artillery no more than about 500m. The size of battlefields was small – sometimes no more than a few hundred metres in any direction – with thousands of troops closely crowded into this small space. Up to about 1500, battle was generally decided by the use of hand-held weapons against people standing within arm's reach. After this, battle was more commonly decided by the use of firearms, although at the distances involved the faces of one's target could often be clearly seen, smoke permitting. War in this period was therefore a very personal thing and a direct experience of killing and the risk of being killed: in this respect at least, all the battles considered here are similar.

Types of Battle

The characteristics of battle discussed in Chapter Two and the definition summarised in Table 2.1 can be applied to all the actions covered here, even though one of them, Linton, is more usually ascribed the status of skirmish or civil disorder. The forces engaged at Linton consisted of regular army units against local militia organised and led in military style, and the fighting took place within a definable geographical space. The aim of the assault was clearly defined, and included the destruction of the rebel force as an effective fighting unit in order to achieve a decision. There was also a mutual agreement to fight, limitations on behaviour and closely ordered movement by all the forces involved. Linton therefore falls happily within the terms of this definition. What is interesting is that other actions considered here, all of which are otherwise generally recognised by historians as deserving of the status of battles, share some attributes not usually associated with battles. The first battle of St Albans, for instance, is less a formal battle than a messy slaughter brought about by a surprise assault. Northampton is characterised by a lack of actual fighting: the result was achieved by deception and treason rather than by combat, and the casualties were the result of panicking troops throwing themselves into a swollen river. Bosworth began as a formal battle, but its decision was achieved by an impromptu skirmish at its edge in which a lucky intervention caused the death of one of the contenders for the crown. At Courtrai and Sedgemoor, as at Linton, professional soldiers met rebel civilians, and at Sedgemoor fighting commenced with a bungled night attack rather than a more organised 'military' advance.

Different types of battle, however, and especially those in different historical periods, can be distinguished in a number of other ways. A focus on technical differences – to be further discussed below – is one such way. A second may distinguish the formations used, such as column or line of troops. A third way may be to identify particular tactics applied in an attempt to achieve victory – such as direct frontal assault, single envelopment, double envelopment, or night attack on encampments. Any and all of these are valid for particular purposes, but none relate directly to the type of ground on which the battle has been fought. The battles we have examined can perhaps be distinguished in terms of the degree of relative movement of either army: those where one army is relatively static in its position, and those where both move. The latter divides into those where each side is fully organised as the action begins (a 'set-piece' action) and those where units of each army are brought into action as they arrive (an 'encounter' battle).

Set-piece Engagements: Offensive–Defensive

Perhaps the simplest form of battle is where one force remains static and the other moves to the assault. This is most evident among the battlefields studied here where fixed defences were built – especially at Aljubarrota, both battles at St Albans, Northampton, Linton and Fontenoy. At other sites, however, this kind of fight is also evident. At Maldon it is possible that the Saxon force remained static at the water's edge rather than advancing against the Norse, and at Stamford Bridge the Danes held the bridge as a defensive location and subsequently allowed the Saxons to form on the high ground above the river opposite their own main force. Similarly, the Flemings, caught with their backs to the city at Courtrai, appear to have remained relatively immobile against the French assault. At Roundway Down, the Parliamentarian cavalry were swept away before they were able to advance and the infantry caught by the Royalists breaking out of Devizes to their rear, and the regulars at Sedgemoor were attacked while encamped. The French at Roliça had occupied a strong hilltop position at which they were attacked, as did the allies at Sorauren. Despite their relative lack of manoeuvre, however, at few of these was the defending force in fact required to remain entirely static. Where the force holding a fixed position was victorious, as at Aljubarrota and Fontenoy, they subsequently moved to advance against a retiring enemy, and at Sedgemoor the regulars subsequently moved out to pursue and outmanoeuvre the retreating rebels, as did the allies at Sorauren. Where the force holding built defences was defeated, however, their movement was always to the rear of their own position: at the first battle of St Albans and at Linton into and through the town, at the second battle of

31. Roundway Down: the Bloody Ditch today.

St Albans out of the town, and at Northampton towards the town and into the flooded river. Other defeated defenders also moved: the Norse to their ships at Stamford Bridge, the Parliamentarian cavalry at Roundway Down into the Bloody Ditch (Plate 31), the Linton rebels over the hills to scatter in the countryside, the Sedgemoor rebels into watercourses and prison, and the French at Roliça out of Portugal and into Spain. Only at Courtrai does the successful defending force appear to have remained relatively immobile, only moving into the town once the fighting was over and the enemy fled.

Where built defences were used, some rise of ground may have been particularly relevant: as at Aljubarrota and the first battle of St Albans where the rising ground below the position would slow an enemy advance; or at Fontenoy where the slight ridge on which the village sits provides a convenient vantage on which to align a position. This does not apply to the defences at Northampton nor necessarily to those at the second battle of St Albans where the ground itself is flat, although here the fall of ground either side at Barnard's Heath provides a convenient edge. High ground provides the site of the defending position at Stamford Bridge and Roliça but failed to provide any security for those positions; the converse was true for the defenders at Sorauren. At Maldon a bank immediately at the water's edge may have provided a convenient position on which to stand for the Saxons. At both battles of St Albans and at Linton the ends of built-up streets mark the site of defences, but, as elsewhere, offered no particular security against determined or sudden assault. At Sedgemoor the Bussex Rhine was the line on which the defenders stood: in this case it provided no protection for the attackers; and at Courtrai the stream in front of the Flemish position hindered and disordered attacking cavalry. Accordingly, offensive–defensive battle appears in all our historical periods and at all kinds of landscape: as a particular tactic it therefore seems to be one that is not dependent upon a particular landscape type.

Set-piece Engagements: Offensive–Offensive

Where both armies advance against each other, neither side is defending: built defences are therefore an irrelevance and even an encumbrance. At Maldon, it is possible that both armies formed opposite one another and then moved to the attack, meeting somewhere in the space between them; the same is probably true of Assandun. At Bouvines different contingents of each force moved to engage the enemy, leading to a wheeling movement of both armies as each had different success. Similarly at The Dunes one flank of each force was able to push back its opponent, although the main fighting took place and the ultimate decision was reached on the seaward flank of both armies. At Tewkesbury and Stoke the armies advanced against each other across relatively even ground, while at Bosworth the mutual advance was downslope for one army and upslope for the other. The ebb and flow of the fighting at Corunna took in the slope of the hills and the low ground of the valley floor as well as the village against the slope, while at Naseby both forces moved from hilltop positions into the valley floor. Accordingly, the usual choice of ground for offensive–offensive battle will be flat ground, whether on the top of a hill as at Bouvines or Stoke, or on low ground as at Maldon, Assandun, Tewkesbury and Naseby. However, this is not determinant or inevitable, as shown by Corunna, where fighting took place against the hill itself, at Bosworth, where forces moved to engage one other part way up the slope of the hill, and especially The Dunes, where forces occupied the tops of sandhills but also fought in the hollows between them.

'Encounter' Battles

While set-piece engagements are carefully arranged and orchestrated, there are instances where more opportunistic decisions for battle were reached. At Cropredy Bridge, the commanders of both armies saw an opportunity to attack the other while in line of march: both then moved down into the valley where fighting took place. At Oudenaarde, the allies sought to bring the French to battle while the French sought to avoid battle: the chance encounter between units of both armies led to a gradual build-up of forces as one force attempted to outflank and thereby defeat the other, while the other sought to support its units in order to allow them to extricate from fighting without heavy loss. In both these cases, battle was in practice a matter of choice for both armies: because of the time involved in mobilising and ordering troops for action, there always remained the possibility of complete withdrawal out of the combat area. Accordingly, such 'encounter' battles never constitute accident or a failure to respond to threat or challenge. They are, however, much less common in the periods considered here than set-piece engagements because of the time and complex manoeuvres involved in getting an army ready to fight. In both of the cases considered here, battle was joined in a shallow valley, which is consistent with the general preference we have identified for this period. At Oudenaarde, one army formed on the line of a low ridge while the other formed along a small stream, with new units joining the line at its end as they entered the battlefield area. At Cropredy, units fought in a more piecemeal fashion, forming separate detachments spread along the valley and each concentrating on the three bridges across the river. It seems likely that encounter actions may be more common in periods of relative mobility of forces and where discipline can be maintained so as to bring troops into action without undue confusion. In terms of landscape, any shape appropriate for the warfare of a particular period will be selected for an encounter battle.

Discourses of Battle and Military Revolutions

All the battles and battlefields examined so far by us are located in western Europe and thus should reflect changes consequent upon what has been termed 'the Military Revolution'. Originally propounded by the historian Michael Roberts (1967), this is the idea that in the century after 1550 significant changes took place in European warfare practice. These included the widespread adoption of firearms (and consequent abandonment of the cross- and longbow), the development of new tactics that meant the dominance of infantry over cavalry on the battlefield, an increase in the size and professionalism of armies especially among the Protestant states of northern Europe (such as Holland and Sweden) and in France, and the support that this gave to increasingly centralised systems of government in absolutist and *ancien régime* states. A modified version of the thesis by Geoffrey Parker (1988) placed the beginning of the process earlier and left the closing date less certain, but gave it general support. Since then, the idea has been modified further into two linked concepts: that of the Military Revolution and of the Revolution in Military Affairs (Knox and Murray, 2001). The Military Revolution is held to comprise those wider changes in politics and society that 'recast society and the state as well as military organisations [and] alter the capacity of states to create and project military power' (Knox and Murray, 2001, 7). Revolutions in Military Affairs (RMAs) are consequent upon these and 'require the assembly of a complex mix of tactical, organisational, doctrinal, and technological innovations in order to implement a new conceptual approach to warfare' (Knox and Murray, 2001, 12). In other words, Military Revolutions concern the realms of politics and ideology, and RMAs represent alterations in warfare practice to accommodate these changes in wider conditions.

Jeremy Black (1991, 2000) has been a critic of the idea of the Military Revolution as generally understood from a number of perspectives. In terms of its specific periodisation, he has argued that a more important and more widespread period of military change can be seen from 1660 to 1760 than in the preceding century (Black, 1991). He has also offered the alternative of a 'long Military

Revolution' from 1450 to 1815, one that sees the rise of infantry power and the projectile weapon as part of the same process as the later adoption of firearms and their refinement (Black, 2001, 104–42) and all as part of the greater project of European overseas expansion. Indeed, it is European overseas conquest that he offers as the real Military Revolution (Black, 2001, 105). In this light, he further criticises the idea of the Military Revolution as essentially Eurocentric in formulation, taking no account of developments much beyond western Europe and assuming a universality of success by European forces in conflict with those of Asia, Africa or the Americas. He also challenges the focus on technology as the driver of change: 'Historians who argue for a technologically driven Military Revolution as the key causative factor behind the European rise to dominance . . . are mistaken, because, first, although the Europeans created the first global empires, this was only partly due to the military developments of the Military Revolution and, second, there was no European dominance. Third, the crucial changes in European armies in this period can be discussed in organisational as much as technological terms' (Black, 2001, 95). These 'organisational terms' include those ideological and political factors that allowed 'polities to incorporate insiders and outsiders' (Black, 2001, 129) and 'to win and retain allies' (2001, 130), which are in turn a measure of 'cultural flexibility that can be regarded as a crucial politico-military resource' (2001, 130). In such a scenario, the adoption of firearms over other projectile weapons (generally taken to be the crucial technological development) becomes less significant. John Lynn (2001, 35–56) has argued a similar point of view in relation to the reorganisation of the French army in the later seventeenth century.

The relevance of the concept of the Military Revolution for our work is precisely that of periodisation. If a Military Revolution (or at least a major RMA) took place during the early-modern historical period – between the late fifteenth and early eighteenth centuries – then it may be reflected in those aspects of warfare practice that we have chosen to investigate. Like Black, we are interested in ideological factors; unlike him, we are also interested in how these are reflected in the contexts of specific battlefields. It would seem that the kind of change in warfare practice that represents an RMA may indeed be evident from our work, especially in the shift from a medieval preference for high ground near towns to the early-modern preference for valley bottoms away from view; the further shift towards a 'utilitarian' view of landscape would represent part of a second Military Revolution and associated RMA (as suggested by Knox and Murray, 2001, 13). Whether these changes represent an effect of modern RMAs, however, depends upon how they are seen. If this kind of change is technologically driven, then it falls within the Military Revolution scenario; if not, then it is an ideological change that is part of wider changes, only some of which are specifically military.

From this perspective it is interesting to note the different accounts of the take-up of firearms available from the literature. For Keegan (1993, 328–34) the story is entirely one of technological advance, albeit beset with difficulties. The intermediary step was the development of the crossbow, which, like the firearm, was mechanical, and contained both a trigger firing mechanism and a wooden stock to rest against the shoulder. Adaptation for use as a gunpowder weapon was relatively simple: it meant replacing the grooved rest for the bolt projectile with a cylindrical barrel for the bullet. The issue thereafter was working out the best combination of arms for use on the battlefield, and various experiences are cited which contribute to this. Keegan (1993, 329) points out the alternatives to firearms available in the late medieval period – the English longbow and the Swiss pike in particular – but subsumes both to the perceived need for mixed forces (which represents the projection of a modern precept back into the past as if the precept is inevitably true, which it may not be). By contrast, Black (2002, 35–6) looks to a more economic reasoning for the adoption of gunpowder weapons. Here, the longbow is seen as pre-eminent on the battlefield in the late medieval period but limited in availability since it required a specific skill-base for its manufacture and use. The increase of the effectiveness of its chief (and more easily manufactured) rival the crossbow by the addition of a steel bow was, however, significantly expensive and required an investment in advanced metallurgical technology and infrastructure. By contrast to both, the early musket was made of iron rather than steel and required no particular specialist skills in use. Accordingly, out of similar materials but alternative frameworks, two different authors construct very different explanations for a single event.

A confusing element is the supposed relative advantage in effectiveness of gunpowder weapons over bows and arrows. As late as the eighteenth century – by which time European armies had been able to come to terms with muskets as weapons – estimates of kill rates are as low as 1:260 (that is, one kill in 260 firings) or even on occasion 1:460 (Duffy, 1987, 209). Assuming that the sixteenth-century arquebus was less effective than its flintlock descendant, then the early model must have been less effective still. In terms of range and rate of fire the musket and crossbow are roughly comparable, although both are surpassed by the longbow (Hardy, 1992); the inevitability of the adoption of firearms and their inherent superiority over other weapons once they become available is clearly questionable. On this basis, it seems more likely that Black's (2002) economic account may carry more plausibility. This, in turn, gives support to the idea that changes in battlefield preference also reflect other, non-technological and non-purely military, factors since the adoption of firearms on its own appears to change very little else. Any explanation for a new set of preferences for fighting terrain must indicate specifically how firearms in particular affect such choices: none are forthcoming in the literature so far. (Having said this, it needs also to be pointed out that our concern with the shapes of battlefields has not been a particular concern of military historians: the issue therefore has not previously arisen. This accordingly becomes a challenge that needs to be met.)

Our preferred explanations for the phenomena we believe we have identified lie in the realm of cultural expectation and ideology rather than of technological necessity. We appear to have some support in this from some interpretations of military change. It is, however, also possible that the changes in battlefield choice we have seen are a part of those changes attendant upon a Military Revolution. The first change we confidently identify takes place somewhere in the period post 1487 (the date of our last medieval battle) and prior to 1643 (the earliest modern battle we examine). This would place the most likely moment of change (although it may not be a sudden change: there may have been a long period of transmission or overlap between battlefield types) somewhere in the sixteenth century. This, in turn, gives support to the Roberts/Parker thesis of a Military Revolution between 1550 and 1650 rather than Black's later alternative. On the other hand, it does not rule out the idea of a 'long' Military Revolution spanning the late medieval and early modern periods, nor indeed an even longer Military Revolution covering the period to 1815. The latter would include our second major shift of landscape preference, to 'featured' space, in which case these changes may be reconsidered as a process of continuous development: from the highly visible medieval landscape reflecting medieval ideology, through its opposite to an appreciation of landscape as a resource like any other. The change is no less ideological in form, but becomes part of a wider and more widely recognised process which may also have some explanatory force.

CONCLUSIONS

This chapter has been a contribution specifically to the academic literature of historic warfare. We have compared and contrasted the landscapes of battle from various periods in various places, and offered ideas about what the differences between them may mean in terms of understanding war in the past.

The focus throughout has been on the similarities between and differences of one space from another, especially where features are shared by battlefields of a particular period. We think this is useful: it opens up the possibility of looking beyond the individual historic event and seeking out regularities in the choice of landscapes to fight in. We also sought to relate, however provisionally, these general findings to broader issues in military history, specifically the idea of one or more 'military revolutions'. These ideas must remain provisional, pending not only further work along the lines we recommend, but also debate and discussion among our colleagues who also study historic battlefield sites and historic warfare more generally. The results of these debates will emerge in the future. In the meantime, our focus shifts from the general to the more particular, as we attempt in the next chapter to tell some stories, of different kinds, about the places we have visited. This will provide a link with an examination of the current status, uses and memory of these places in Chapter Six, which will return us from the past into the twenty-first century.

FIVE

EXPERIENCING BATTLEFIELDS

As indicated in Chapter Four, this chapter moves us towards the more experiential aspects of our subject as required by the adoption of a 'phenomenological' approach. This chapter is therefore not about correlating information and data about all our sites as an assemblage, but concerns the specifics of the individual places we have visited and what we can learn from examining them in the particular way we advocate. Accordingly, rather than treating such places as sets of separate features and elements, here we endeavour to consider each of them as a whole, and, indeed, especially as a whole experience. In part, this chapter – and indeed our entire project – is a challenge and response to what we take to be the most common manner of approaching a historic battlefield in the present: that of the 'battlefield walk' (e.g. Guest and Guest, 1996; Holmes, 1996; Keegan, 1996), although we remain aware that we too walk these spaces. Frequently, battlefield walks invite one not to walk through the battlefield space – as we have usually done – but to walk around its boundaries and gaze upon it from the outside. This is what is offered to those interested in battle sites, especially in Britain, and is particularly noticeable among our sites at Roundway Down (Colman and Coupe, n.d.), Naseby and Tewkesbury (Plate 32). In contrast to these, we offer here an indication of what we experienced by being 'inside' these sites and its impact upon our appreciation of them.

Although we can perhaps claim to be the only battlefield archaeologists taking an explicitly phenomenological approach, we are not the only students of war to concern themselves with experiential aspects. Even the highly philosophical Clausewitz made his point about the battlefield as a province primarily of danger by emphasising its experiential aspects:

As we approach, the rumble of guns grows louder and alternates with the whirr of cannonballs. . . . Shots begin to strike close around us. We hurry up the slope where the commanding general is stationed with his large staff.

32. Tewkesbury: battle-route signs.

Here cannonballs and bursting shells are frequent and life begins to seem more serious. . . . Suddenly someone you know is wounded; then a shell falls among the staff. You notice that some of the officers act a little oddly; you yourself are not as steady and collected as you were: even the bravest can become slightly distracted. Now we enter the battle raging before us, still almost like a spectacle, and join the nearest divisional commander. Shot is falling like hail, and the thunder of our own guns adds to the din. Forward to the brigadier, a soldier of acknowledged bravery, but he is careful to take cover behind a rise, a house or a clump of trees. A noise is heard that is a certain indication of increasing danger – the rattling of grapeshot on roofs and on the ground. Cannonballs tear past, whizzing in all directions, and musketballs begin to whistle around us. A little further we reach the firing line, where the infantry endures the hammering for hours with incredible steadfastness. The air is filled with hissing bullets that sound like a sharp crack as they pass close to one's head. For a final shock, the sight of men being killed and mutilated moves our pounding hearts to awe and pity (Clausewitz [1832], 1976, 113).

This is a generalised account rather than a description of what it was like to be present at a particular battle in the past, although firmly grounded in the author's own experience of early nineteenth-century warfare in Europe. It serves nevertheless to emphasise aspects so often left out of the academic discourse of war. The first element is *fear*. Clausewitz's account is one that is rarely referred to in discussions of his work, but it is a passage crucial to his argument that war is, above all else, a province of danger; indeed, the passage comes from the chapter called 'Of danger in war'. The second element is *confusion*, since the observer has a very unclear idea of what is going on or the broader picture. The third element is *movement through space* as the author approaches the front line of action. The reality of battle as thus experienced is one of confusion, terror and movement through a landscape where these things take tangible shape.

Our own modern experience of these spaces is not that of combat. As outlined in Chapter Two, it is a sense of the historicity of a place where combat once took place. In some cases, we used our experience of the place to consider what it meant for our understanding of the events of the fight there. These led to some small but interesting and sometimes significant alterations to our conception of the historic event. At others, the experience was one where we were able to focus upon more general aspects of the battlefield in the light of what became our emerging idea of what was most common for battle sites of that particular historical period. At others again, we were able to sense the historicity of the place as evident in its shape and form. Throughout, achieving a sense of place was a crucial factor in making sense of the space of the battle. Where our concerns were particularly those of intellectual curiosity, we sought to relate the landscape as it is or was to events of the fight. A strong feeling of general affinity of the landscape today with its form in the past led to particular understandings of the place in the present, and this contrasted to those places where specific features or structures 'spoke' of the past in that location but where a more general affinity was lacking. At other places – not always those we assumed would be the case – so different are they today that gaining a clear impression was difficult if not impossible.

NOTICEABLE FEATURES

A key experience for us at some of the battlefields we have visited is linked to very particular features of the space. In some cases this is literally one key feature which strongly defines the experience of being there. At others it is a single central attribute or characteristic of the place which dominates all others. In all cases, they provide some kind of insight into the space as a historically constituted place, and the role of the fight that took place there in creating that sense of its history.

Roads

Corunna

The battle of Corunna – or as it is known locally, Elviña – was fought by Sir John Moore's retreating British army prior to taking ship from Spain in 1809. The contending armies were formed on two parallel ridges about 6km south of the city, and most of the fighting took place on the slopes of the higher and steeper southern ridge on which the French army stood (Plate 6). The fiercest fighting took place in and around the village of Elviña, which changed hands several times. The vernacular stone buildings of the village still hug the steep slopes of the hills, and the original core of the settlement remains much as it must have been on the day. From within the settlement, due to foreshortened lines of sight and impeding buildings, a sense of the surrounding landscape is difficult to grasp: little can be seen except the village itself. Modern visitors may find themselves confused by the change of names of the small villages here: the entire area now carries the name of Elviña, although at the time of the Peninsular War this was limited to the group of habitations hugging the slopes of the southern ridge. The modern Elviña church (Plate 48) lies across the valley (in what was the village of Eiris), providing a view of the main area where fighting took place. From here it is possible to gain a good view across the flat ground of the valley between the two main ridges and the arable fields occupying it. The small size of the fields and the vernacular buildings set among them indicate little change in this landscape since 1809, although on the hills above, the encroachments of the expanding city and especially the new university (Plate 6) are very clear.

In general, interpretations of the battle have emphasised the use of high ground and its defensive advantage; they have drawn the focus of the fight as an attempt by the British to halt the French advance by holding on to the high ground of the northern ridge. This interpretation is plausible, but only if the northern ridge would provide an effective block to the French advance, and from a map it looks quite likely. On the ground, however, it becomes evident that this interpretation really does not work so well. First, the tiny village of Elviña clings very tightly to the foot of the southern ridge (Plate 6): gaining control of the small cluster of buildings there would not prevent a French advance on either side of it. Second, the valley between the two ridges is too wide to allow troops on one ridge to impede movement from the other. The valley is, however, reasonably flat; and it is criss-crossed by a series of roads and tracks. These roads and tracks meet at a number of points, allowing ultimately any army in control of these routes to bypass troops on the northern ridge and enter the city. It therefore seems much more likely that the fighting was meant not to secure a firm position on high ground but to secure the roads and their junctions in the valley: to achieve this, control of the village of Elviña would have been vital. This would explain Moore's focus on Elviña and, indeed, on the lower slopes of the higher ridge, as well as his choice of fiercely offensive (rather than defensive) tactics. Paradoxically, perhaps, it also turns Corunna from an event similar to a rather static eighteenth-century set-piece battle to a more mobile one akin to those of our own age.

Sorauren

The two battles of Sorauren were fought by Wellington's army four years after Corunna. They too were fought in northern Spain on two lines of ridges facing north–south, and small settlements (this time located on the lateral edges of the battlespace) again provided the foci for action (Plate 21). Sorauren itself (Plate 33) stands at one end of the bridge over the River Ulzama which marks the western extent of the battlefield. From this bridge Wellington first surveyed the French forces and the view past and over the village church is relatively unchanged. Sorauren is a moderately sized settlement, rapidly suffering embourgeoisement, of stone buildings and narrow alleys. Zabaldica at the other side of the battlefield – hidden from Sorauren by rising ground – is much smaller, remains a farming community, and consists of very few buildings and no church: its bridge over the River Arga, which marks the eastern extent of the battlefield, is about 500m distant. The space between the two villages consists of a narrow valley containing a stream which enters the Ulzama by Sorauren. The valley sides are steep and rocky as well as overgrown, and at the eastern end above Zabaldica the two ridges are joined by a linking saddle with sides even steeper than those of the valley itself (Plate 26).

Apparently topographically accurate plans of the battlefield (e.g. Oman, 1902c, 652–3) reveal a central circular hill forming the allied position and a wide enough linking saddle between the eastern slope of this hill and the French-held ridge to the north to allow attacks along it in force. On the ground, however, the central valley is experienced not as a linear ridge opposite a dominating hill but as two opposed linear ridges of roughly equal height. The linking saddle between them measures only three or four metres across its top, barely wide enough for a decent footpath, and the steep inclines on either side provide little space for deployment. This main area of fighting is experienced as a very contained space with restricted sightlines within the battlespace and none beyond except beside

33. Sorauren: village and French hill-top position as seen from bridge, the allied commander's first viewpoint.

the two main rivers to east and west (Plate 21). Overall, this battlefield landscape is unsuitable for mass movements and instead would suit much more the use of skirmishers in small groups or as individuals, taking cover among rocks and shrubs. Only the main river valleys to east and west provide wide enough open ground for the movement of troops in good order. This suggests that the two battles of Sorauren as fought may have been confused affairs, relying less upon the regular discipline of troops in line or column than upon individual initiative and skirmishing skills. Where the French centre took the offensive against troops in line standing upon the top of ridge and hills, the disadvantages they faced become clear: the ordered linear allied formation would be able to focus their fire against disordered groups of small numbers of French soldiers.

The fights at Sorauren did not involve roads to the same extent as at Corunna, but were nevertheless fought for access by road. After the French withdrawal, the allies were able to advance deeper into the Pyrenees and closer towards metropolitan France itself. Previously in the campaign, in order to avoid French-held garrison towns such as Pampeluna and the French-held routes between them, it had been necessary for the allies to construct their own roads for heavy supply trains and artillery. We believe we located part of this *camiño des inglés* on the Sorauren battlefield. A farm track a few metres wide (Plate 27) runs along the top of the southern ridge and obliquely down its steep forward (northern) slope towards Sorauren, ultimately joining the modern track which runs the length of the valley beside the stream at its foot into the village itself. The track is of a width to accommodate a gun carriage or a cart, does not appear to be Roman or medieval in origin and although now in poor repair as a road, does show evidence of former metalling with flat stones. It is certainly in the right location for a part of the *Camiño des Inglés*, joining as it does the main route at Sorauren but originating from the south and not leading from or to the city of Pampeluna.

Heights and Depths

Roundway Down

The landscape of Roundway Down is typical of its region in the southern part of Britain: rolling chalk downland with mostly gentle slopes although cut by steeper scarps (Plate 17). Roundway Hill itself is orientated east–west: it is a rough isosceles triangle in shape with two long sides to north and south and the higher and broader eastern end immediately above the battlefield. To the south lies the town of Devizes, masked by a lower rise of ground, and linked by a route that climbs the steep southern slope of Roundway Hill. The land was mostly open grazing in the seventeenth century, looking much as the small preserved patch of downland on the southern slope of Roundway Hill does today: the ploughed ground that makes up the rest of today's landscape is much more recent in origin. Roundway Down is today peaceful countryside: agricultural, tamed, gentle and empty. To see the battlefield you must walk around it and gaze at it from some distance away, for there is no right of way through it.

The area is rich in older remains which are, for a modern viewer, difficult to ignore. An Iron Age hillfort erroneously called 'Oliver's Camp' (a reference to Cromwell) stands above the scarp at the western end of Roundway Hill. The fort is circular in plan, surrounded by the remains of its earthen ditch and bank: inside the ground is relatively flat, revealing little of its ancient use, although most visitors will assume a military one. On the top of Roundway Hill immediately above the battlefield are several large Bronze Age burial mounds, and more lie on the hills surrounding the low ground on which the armies formed. King's Play Hill to the north has an even older burial monument on its summit in the form of a neolithic long barrow. The battlefield itself is approximately equidistant from the great henge monument at Avebury to the north-west and Stonehenge to the south. None of these features played any part on the day of the battle, however, and may have been effectively 'invisible' to participants: the days of strong antiquarian interest in landscape features were yet to come.

For 2km above the eastern scarp the ground rises gently along the top of Roundway Hill, but suddenly beside Oliver's Camp it falls almost sheer for 100m: down this near vertical slope, fleeing cavalry tumbled and fell, horse and rider, unable to stop or rein in. Walkers today going slowly on foot also come across it with frightening suddenness: one moment the ground is flat, the next it falls away into bottomlessness, hidden by trees (Plate 31). What it was like for fast-moving riders – the panicked screaming of horses and riders; the attempt to pull up only to be pushed on by those coming from behind; the fear, confusion and noise – can at least be guessed at when you are there. The bottom of the slope still bears the memory of the event: it is today called the Bloody Ditch.

Sedgemoor

The landscape of the Somerset Levels – flat, cut by waterways and drainage ditches (Plate 20) – gives you a good impression of the landscape in 1685, although the main water obstacle of that period, the Bussex Rhine, is no longer extant. The Polden Hills to the north and the rising ground to the south and west enclose the space of the battlefield, and the church tower of Westonzoyland is visible only a few hundred metres away. A ditch immediately to the north of the battle site, about a kilometre away, is curved like those of the seventeenth century and may well mark the line of the Moor Drove into which fleeing rebels fell. Here, one achieves in particular some sense of the history of the location: it feels very low and isolated, and routes out of the Levels are not easily evident.

The story of Sedgemoor has passed into local knowledge and folklore, and it is an interesting site for the student of heritage places because – unlike so many other historic battlefields in England – it has been so readily incorporated into local and national historical knowledge and importance. The battlefield is well marked, it is part of a 'historic' route you can drive along and is recorded by a small exhibition in the local church. It has been adopted as the local memorial site for the dead of all wars, where these memorials on the site of the action create a sombre atmosphere (Plate 34). It is largely assumed that visitors who pass through the district – whether in nearby Bridgwater or the villages of Westonzoyland or Chedzoy, between which the battle was fought – are visiting the site of the battle; if not, they are directed there. Partly this represents the importance of the event of the battle to the locality (as represented by the public house in Westonzoyland, Plate 34): those who fought and died on the rebel side were largely drawn from the region. Partly it is the national historical importance of the event, and partly it is the fact that this was the last event of its kind in England.

34. *Sedgemoor: a pub sign celebrating the battle, Westonzoyland.*

Structures

Northampton

Although included in the English Heritage (1995) *Register*, Northampton battlefield today is relatively unacknowledged. It is not marked as a battlefield – certainly not as a historically important one; and staff in the local Tourist Information Office showed no knowledge of it. The ground on which it took place is now a municipal golf course (Plate 14). Between it and the river lies a disused industrial estate and railway line. Until recently, the actual site of the battle was thought to be where the disused railway line and factories are. These are sufficiently close to the current line of the river to make sense of the flooding of the entrenchments. Also, they are further away from the high ground on which one of the contending armies encamped. Modern military sense would dictate that – if indeed somewhere close to the river was where the royal army camped – this place ought to be the site. Work by Glenn Foard (n.d.), then Northampton's county archaeologist, has located the buried remains of the 'Battel Dike', the earthwork that surrounded the royal forces. It is on the golf course and adjacent to the modernised buildings of the (then) nunnery now called Delapre House (Plate 30).

Northampton is quite typical of battles of the Wars of the Roses in some ways, but seems untypical in others. Its typicality lies first in the highly *political* nature of the event. Treason, betrayal and the changing of sides are the stuff of this conflict, which lasted for nearly fifty years intermittently. Although the high casualties are reflected elsewhere, at Northampton they were not due to high levels of butchery as at other battles but to a natural phenomenon and to disorganised panic. Also typical is the proximity to urban space, although lying on low ground, and the way in which other features present in or adjacent to the battlefield space were ignored. Rather than occupying Delapre Abbey, both sides bypassed it; the wounded and injured were taken there after, but otherwise it played no part in the action despite its apparent suitability for military defence.

Tewkesbury

Tewkesbury (1471) was one of the bloodiest fights of the Wars of the Roses. After very fierce fighting in fields south of the town and within sight of the great Abbey church (Plate 24), a contingent of fleeing soldiers was trapped in low ground beside a stream. There, they were mercilessly cut down despite attempts to surrender: this place bears the name of 'Bloody Meadow' to this day. The very final stage of the battle was fought immediately adjacent, possibly even inside, the great church.

The battlefield is included in the English Heritage (1995) *Register*, but in practice it has not been well protected from alteration as part of the battlefield area has since been built upon. Today, Tewkesbury is visited by many tourists and makes much of its medieval past. In particular, its streets are hung with heraldry, its museum boasts the town's aristocratic connections, many of which relate to the battle which is celebrated there by a rather romanticised diorama of the event. The battlefield itself has also been incorporated in the tourist appeal, and is marked by a battlefield trail to be walked. Typical of such walks, it is circular: it ends where it began, as indicated by the signs which direct two ways at once (Plate 32), and to join the walk at any point along its route and to go either way is equally valid. The route itself takes you through various parts of the battlefield in the form of a gentle, sometimes countryside, stroll. The signs themselves remind you what route it is you are walking, and along the route are other reminders of the event it commemorates. Other aspects of the local historic environment are also included.

One particular nineteenth-century memorial of the event, located in an area known as 'The Vineyards', now stands on the edge of a housing estate but has found uses other than that of historical marker – such as a place to park one's bike (Plate 43) – and yet also has kept its status of 'tourist viewpoint' in the other direction. The walk takes you past this point to emphasise that *this place* is part of a significant historical event. The point is emphasised by the inclusion in the route of other 'historical' places. One is a medieval moated site, most likely abandoned as a habitation well before 1471 but glorying in the name 'Margaret's Camp' (Margaret being Queen Margaret, the Lancastrian commander during the battle) which links it to a battle of which it was never, in fact, a part. From here, the walk passes *across* the battlefield space, via a preserved medieval field system, towards its main site. A plinth here records the events of the battle by use of a map of the battlefield, pointing out its historical importance as an event. The plinth stands on the edge of the area called 'Bloody Meadow'. The Bloody Meadow is experienced today as a haven of nature, planted with trees and shrubs which produce red flowers in spring and summer, to match the name of the place where they stand: it is one of the places which has given its name to the Bloody Meadows Project itself.

A SENSE OF PLACE

There is a sense in which the distinction between locations that offer 'a sense of place' and those that do not is meaningless: if a place cannot offer a strong sense of its identity, then that is part of the experience of being there. On the other hand, people are best at remembering those locations where a sense of place is strongest. Among the sites we visited for this project, most offered a strong sense of their history. Others, however, had any such sense removed from them, and these are discussed in the next section. One way of using this sense of place is in choosing between possible but disputed locations for a historic event. Elsewhere, it is a particular kind of experience that one encounters at particular places.

Disputed Place

Assandun

We visited two possible sites for the battle of Assandun fought between Edmund Ironside and King Cnut of Norway. The most commonly accepted site (Smurthwaite, 1993, 46–9) is that in southern Essex, on the low ground between the hills on which stand the modern villages of Ashingdon and Canewdon (Plate 3). The name Ashingdon represents a good modern rendition of ancient Assandun, while Canewdon is a modern version of Cnut's Don

(Cnut's fort or stronghold). An alternative site was, however, offered by Rodwell (1993) in north Essex at Ashdon, especially because of the area of that village referred to in tithe maps as 'Old Church' (Plate 2). Since it is reported that Cnut built a church on the site of the battle to celebrate his victory and conquest, this 'Old Church' could be that to commemorate Assandun. Both sites are adjacent to rivers and would have been accessible by boat. Both therefore represent plausible points of rest on routes between the east coast and the Midlands. The regions of both provide evidence of occupation in the Roman and later periods: in particular, near Ashdon is the Cambridgeshire village of Bartlow, whose 'hills' are in fact Romano-British burial mounds. About 500m south of these at Hills Farm is evidence of an earthen bank which could date from the Saxon period, and possibly be related to defences built by Edmund.

The two landscapes are, however, quite different. The ground between Ashingdon and Canewdon is flat and open (Plate 3), and the hills on which the two villages stand rise out of this about 2km apart. At Ashdon, the area of 'Old Church' is not at all flat but falls to the river with increasing steepness (Plate 2). While the Ashingdon landscape is wide and unconstricting to view, the Ashdon space is claustrophobic and constrained. Neither would be impossible space on which to fight a battle, especially with the relatively small forces typical for the early eleventh century, but the Ashingdon location feels more like a battlefield should. There is space to manoeuvre, to form bodies of troops, to disembark, and hills on which to stand to oversee the space and to watch for an encroaching seaborne enemy. Ashdon provides none of this: the space is narrow and not overlooked, and visibility is restricted by the slope of the ground. It is difficult to see either Saxon or Norse choosing this place to decide their differences. By contrast, at Ashingdon the result would be clearly visible to watchers on the hills, and indeed to those by the riverside. On balance, therefore, and based on our experience of these two places, we feel the more likely site is that more generally accepted.

Public Space

Bosworth

Bosworth is the only battlefield in England with a dedicated visitor centre, at the time of writing (2004) undergoing refurbishment. The building housing the centre lies on one side of Ambion Hill, out of site of the main battlefield space.

The focus of the site is upon Ambion Hill itself, where the royal army stood. On the lower ground below, a hedge marks the line where the opposing forces supposedly formed. From the marked track around the battlefield space – and especially from higher on the hill – tall flagpoles mark the more distant positions of other forces who waited the opportunity to intervene on one side or the other (Plate 4). At the foot of the hill and across a road lies the area marked as the site where a cavalry skirmish decided the final outcome of the action. A stone memorial records the death of the last Plantagenet king of England (Plate 35). Nearby is the nineteenth-century railway station, from which many visitors approach the site, and rising above is the channel of the Oxford Canal, providing a rear boundary to the site.

There is a strong sense of claustrophobia and the smallness of the fighting area at the foot of Ambion Hill where the hedge lies: the few hundred metres of visible space in any direction serve to emphasise the closeness of soldiers to one another in medieval warfare. The views from the hill distract from this sense of place: the flags marking other positions feel very distant and unconnected to where one stands (Plate 4). The site of the skirmish is by contrast highly atmospheric: the modern intrusions of railway and canal do not interfere with a sense of entrapment in a small space with no escape, and the rather romanticised memorial adds to the emotional impact (Plate 35). Nevertheless, as a site

35. Bosworth: stone monument to Richard III.

165

designed for visitors, it is highly orchestrated and organised: the place is not experienced but imposes itself upon the visitor. Although 'historic' in several senses, the site loses a feeling of historicity.

Empty space

Oudenaarde

Oudenaarde, fought in 1708, is one of the Duke of Marlborough's four great allied victories against the French. Typically for its period, the battle was fought in a shallow valley with few noticeable landscape features (Plate 15). Especially as experienced today, the site apparently offers little in the way of interest and is really a rather unexciting piece of Belgian landscape. The low mound representing all that is left of Breween castle where Marlborough positioned himself is undistinguished and inaccessible by right of way (Plate 29). Lines of sight along the valley are unencumbered apart from occasional trees and slight undulations in the ground. The location is highly rural, open and quiet; the town of Oudenaarde is a very short distance away and yet one feels entirely cut off from urban bustle. What is also felt, however, is a strong sense of the battlefield as a place. It is experienced as an open shallow valley but with external lines of sight impeded by rising ground in all directions. This creates a paradox that gives the place a strong character: it is separated from the surrounding territory and enclosed, but because it is also an open space it is not constricted.

The French occupation of the line of the ridge at the western side of the valley is often interpreted as their adoption of a strong position on high ground, in contrast to the allied occupation of low ground along a stream. On the ground, however, it becomes apparent that the ridge is not very high, that the slope from which it rises is not steep but shallow and gentle, and that it offers no obstacle to advancing troops. The same is true of the stream along which the allies formed: it is no more than a few tens of centimetres deep, and is less than a metre across. It provides no obstacle to movement to front or rear and no protection from a determined enemy advance. This raises the question: what were these features good for if not strength of position and solid defence? The answer is that they both offer rather nice straight lines: the ridge is fairly straight for a kilometre and more, and the stream runs parallel to it until it curves slightly away from the ridge. In other words, rather than being good positions from which to defend against attack, they offer good positions on which to form troops as they come into action, so the battle line remains linear and well ordered as required by the tactics of the day. This is not a significant change of interpretation from a military historical point of view, perhaps: both ridge and stream remain 'good positions' and our understanding of the tactics and outcome of the battle are not subject to revision. What does change is the emphasis: no longer on functional utility for defence, but on other decision-factors which may have been just as important at the time. It demands that we address some of our ideas about the way people thought in the early eighteenth century and acknowledge that they did not think like us.

Stoke

Stoke or Stoke Field (1487) today is largely agricultural land on high ground above the main A46 road running north to Newark (Plate 23). The village of East Stoke (which gives the battle its name) was for a while the home of our forerunner Richard Brooke, and his drawing of Stoke Church (Plate 52) forms the frontispiece to his book (Brooke, 1854). Beside the church stands the modern memorial to the battle (Plate 42), replacing a much earlier one. On the other side of the road from the church – almost on the edge of the battlefield – lie the earthwork remains of the medieval village of Stoke.

Access to the battlefield is via a path following the line of an ancient trackway which peters out – along with the public right of way it represents – when you reach the centre of the battlefield itself. There is a good sense here of the height of the battleground above surrounding land. From this spot on a good day you can clearly see the town of Newark, 6.5km away, which means the battlefield was visible from Newark. Further across the battlefield and 14km to the south-west on the extreme edge of visibility lies Nottingham, and the extreme northern edge of the battlefield hill provides a clear view to the small village and ferry of Fiskerton on the River Trent. Between the road to the ferry and the battlefield itself is an obvious way down: a slight cleft in the side of the hill. This carries the name today of 'Red Gully' – partly because of the soil colour; but also because by tradition so many of those fleeing the battle were cut down until the soil ran red with their blood. Today, the countryside quietness of Stoke belies its violent past but offers a good canvas for the historical imagination.

Bouvines

Bouvines is one of the founding moments of the French nation, and yet its actual site is unmarked (cf. however Chapter Six). The entire space is bounded by falling ground in all directions, although the fight itself occupied only part of this: human military architecture may therefore have been more important than landscape features for the shape of events.

From the flat ground that is the site only the red rooftops of nearby settlements are highly visible (Plate 5): the modern church at Bouvines village is the sole building standing high enough to be seen in full. The ground falls away gradually in all directions giving a sense of openness: there is no true horizon here, only the fading edge of vision. A modern stone cross at a road junction is the only feature in this space, which is otherwise an empty rural landscape. The Roman road that ran across this space is today marked by a track, and the main modern intrusion is the railway line that marks the eastern extent of the battlefield. The farm on the site of the monastery adjacent to the Roman road and on the edge of the eastern slope is hidden behind trees, creating another edge to the space. All around is emptiness and silence. Accordingly, like Stoke, this space offers a clear canvas for the historical imagination with little to impinge upon it.

Cropredy

The modern bridge across the Cherwell at Cropredy stands on the same position as its predecessor fought over in the seventeenth century (Plate 36), as do the others involved at Slat Mill and Hays Bridge. On one side of Cropredy Bridge lies the small village, on the other the floodplain opens up in front and to either side (Plate 8). From the plain there is a clear view across and along the wide flat valley, while the steep hills either side are high and block any line of sight beyond them. The initial positions of the two contending forces can be easily identified – the Parliamentary army on the western scarp beyond the village, and the modern road on the slope of the eastern hills marking the route of the Royalist forces. Their respective routes down into the valley where the fighting took place can be traced both by eye and on foot. As a place, it has no particularly strong identity but the landscape allows a clear picture of battlefield events unfolding.

Naseby

The same is true of Naseby, fought in 1645. Here, the valley itself is one not to stand inside but to gaze upon from above – most conveniently at the site of the monument and information board marking the initial position of the

36. Cropredy Bridge: memorial tablet on the bridge with flowers in remembrance of the dead.

Parliamentary army (Plate 13). The relatively shallow fall of ground to the small stream at the valley foot is evident, as is also the similarly gradual rise towards the Royalist position on the ridge approximately 1km opposite. To the rear of the Parliamentary position lies a modern motorway link, but despite opposition to its construction this does not impose upon an experience of the actual battlefield space. It does, however, separate the main battlefield from Naseby village, which was the site of one of the baggage parks, and also from a separate monument nearby. Although the on-site monument and interpretive panel invite visitors, the overall experience at Naseby is very typical of most battlefield visits: it is very clearly a site to be gazed upon rather than walked into.

Between Rural and Urban

Fontenoy

While most battlefields present a reasonable sense of unity in terms of experience, the site at Fontenoy is more mixed. Fontenoy village – the centre of the action on the day of battle – lies to the west of an extensive plain flanked to the north by a small wooded area which was much more heavily wooded in 1745. This plain is open and wide (Plate 10), falling very gradually away from the village and presenting clear lines of sight from it, broken only by modern incursions such as the railway line that now lies across it, modern house construction and field boundaries. Above and behind the village, further to the west, a quite steep slope rises to flat high ground, topped by a conical Iron Age burial mound and souterrain from which the roofs of the village may be seen but which cannot be seen from the village. The north–south road that runs through the village lies upon a slight ridge dominating the battlefield plain: it leads north past a small modern cemetery also providing a good overview of the central battlefield area. The impression is of openness, clear lines of sight and room for manoeuvre.

A very different experience of the battlespace is provided at Antoing, 2km to the south of Fontenoy and standing on high ground above a gorge of the River Escaut. Here the defensive battle line turned 90° to the west, facing south across the river. Antoing itself is a sizeable town of steep streets centred upon a large and imposing chateau surrounded by high walls. The impression is of a highly urban space with restricted space for movement and limited views: the only clear view across the battlefield would be either from the high windows of the chateau or from a point on the northern edge of the town, leading now to a public park and beyond to countryside. This is perhaps more than a matter of the presence of buildings: the buildings at Fontenoy village – especially the church, and the great barn nearby (Plate 28) – would have been present on the day of the fight, and indeed were fortified as part of the defensive arrangements. The streets of the village, apart from the rather incongruous (for France) village green, are not especially wide. The impression is, however, of being in the countryside rather than a town and of open vistas around one, even though not immediately discernible by eye. It is noticeable here that fierce fighting took place around Fontenoy, but not in or around Antoing: apart from the defensive strength of the Antoing position – although possibly not that much stronger than that at Fontenoy – it may be that feeling of space which contributed to the allied decision to attack in the centre at Fontenoy rather than the Antoing flank.

Linton

Linton (1648) is a less obviously schizophrenic experience than Fontenoy, although sharing some characteristics and also highly disjointed. Half of the space – around Haw's Hill to the south – is highly rural; the other half through the streets of Linton itself is essentially urban (Plate 11). The fight at Linton, as mentioned in Chapter Four, is technically not considered a battle although it meets certain of the criteria for such an event, and covers a larger area than most battles of its period proportional to the numbers of fighters engaged.

Haw's Hill rises 2km south of Linton itself, overlooking the town but providing no place from which to fire into it directly. Of more relevance is the hill's dominance of the road from Saffron Walden, which provided access to Linton. It is possible to gain a good sense of this from the site today, crossed by rights of way which allow clear lines of sight and access to the hill and the road below. From here it is easy to trace the sequence of the event into the town and beyond. On the opposite side of the space of the fight – on the slopes of Rivey Hill above Linton and the slope beyond to the Roman road – is an equally rural area. Entry into Linton from the south is by the same road as was barricaded and it follows the same path as the fleeing rebels took from the assault. Some buildings in the streets survive from the seventeenth century, although altered, giving a sense of the place as it was. Modern roads and footpaths allow good access to what were escape routes for the rebels to the surrounding high ground and the Roman road.

Urban Space

St Albans

For the first battle at St Albans in 1455 Henry VI gathered his forces in the centre of the town, where the wide main market street, as today, was suitable for the mustering of an army. The opposing army launched an attack that travelled up the narrow streets towards the centre of the town. Barricades along the old town ditch – a line still traceable as modern roads – were thrown down and the defenders retreated towards the town centre. Some of the buildings present today were those standing on the day of battle, and passing up these streets today, you still enter the town centre suddenly, going from quiet residential side streets into the bustling market area (Plate 18). The effect is somewhat similar to that likely to have been experienced on the day of battle. As you pass up these streets, memorials to the dead of other, more recent, wars remind you what war and battle is all about, since St Albans is one of only two towns in England where the First World War dead are commemorated in the individual streets from which they came (Plate 37), and nearby stand the alms houses built by Sarah Churchill, wife of the Duke of Marlborough.

37. St Albans: First World War memorial in Hopewell Lane.

The second battle at St Albans also began in the streets but moved beyond them. Unlike the first action, troops mustered in the Roman remains at the foot of the hill on which the town stands, moved up past the great Abbey church and penetrated once again the main market area. Thereafter, the fight moved some 2km away to Barnard's Heath (Plate 19), dropping out of the centre of the town by a steep road to the east and rising again a little further on. This area is today part of the town itself: the only evidence of open ground is the lawn that occupies one side of the road. Opposite stand late nineteenth-century houses forming, in memory of the event, Battle Row and Archer's Fields: Boundary Road, running perpendicular to the main street, marks the original edge of the town demesne and the likely site of the barricades set up. A small diversion to right or left down modern suburban streets indicates the steep slope that lies either side. From there, it is a further 3km to the slight hill on the north side of Sandridge village and the final site of the battle (Plate 25).

Neither battle of St Albans is included in the English Heritage *Register*. The reasons relate to the difficulty of controlling development and maintaining 'landscape character' in a busy modern town centre. But St Albans is also well enough protected under other procedures – as a conservation area, under development control arrangements, and so on. Also, the construction of a 'circular battlefield walk' is just what would interfere with other legitimate current uses for the same spaces. The experience of being in an urban space here is similar to that on the day of battle: bustle and busyness, lines of sight blocked by buildings, vehicles and other human beings, and confusion as to which way to turn oneself and as to the activities of others. Accordingly, what is

38. Roliça: view from the French second position over Columbeira village; the French first position is in the middle distance.

experienced – and partly because there is no deliberate attempt to determine how one should experience the place – is a sense of the historicity of St Albans as a place once of ordered mass violence.

DENIAL OF PLACE

All places offer some kind of experience of themselves, but at some the experience is stronger. The difference can also be measured in terms of the temporality they contain: some places are irredeemably of now, while others impart an idea of their pasts. Where the experience is one of the now, the past has often been overlain or masked by more recent intrusions. These changes – usually in physical form – may be massive, in terms of an entire recasting of the landscape, or smaller but equally affecting.

Coastal Change

Maldon

The Battle of Maldon (AD 991) is the earliest event in English history to which the term 'battle' can be applied and of which the location is securely known. We know of the battle from a large fragment of Anglo-Saxon poetry that has survived, along with entries in various contemporary and near-contemporary chronicles. The story of the event is simple: a band of Vikings landed on the Essex coast, and were met by armed men drawn from the surrounding region. The Saxons drew up on the shoreline before the Vikings crossed from Northey Island where their ships lay. After an exchange of bravado speeches (conveniently recorded for posterity), there was a tough fight in which the heroic leader of the Anglo-Saxons was killed. The Vikings were victorious but, due to heavy losses, unable to exploit their victory beyond the demand of payment, after receiving which they went home. The site of this action as described in the various literary references was finally identified in 1925 and is generally regarded as the correct spot (Cooper, 1993; Swagg, 1981).

Incorporating this story as part of English history and making sense of the place where it happened, an additional event was added to the tale, of which the contemporary literature makes no mention. Supposedly, after the exchange of speeches, the Saxons gallantly and honourably withdrew to allow the Vikings to cross the causeway from Northey Island and form on the dry ground of the mainland. Then the fighting could start. This withdrawal was understood to be necessary because the ground as experienced today is very marshy (Plate 12) and would not allow for large numbers of heavily armed men to move easily. Only withdrawal to higher and dryer ground would allow fighting. This voluntary withdrawal by the defending Saxons has been incorporated in virtually every telling since 1925 and still persists (cf. Guest and Guest, 1996, 8–11; Smurthwaite, 1993, 43–5). Work by Petty and Petty (1993, 159–69) in the 1970s, however, established that in the tenth century the ground at this spot was not marshy but dry and firm. Over the past 1,000 years or so, the sea level has risen by nearly 2m to create the landscape we see today; but this is not the landscape on which the battle was fought.

The site itself is interesting, however, from the point of view of trying to understand Anglo-Saxon attitudes to warfare. Much is made of 'warrior' ideologies for the post-Roman and early medieval periods (Hawkes, 1989) and the literary sources make much of 'honourable' warrior behaviour. But it would seem that the reconstructed landscape of the Maldon battlefield – as interpreted with the aid of contemporary texts – tells a different story. Instead of bands of warriors bound by codes of honour and courage determined to fight on equal terms, the Saxons simply tried to slaughter the Norsemen as they stood at a disadvantage on the shoreline. In return, the Norsemen tried to kill those Saxons who stood in their way. As a style of battle it represents what might be called a 'swarming' of an enemy. This is a kind of relatively disorganised warfare involving relatively unformed bodies of armed people, a style of combat from the very earliest periods of organised warfare that we know about (Carman, 1999a, 49). There was nothing honourable here: no formal exchanges of speeches, nor any gallantry, nor any particular discipline. Pre-battle organisation among those involved was probably not very unlike post-battle disorganisation. The time between consists simply of butchery without mercy. The literature of the day justified and reordered the events afterwards, turning it into a tale of courage and honour to meet the expectation of what warriordom was about, but on the day it was just mutual disorganised slaughter. Literary retellings aside, the reality of early medieval warfare as represented at Maldon, it seems, had nothing to do with warrior ideologies and may have been instead merely about blood and death.

The Dunes

The Dunes (fought in 1658) is well named, since most of the landscape consists of just that – large sand dunes on the northern coast of France (Plate 9). About 2km inland lies a flat area of arable farmland bounded by a canal, but this strip is no more than 500m wide. The seaside beach is only a hundred or so metres deep at most, so most of the battlefield consists of the 10m-high dunes, standing at varying distances apart but rarely more than 50m at the top and considerably closer at their foot. The ground is therefore difficult to walk and lines of sight are few at ground level, although clear all-round vision is possible from the very tops of the sandhills themselves. Accordingly, gaining an overall sense of the site as a seventeenth-century battlefield is difficult. By contrast, the specifics of certain very restricted areas – at the foot of dunes, or part way up their side – give a strong idea of the problems of soldiers on the day, unable to move without difficulty, unable to see clearly ahead or around, and with no sense of events more than a very few metres away.

The difficulty of gaining an overall experience is compounded today by the continuing presence of debris from the Second World War. Everywhere under the sand, strips of rusting barbed wire impede movement and entangle feet, and most notable is the large and ruinous concrete gun emplacement standing immediately above the beach. It is in general this twentieth-century experience that dominates. The nearby Fort des Dunes is a testimony to twentieth-century warfare in the vicinity: during our visit it was reoccupied by the French military as a firing ground for training for counter-terrorism operations. On its wall is a monument to those shot during the Second World War for resisting the German occupation. Adjacent is the French military cemetery for those killed in 1944 and 1945. Between the fort and the dunes themselves is a railway line that must be crossed. All this – plus the focus in nearby Dunkerque on the events of 1940 – overlies any experience of the site as a place where seventeenth-century soldiers once fought. One nevertheless receives a strong sense of place here – but it is a twentieth-century place rather than a seventeenth-century or exactly contemporary one.

Rural Space

Aljubarrota

The site of the battle of Aljubarrota lies some distance from, and completely out of sight of, the place of its memorialisation. The latter – the town of Batalha with its great cathedral (Plate 46) – provides a strong experience of medieval piety in memory of a historic event of national significance to Portugal. The battle site itself occupies a more rural location (Plate 1), heavily encumbered with militaristic intrusions (for a discussion of which, see Chapter Six) which interfere with any sense of the location as a historically constituted place other than in the twentieth century. An excavated feature – the *fosse* or ditch which

39. Aljubarrota: monument on the battle site.

covered the front of the Portuguese position – is revealed only by the lifting of a metal cover, designed to protect it from weathering. Other features were excavated away and are only evident in the brief report contained in information boards on site. The view down the valley towards the direction of the Spanish and French attack is impeded by the concrete memorial (Plate 39), and although a road leads this way, high walls and trees interfere with lines of sight. Overall, the experience of Aljubarrota as a landscape is overlain by militaristic symbolism which would rather be forgotten.

Roliça

From a distance – as for example from the medieval walls of Obidos which overlook the wide plain (Plate 16) – the battle site at Roliça appears to offer a strong landscape experience. The ground over which the contending forces moved prior to engagement – broken by wooded and rocky hillocks – is not overly encumbered with modern intrusions, and the line of heights above the villages of Roliça and Columbeira beyond rises clearly out of the lower ground, with the white-walled villages clustered at its foot (Plate 38). From this distance, the landscape takes on the appearance of what a battlefield should look like, and closer in this does not change. The village of Roliça provides a second vantage point from which to examine the battleground, with clear views to the heights across the intervening plain. Closer still, at Columbeira, the heights themselves dominate, rising almost sheer at the end of the village street: the great cleft in the chain of hills that provided access to British troops on the day is highly visible. Climbing the hills themselves, a process of scrambling over rocks and through undergrowth, a good sense of the confusion of troops on the day may be had.

It is at the summit that the experience begins to break down. There is a very strong sense of the height above the plain, together with clear views across to neighbouring hills and along the valley below to the citadel at Obidos (Plate 38). The monument to Colonel Lake stands alone and lonely on its hilltop (Plate 49), and views around are blocked by the lie of the ground: this may be a true summit, but it feels dominated by other ground nearby. To gain a sense of the real height, it is necessary to walk 50m or so from the monument, where the ground falls away and drops down to Columbeira, which is seen almost from directly above (Plate 38). The summit opposite was the main French position on the day, and it is here that the experience is weakest. The construction of a viewpoint and camping ground for those who come to visit the site for its ecology rather than its history interferes with any sense of the cultural significance of the place. The views are spectacular in all directions, but the effect is the same as if a housing estate had been built here: it strips the place of any particular historical connections that may be experienced.

Urban Space

Courtrai

The modern city of Kortrijk offers itself as a tourist experience, replete with interesting buildings and features. These include several churches, a cathedral, market places, the defended medieval bridge with a pleasant riverside walk to reach it, a number of museums in historic buildings, and parks. One such park marks the spot immediately outside the city wall where Flemish rebels on foot met mounted French knights in combat in 1302 (Plate 7). The gate to the city that was closed to the rebels still stands as an impressive monument as an entry to the park area, and at the centre of the park lawn rises the modern monument to the event of 1302. Apart from this, the landscape today has changed entirely. A main road cuts across the line of vision from the battlefield space, the marsh and stream that played a vital part in slowing the mounted charge have been replaced by the park and the road, and modern housing occupies what was the opposite side of the stream. Although, as will be discussed in Chapter Six, the monument places the battle high on the cultural landscape of modern Belgium, the landscape of the battle itself is no longer evident.

Stamford Bridge

The same is true of Stamford Bridge, although in a more complex manner. The battle here had two key locations: the bridge across the Derwent, which was held by a body of Norsemen assaulted by the Saxon vanguard, and the high ground beyond the river on which the main forces clashed. The original bridge has now been replaced by a more modern roadbridge 100m or more upstream from the original location. It leads into the centre of the modern settlement, which is busy with shoppers, visitors and traffic, although the road through the town follows the line of the original Roman road that brought fighters in 1066. The way up to the ground beyond the river is still steep, and the modern streets most likely follow an original route. At the top, however, instead of open moorland there is modern building, and an estate ironically called 'King's

Meadow' occupies the site of the main fighting. To be fair, the battle is acknowledged in the naming of some of the streets in the estate – 'Saxon Way', 'Norse Drive', etc. – but no sense of the landscape of 1066 has survived (Plate 22).

CONCLUSION: EXPERIENCE OF PLACE AND PLACES OF EXPERIENCE

This chapter has sought to order our sites not by alphabetical listing as in Chapter Three nor by their components as in Chapter Four, but in terms of the kind of experience they have offered. A methodological distinction was drawn between those sites where the presence of particularly noticeable individual features or attributes dominated other aspects, and between those which offered the presence or absence of a feeling of 'place'. There was no particular standard for what kind of a sense of place was felt: some were rural, others urban, some a mixture of rural and urban, and at least one an overwhelmingly public space, while the significant aspect of some sites was that of change over time. In general, however, there is a hierarchy of 'placeness' which becomes evident: some sites offered a very strong sense of their history, while others presented a weaker sense, and at others that sense had been lost completely. These differences are the result of a number of factors, but of these perhaps three stand out from these examples and will serve to lead us conveniently into the concerns of Chapter Six, which examines our sites as examples of contemporary 'heritage'. These three are: the presence or absence of surviving features; the domination of the visual over other senses; and the persistence of memory over monumental memorialisation.

The presence at some sites of features dating from the battle contributed to the experience of being there. In particular, topographical features such as the Bloody Ditch at Roundway Down (Plate 31), the Red Gully at Stoke and the Moor Drove at Sedgemoor served to strongly define these sites. In a similar vein, the retention of road and street plans at urban sites – especially St Albans (Plate 18), Linton (Plate 11) and Fontenoy (Plate 28) – together with the existence of buildings dating from the day of battle at these places, assisted in maintaining a sense of the site's history. The continuing presence of a much-altered Delapre Abbey at Northampton (Plate 30) nevertheless gave an insight into the battle site, while discovery of the *camiño des inglés* at Sorauren (Plate 27) added much to the experience of the site. Major landscape change at Maldon (Plate 12) required a change in interpretation to give meaning to the site, while more recent building at Courtrai (Plate 7) and Stamford Bridge

(Plate 22) has irrevocably damaged any sense of the battlefield space. Less radical change elsewhere – whereby the Bussex Rhine at Sedgemoor and the 'Battel Dike' at Northampton survive only as buried features, for instance – also has an effect on our response to the site as a place of history: as at Maldon, where the site itself as seen today says little and requires reinterpretation.

The concept of the modern 'gaze' as the means by which space is experienced is well covered in the literature of landscape studies. At historic battlefields it manifests itself in the form of the 'viewpoint' overlooking the battlefield space; where a route around the space has been created, this distanced 'looking into' the space is encouraged over other forms of engagement. Among our sites, Naseby (Plate 13) and to a slightly lesser extent Bosworth (Plate 4) offer themselves for this kind of experience. The Naseby monument is sited so as to look into the arena where the fighting took place from above, while at Bosworth the general perspective is one of looking at positions in space where troops once mustered. Although at Cropredy and at Roliça entry to the actual space of the fighting is encouraged, it remains the case that the primary sense used is that of sight, and especially at Roliça long-distance vision (Plate 16) is able to inform more than standing on the ground itself.

These sites contrast with those where an experience is acquired. Urban sites provide particularly strong experiences, both in terms of a place in the present and its history. St Albans stands out among our sites in precisely this manner, offering a strong sense of place in the present as well as some notion of the experience on the days of battle. To a lesser extent, Fontenoy and Linton are able to do the same, although the experience here is more mixed. This apprehension of 'placeness' is not, however, limited to townscapes. Among our sites, the very empty rural landscapes of Bouvines (Plate 5), Oudenaarde (Plate 15), Stoke (Plate 23) and Sorauren (Plate 21) provided powerful experiences of place. To some extent this might have been due to a perceived sense of isolation from a surrounding world, since long-range vision was effectively limited by the rise or fall of ground. Within this sense of closure, however, they were also open spaces with clear lines of internal sight where locations within the space could be marked from a number of different points: this was also, paradoxically, largely the case at St Albans. To that extent all these sites are at once enclosed but also internally accessible, and this too may be a factor in creating a strong sense of place and of historicity.

A strong sense of place often goes together among our sites with a strong sense of specific histories. This is certainly the case at St Albans (Plate 40), but also at Corunna (Plate 6) and Sedgemoor (Plate 20), and to a lesser extent at

40. St Albans I: plaque to the Duke of Somerset.

Maldon (Plate 12), Roliça (Plate 16), Tewkesbury (Plate 24) and The Dunes (Plate 9). All of these sites are specifically remembered as battle sites by some kind of marking, but such marking is not necessarily monumental. By contrast, Bosworth boasts a dedicated visitor centre, Aljubarrota (Plate 39) and Courtrai (Plate 7) have significant monuments raised to them, and Stamford Bridge is marked by a memorial in the town's central square (Plate 51). In these cases, however, other factors – urban development at Stamford Bridge and Courtrai, tourism development at Bosworth, and excessive monumentalisation at Aljubarrota – have conspired to remove that sense of history from these places. At these sites, memory contrasts with memorialisation, and memorialisation overwhelms memory. None of this goes to explain the differences they all have, however, with sites such as Oudenaarde and Sorauren where a strong sense of place is unconnected with any kind of formal memorialisation. This is a matter to be addressed in Chapter Six.

Six

MARKING BATTLEFIELDS

Whereas Chapters Four and Five considered locations from the perspective of their use as battlefields in the past, this chapter takes a deliberately more contemporary perspective by considering them as aspects of modern heritage. We are concerned here not with how these places were perceived and understood in the past, but how we conceive and especially use them today. In the sometimes considerable time that has elapsed since the use of the spaces considered here as battlefields, and as discussed in Chapter Five, there have been inevitable physical changes to the locations. These are summarised briefly here before we go on to examine memorialisation and memory at these sites and the issues arising.

LANDSCAPE CHANGE

One of the themes underlying the descriptive and experiential approach taken in Chapter Five is that some battlefields have seen considerable alteration in their form since armies fought over them. Some have seen reuse for the same purpose in more recent times. Others have been subject to changes wrought by natural or semi-natural processes. Others have been affected by the results of human action and intervention, although as Darvill (1987) points out, in England at least, no change is entirely natural. By contrast, others have seen relatively little obvious alteration in their form.

Following Darvill's lead, any distinction between 'natural' and 'made' change is inevitably arbitrary, but there are certainly some kinds of landscape change where the role of humans is at least limited and their capacity to prevent change more so. At the sites of the battles of Maldon (Plate 12) and The Dunes (Plate 9), changes in coastal morphology over the past centuries have been largely the result of the action of the sea. At Maldon the rise in sea level has caused a change from dry strand to salt marsh: what was in AD 991 a safe place to stand has become a wet and boggy mire, with consequences for our understanding of the battle as set out in Chapter Five. At The Dunes, repeated tidal and wind action will have modified the shapes and positions of the dunes to alter the space, but in general the ground gives a good impression of the kind of landscape it was in 1658. The heights of the dunes themselves tend to hide from view more obvious human intervention: the railway paralleling the line of the canal, the late nineteenth-century Fort des Dunes and the mid-twentieth-century gun emplacement (now ruined) built at the water's edge. At Sedgemoor (Plate 20), the drained wetland has seen alterations in the positions and shape of watercourses since 1685 and alterations in land use patterns, but some original watercourses may remain and the overall flatness and the watery landscape still provide a feel of three centuries ago.

Other sites provide more immediate and tangible evidence of human interference. The original bridge at Stamford Bridge has been replaced by a much later construction built some way upstream. The heights above the river where the battle was fought have also been built upon (Plate 22), as has also happened to the sites at Courtrai (Plate 7), the Barnard's Heath area of St Albans (Plate 19), and parts of the Tewkesbury battlefield (Plate 43). Change in agricultural use and the imposition of new field systems at Bosworth (Plate 4) and Naseby (Plate 13) have affected the landscapes there – ironically, since there are concerted efforts at both to actively promote the battlefield as a visitor resource. Northampton,

41. The Dunes: crest of Leffrinckoucke village.

Aljubarrota and Roliça are also subject to use as a public amenity, the first as a municipal golf course (Plate 14), the others as tourist sites: Aljubarrota suffers massively from monumentalisation (Plate 39), while Roliça is altered by the creation of amenities for campers and walkers. The university construction at Corunna (Plate 6) inevitably changes the appearance of the battlefield heights, but the villages remain small with existing buildings intact, and the general experience of the space is ironically one of 'authenticity'. A feeling of relatively little change is also evident at other battlefield sites. The streets of St Albans (Plate 18) and of Linton (Plate 11) follow the lines of those in earlier centuries and the shape of the ground has altered little at either location. The rural sites of Bouvines (Plate 5), Stoke (Plate 23), Roundway Down (Plate 17), Cropredy Bridge (Plate 8), Oudenaarde (Plate 15), Fontenoy (Plate 10) and Sorauren (Plate 21) have seen alterations in land use and in field shape over time but retain much of their character. In a number of these sites, structures and features from the time of the battle survive to add to a feeling of continuity.

From an archaeological perspective – the field from which this work ultimately derives – all of these sites have seen considerable alteration. A more usual battlefield archaeology – one based around the search for artefactual evidence and detailed ground survey – would almost certainly emphasise the changes time has wrought. Their significance would be considerable, since unnoticed changes in topography, in land use, vegetation or soil chemistry could alter the chances of retrieving useful data from the soil and identifying specific areas of ground from contemporary battle reports. From the phenomenological perspective adopted by us, however, these small changes are of less significance: what is evident, from this summary and from the descriptions in Chapter Five, is that alterations in landscape character and apprehension do not necessarily reflect the degree of actual change undergone. The relative quietude of a grassy and lightly wooded golf course or of a 'natural' mountainscape can deny any sense of history; by contrast, the busyness of a modern city can still provide a feeling of its past, and the construction of a brand new institution can enhance a sense of history.

PLACES MARKED AND UNMARKED

There is a sense in which all of the sites we have studied are marked as historic battlefields: for if there were no memory of the event and no recording of it by historians we would have no knowledge of it. As such, all our sites are remembered and all marked as significant. Some are, however, marked in a more concrete manner than others by having some kind of monument raised to

Table 6.1   *Memorialisation of some western European battlefields*

Battle	Date	Country	Memorial Contemp.	Memorial Modern	Plaque	Monument	Related to Twentieth-Century War Memorial	Type of Memorial Church Building	Church Interior	Museum/Heritage Site	Military Site	Street Names	University Building
Maldon	991	UK		•	•					•			
Assandun	1016	UK	•					•					
Stamford Bridge	1066	UK		•		•						•	
Bouvines	1214	France		•		•	•		•				
Courtrai	1302	Belgium		•		•			•	•			
Aljubarrota	1385	Portugal		•		•		•	•	•			
St Albans I	1455	UK	•	•	•								
Northampton	1460	UK											
St Albans II	1461	UK		•		•							
Tewkesbury	1471	UK		•		•				•		•	
Bosworth	1485	UK		•		•				•			
Stoke	1487	UK		•		•			•				
Roundway Down	1643	UK											
Cropredy Bridge	1644	UK		•	•								
Naseby	1645	UK		•		•							
Linton	1648	UK											
The Dunes	1658	France		•			•				•		
Sedgemoor	1685	UK		•		•	•		•				
Oudenaarde	1708	Belgium											
Fontenoy	1745	France		•	•	•							
Roliça	1808	Portugal	•	•		•						•	
Corunna	1809	Spain	•	•	•					•			•
Sorauren I and II	1813	Spain											

185

or upon them. As indicated in Table 6.1, only five of our sites – Northampton, Linton, Roundway Down, Oudenaarde and Sorauren – are currently left unmarked in this very restricted sense; and although the site of Assandun may be added to this list because it is currently unmarked, it was nevertheless powerfully marked shortly after the event.

Marking Sites

The construction of memorials on battlefields has a long history reaching back at least to the classical eras of Greece and Rome (Borg, 1991; Carman and Carman, 2005a, 1:1). None of the battlefields discussed here is of that period, but five of our sites were nevertheless marked at the time or immediately after. The two medieval sites of Assandun and Aljubarrota saw the construction of churches in commemoration of the fighting. At both, the purpose was to thank God for victory. Cnut's church at Assandun has since been lost and its location disputed: it may have stood either in the 'Old Church' area of Ashdon in northern Essex (Plate 2) or at Ashingdon or Canewdon in southern Essex (Plate 3) on the site of either of the surviving later churches of these settlements. Aljubarrota is distinctive in having two churches built to commemorate the Portuguese victory. The smaller and plainer fourteenth-century building, which was constructed almost immediately after the event, stands on the battlefield itself (Plate 1), adjacent to much more recent and military brutalist-style monuments. The larger and more impressive took substantially longer to build – over a century in fact – and this is evident in its style and form: the great Gothic monastery and cathedral to Our Lady of Victory (Plate 46) stands some 2km from the battlefield itself, forming the core around which the town of Batalha ('the Battle') has since grown. In both cases, a grateful and successful monarch raised the monument.

There is no evidence from our sites of any interest in marking battlefields through most of the seventeenth and early eighteenth centuries. In part this may be due to the nature of the conflicts of which they were so often a part: civil wars such as those in England leave scars that need to heal, and in many ways the most appropriate form of healing is forgetfulness; the embargo on memorials extended also to international conflicts. However, Fontenoy represents such an international conflict, and in particular a rare French victory against British arms, making it perhaps worthy of commemoration. The battlefield itself, however, remained unmarked: instead an obelisk was raised at Cysoing several kilometres away to mark the place where the French king slept

42. Stoke: replacement monument to the dead of battle, on the wall of Stoke church.

the nights before and after the battle (Plate 47). Individuals are also commemorated at the later sites of Roliça and Corunna. Colonel Lake of the 29th Regiment – who died on the slopes above Columbeira – has a small stone cross raised to him at the spot where he fell (Plate 49). At Corunna, the monument is to the commander of the British army and is also located at the spot where he fell. The monument at Cysoing was raised by the French state to its king, representing an 'official' marking. At Corunna and Roliça, however, the monuments were more personal: soldiers who fought in the action or others representing their military unit returned to the site of action to raise a memorial to people they explicitly remembered. Contemporary memorialisation accordingly reflected memory in a very direct manner, whether the memory was that of an institution – a state or a military unit – or of specific individuals.

Such direct memory plays a less significant part in later commemoration: by the nineteenth century such sites have become part of 'history' rather than places of contemporary experience. Only five of our sites were marked in the nineteenth century: Bouvines, St Albans II, Tewkesbury, Naseby and Fontenoy, all but St Albans by the erection of stone obelisks; and these four have seen further acts of commemoration in the twentieth century. The remainder of those commemorated in modern times by the construction of a monument had to wait until the twentieth century, reflecting the growth of the idea that such places were worthy of note. Of those commemorated immediately after the event, Aljubarrota, Fontenoy, Roliça and Corunna have all also seen twentieth-century monuments raised: only Assandun is today unmarked, although the location of this site is still disputed, which goes far to explain this. As will be discussed below, the form of modern monuments varies but is patterned: there may be alternative possible forms of commemoration that are deemed inappropriate. Only three sites are specifically made available to the modern tourist industry: Aljubarrota, which houses a museum and spectacular monument; Bosworth, which has a dedicated visitor centre; and Tewkesbury, with a marked battlefield walk. Walks are also available at St Albans and at Roundway Down (Colman and Coupe, n.d.) but the walks are otherwise unmarked. Of the sites we have examined, a small majority can be considered as memorialised in terms of a local or direct interest, and the remainder by more detached and distant interests.

Obelisks and Others: Forms of Commemoration

The most common form of marking a battlefield – as evident from Table 6.1 (see p. 185) – is the free-standing monument of concrete or stone, and of these the most popular form is that of the obelisk (see also Barnes, 2004). The earliest example from our sites relates to Fontenoy: the tall and slender eighteenth-century monument in classical style raised at Cysoing is of this form (Plate 47). Nineteenth-century versions – at Bouvines, The Vineyards at Tewkesbury (Plate 43), overlooking Naseby and at Sedgemoor – adopt the more typically Egyptian style of a 'Cleopatra's Needle', square in lateral section and topped by a pyramid. At Courtrai (Plate 7) a monumental base is capped by a very large golden statue of victory. The plainer stone cross is evident at Roliça to commemorate Colonel Lake (Plate 49), and the monument in Fontenoy village raised in 1874 by the Irish Military Historical Society to celebrate the contribution of Irish soldiers to the French victory by halting the British advance takes the form of a Celtic cross, echoing ancient Irish tradition (Plate 28). Plain inscribed stones mark the supposed site of Richard III's death at Bosworth (Plate 35), stand in Stoke churchyard to commemorate that battle (Plate 42), and in the town centre at Stamford Bridge (Plate 51). At the centre of the village of Roliça stands a large ceramic representation of the battle, while Aljubarrota competes with these with its wide and tall concrete frieze depicting medieval knights in combat, banners flying, with the names of the main battles of Portuguese history emblazoned above (Plate 39).

43. Tewkesbury: Vineyards monument.

Plaques upon walls fulfil two kinds of mutually exclusive function. At Maldon and St Albans the mounted plaques are there to provide information. St Albans has two blue ceramic plaques indicating a historic location: one is positioned at a street corner where the Duke of Somerset fell in the first battle (Plate 40), commemorating at once his death and the battle; the other stands outside the location of the 'Old Hall' where the king spent his time that day. At Maldon, the plaque is attached to a farm gate, the only convenient vertical structure, and provides information about the battle and the nearby bird sanctuary on Northey Island. At Cropredy Bridge, Fontenoy and Corunna, plaques serve to commemorate those who were present at the battle. The plaque at Cropredy is built into the twentieth-century bridge occupying the site of that fought over in the seventeenth century, remembering all those who were present on that day. Our own visit to the site coincided with the day after the annual re-enactment of the event, and on the bridge below the plaque were laid flowers in remembrance of one of the individual units who fought there, placed by the members of the modern descendant of that regiment in memory of their dead (Plate 36). On the wall of the modern cemetery along the road from Fontenoy is attached a memorial to the Irish soldiers who fought on the day, placed there by an American benefactor, and it is also on the wall of Elviña church that successors to the British units that fought there placed a commemorative memorial 190 years after the event (Plate 48). In some locations, references to the battle are included in other memorials: at Bouvines (Plate 44) and at Sedgemoor commemoration of twentieth-century conflict is directly related to the historic predecessor, and The Dunes is commemorated together with the memory of twentieth-century conflict in the village crest of Leffrinckoucke (Plate 41).

Place names recall battlefield events at four of our sites. The modern building directly on the battle site at Stamford Bridge is called 'King's Meadow', although it is not clear whether this is intended to recall the meeting of Saxon king Harold and Norse king Harald: other such new housing carries similar names elsewhere. Within the estate, however, street names such as 'Saxon Way' are clearly intended to commemorate the event. In similar vein, at Barnard's Heath in St Albans the nineteenth-century houses of 'Battle Row' commemorate the second phase of the second battle of St Albans, together with nearby 'Archer's Green', and other places named for the event. At Roliça, adjacent to the location of the ceramic monument, are streets named for both French and British protagonists. In an interesting variation not seen elsewhere, the battle of Corunna is commemorated on street furniture in the form of the lamp-posts of

44. Bouvines: war memorial dated 1214 and 1914.

the Corunna tramway system. All are overlain, however, by the settlement that grew up around the great cathedral to victory at Aljubarrota: the town of Batalha ('the battle') has become the main testament to the event.

Buildings mark a number of sites: in the modern period some were specially constructed, while others have been adopted as places of memorialisation. The Fort des Dunes at Leffrinckoucke was not built specifically to commemorate the 1658 battle, and its choice of location near the site will have been made on military grounds rather than historical ones, but its name directly references the earlier event. The university buildings at Elviña (Plate 6), however, were located at that place specifically in memory of the battle in reflection of its local significance. The visitor centre at Bosworth was originally adapted from existing farm buildings at the site, but are at the time of writing (summer 2004) being rebuilt. It houses an interpretation centre as well as the usual visitor facilities of shop, restaurant and toilets: while one car park is immediately outside the visitor centre on the reverse slope of Ambion Hill out of site of the battlefield area, the others are some distance away to avoid any encroachment on the site itself. At Aljubarrota a custom-built museum in modern 'brutalist' style stands adjacent to the site and its concrete frieze: it houses the Portuguese national military museum, and was constructed in the early 1960s while Portugal was ruled by a militaristic regime. It is currently closed 'for refurbishment' but shows no likelihood of reopening in the near future.

At Maldon, Corunna, Courtrai and Tewkesbury, local displays commemorate the battles off-site. Tewkesbury museum houses a display of the battle, telling the story of the event and featuring the heraldic devices of main actors: against the opposite wall a glass case encloses a diorama of the event. In the Castle of San Antonio guarding the entrance to Corunna harbour is the local museum, containing an entire room devoted to the battle at Elviña. Here are displayed maps and plans of the battle, images of events such as the death of the British commander, and artefacts such as an artillery piece used in the action. The Groeningeabdij Museum in Kortrijk, in a former monastery within but on the edge of the city near the battle site, houses a model of the city on which is marked the extent and location of the battle. The Maldon Heritage Centre contains the Maeldune tapestry, made to commemorate the 1,000th anniversary of the battle. Like the Bayeux and the later Overlord tapestries (which it is designed specifically to reference), it tells the story of the event in a series of panels.

Church building on sites and to commemorate battles has been discussed above. The Assandun church has been replaced or been lost, but at Aljubarrota two church foundations remain. Inside the battlefield chapel there is a notice of the excavations carried out in advance of development of the site, with a plan of the features – especially the defensive *fosse* and the stakeholes marking the *chevaux de frises* – found and excavated. At Batalha, the great church dominates. Inside is the modern Tomb of the Unknown Soldier (Plate 45), permanently guarded by soldiers; and in a side chapel the tomb of the victor at Aljubarrota, guarded by the tomb of the soldier who saved his life on the day. At Stoke, Cropredy Bridge and Sedgemoor the battle is commemorated by small exhibitions: Sedgemoor contains a contemporary description and plan, while Cropredy has a display of replica armour from the period. Bouvines church, dating from 1890, was not present on the day of the battle it commemorates, but it contains an interpretive panel with plan for visitors. The greatest memorialisation is, however, elsewhere in the church: the twenty-one stained-glass windows installed in 1906 tell the story of the battle and its aftermath in a series of tableaux.

The Event or Persons: Objects of Commemoration

The literature of the commemoration of war sites generally takes one of two perspectives on the dynamics of memory (as outlined by Ashplant *et al.*, 2000, 3–85): either that battlefield memorials serve to support nationalist narratives and discourse by creating myths of heroism (e.g. Bushaway, 1992, 136–67; Hobsbawm and Ranger, 1983); or that they represent community and, indeed, personal responses to trauma and loss as mourning (e.g. Tarlow, 1999; Winter, 1995). The sample of battlefields considered here provides indications of a more complex set of cultural processes at work, in which a range of different objects of commemoration may be selected.

The main focus of memorialisation at English battlefields, including especially those from past civil wars, is upon the event itself, as a historical phenomenon. British, and especially English, national ideology treats civil unrest and foreign invasion both as parts of a series of events culminating in the modern democratic British state. Accordingly, although individuals may consider one side or the other to have been more desirable or more 'right' at the time, their victory or defeat is held to be of greater significance in terms of the ultimate contribution it made to the development of the modern British state. Individuals therefore tend to hold no particularly strong cultural ties to one side or another in these conflicts except as part of a general 'recreational' attitude. As such, the defeat of Saxons by Norse invaders or vice versa, of

Table 6.2   *Commemoration at some western European battlefields*

Battle	Date	Country	Commemoration of			
			Event	Persons Killed	Persons Present	Nation
Maldon	991	UK	•			
Assandun	1016	UK	•			
Stamford Bridge	1066	UK	•			
Bouvines	1214	France	•			
Courtrai	1302	Belgium				•
Aljubarrota	1385	Portugal				•
St Albans I	1455	UK	•	•		
Northampton	1460	UK				
St Albans II	1461	UK	•			
Tewkesbury	1471	UK	•			
Bosworth	1485	UK	•			
Stoke	1487	UK		•		
Roundway Down	1643	UK				
Cropredy Bridge	1644	UK	•			
Naseby	1645	UK	•			
Linton	1648	UK				
The Dunes	1658	France	•			
Sedgemoor	1685	UK	•			
Oudenaarde	1708	Belgium				
Fontenoy	1745	France			•	•
Roliça	1808	Portugal	•	•		
Corunna	1809	Spain	•	•		
Sorauren I and II	1813	Spain				

Lancastrian by Yorkist or vice versa, or of King by Parliament or vice versa all become part of a common story – that of the invention of England and beyond that, Britain. The same may not be true of battlefields in other parts of the British Isles – in Scotland or Ireland, for example – where other political and cultural matters were and may remain at issue. English battlefields therefore have a historical significance, but rarely carry a contemporary cultural meaning beyond this. To that extent, the memorialisation of the sites at Maldon, Stamford Bridge, St Albans, Tewkesbury, Bosworth, Cropredy Bridge and Naseby may represent a national ideology, but it is of a particularly safe and anodyne kind.

The exception to this apparent rule for English battlefields is Sedgemoor, where memorialisation is more closely associated with a sense of the locality and its difference and separation from an England as seen from the metropolitan centre. The focus here is upon local involvement and local opposition to centralising authority from London: monuments to locally raised regiments of the British army and memorials to the two twentieth-century world wars placed alongside the battlefield memorial on the site of battle itself

45. Aljubarotta: Tomb of the Unknown Soldier, in the Monastery Church of Our Lady of Victory, Batalha.

emphasise above all else this focus upon the locality (Plate 50). This kind, and especially intensity, of association with later history is perhaps more common elsewhere. Bouvines was a significant French victory and one that marks the emergence of France as a nation to be reckoned with; the location was also on the route of march of the retreating French army in 1914, on its way to regroup on the line of the Marne river. The battle of the Marne was a turning point in that war, halting the German advance, and the modern war memorial in Bouvines makes the connection clear: unlike most monuments to the First World War, it is not dated 1914 to 1918, but 1214 and 1914 (Plate 44). A panel on the monument quotes a French general: '*La bataille de la Marne était la bataille de Bouvines renouvelée*' [the battle of the Marne was the battle of Bouvines renewed]. On the battlefield itself is a small stone roadside monument marking the place where a local teenager was killed (presumably murdered) by retreating German troops ('*les hordes Nazis*') in 1944. In similar fashion, the area around Dunkerque is another where the events of twentieth-century conflict are difficult if not impossible to ignore: the site of the battle of The Dunes is located within the perimeter of the Dunkerque enclave where Belgian, French and British troops waited for evacuation to England after their defeat in 1940.

Various monuments have been raised in the area to the events of 1940, and the dates of both 1658 and 1940 are included in the crest of the village of Leffrinckoucke (Plate 41), near to where the battle of The Dunes took place. Accordingly, these sites all find their meaning in association with more recent conflicts: Bouvines with the events of the First World War, The Dunes with the events of the Second World War, and Sedgemoor with the actions of all local military units; but the association also works the other way. There is a sense in which the First World War can only have meaning in terms of Bouvines: if the battle of the Marne was indeed 'Bouvines renewed' as the general claims, then an appreciation of Bouvines is integral to appreciating the Marne. Similarly, the juxtaposition of two crucial dates – 1658 and 1940 – at Leffrinckoucke creates a commonality between them. At Sedgemoor, the local tradition of service to history is strongly asserted. Although it is primarily the event that matters at these places, the significance it carries goes beyond the merely historical.

Remembrance of individuals killed is relatively rare on battlefields, but one of the wall plaques commemorating the first battle of St Albans is erected in memory of the death of the Duke of Somerset (Plate 40). At Bosworth a stone monument erected by the Richard III Society – dedicated to restoring the reputation of one whom they consider a much-maligned historical figure – marks the supposed place of death of 'the last Plantagenet King of England' (Plate 35). A monument at Corunna marks the spot where the British commander fell, close to the village of Elviña, and at Roliça a stone cross raised by his regiment commemorates the courageous death of Colonel Lake (Plate 49). Contrasting with monuments to the dead is the contemporary obelisk raised at Cysoing in memory of the presence of the French king at the battle of Fontenoy (Plate 47). Monuments are also raised to groups of people: at Elviña church remembering military units present at the battle of Corunna (Plate 48), and in the churchyard at Stoke commemorating all those killed, and especially the foreign mercenaries, fighting on the Yorkist (defeated) side (Plate 42).

Three of our sites are marked particularly as monuments to national pride. Aljubarrota is regarded as one of the founding moments of Portugal as an independent kingdom and state, and this is reflected in its later re-memorialisation during the 1950s and 1960s. Under the military regime then ruling Portugal, the site was excavated by archaeologists (do Paço, 1962, 115–63), who discovered not only a mass grave of the dead but also key landscape features from the battle. On the basis of these findings, the site was marked out as a small park (Plate 1), new monuments were erected (Plate 39), and the site now houses the national Military Museum. Together with the monastery at Batalha (Plate 46), Aljubarrota is the premier national shrine of Portugal. The site of the battle of Courtrai is also a small park and dominating it is a large plinth on which sits a gilded statue to Victory (Plate 7). This site is treated less obviously as a national site of pilgrimage than Aljubarrota, but it is clearly a site of some significance both nationally and locally. The main French monument to the battle of Fontenoy is the obelisk to the king at Cysoing (Plate 47). In Fontenoy itself, there is no French monument at all. Instead, the monument – no less nationalistic perhaps – is dedicated to the Irish troops who on that day fought for the French (Plate 28); a second and more recent monument to the Irish troops is attached to the wall of the village cemetery a little way along the road from the village.

While to some extent all our sites represent an ideology of nationalism attached to historic battlefields, the sites of Aljubarrota, Courtrai and Fontenoy are all classic examples of the battlefield as national shrine. Aljubarrota is clearly the most obvious of these: a national shrine was created almost immediately by the building of the great monastery at Batalha, and the inclusion of the Tomb of the Unknown Soldier in the twentieth century continues that tradition. This status was renewed and reforged in the 1960s by

46. *Aljubarrota: Monastery Church of Our Lady of Victory, Batalha, built to celebrate the victory.*

47. *Fontenoy: monument to Louis XV at Cysoing.*

the conversion of the space of the battlefield itself into a shrine to militarism. The latter has, under democracy, since been abandoned but the architectural and monumental forms remain. Courtrai is also something of a shrine: the great statue that dominates the space of the battle testifies to the historic importance of the event and the meaning it should carry for the people of Flanders and Belgium. Fontenoy is an interesting variation on this theme. The French monument – raised not long after the battle itself – stands at some distance from the battlefield, and commemorates less the event than the monarch in whose reign it took place. The major monument on the battlefield, raised over a century later, refers not to French but to Irish involvement in the battle. Fontenoy is, accordingly, not a French national shrine, despite being a French victory on what is now French soil, but rather an Irish national shrine. This is perhaps as nationalist as either Aljubarrota or Courtrai contrives to be, but it serves a different audience.

To Front and Rear or to the Side: Locations of Monuments

Not all battlefield monuments stand upon the actual site of conflict: some are located instead within the vicinity but out of sight of the battle area itself, and others overlook but are not directly upon the site. The choice does not appear to be a factor of chronology: some modern monuments stand upon the battlefield, while others overlook it and others yet are located nearby; some contemporary monuments can be a distance away. What conditions the choice is not immediately clear.

The site of Assandun remains disputed, but what is not in dispute is that the victorious Cnut built a church in commemoration of the event. If either of the two existing churches at Ashingdon or Canewdon in south Essex stands upon the site of his foundation, then it is most likely that it was built to overlook the place of his achievement rather than sit directly upon it. Both churches are located on the tops of hills, and the low ground between them adjacent to the river is the most likely site of the battle (Plate 3). Alternatively, if the battle were fought in north Essex at Ashdon then the site of 'Old Church' marks the spot (Plate 2). This may represent the place where the two armies clashed, in which case the commemorative structure was positioned on the battlefield itself; but it may have been placed so as to overlook the site. The nineteenth-century monument at Naseby sits on the ridge forming the initial position of the Parliamentary forces, overlooking the valley below where the fighting took place (Plate 13): it provides a convenient viewpoint for the visitor. The other

Table 6.3 *The location of memorials at some western European battlefields*

Battle	Date	Country	Location of Memorial(s)		
			Overlooking Battlefield	Vicinity of Battlefield	On Battlefield
Maldon	991	UK			•
Assandun	1016	UK	?		?
Stamford Bridge	1066	UK		•	
Bouvines	1214	France		•	
Courtrai	1302	Belgium			•
Aljubarrota	1385	Portugal		•	•
St Albans I	1455	UK			•
Northampton	1460	UK			
St Albans II	1461	UK			•
Tewkesbury	1471	UK			•
Bosworth	1485	UK	•		•
Stoke	1487	UK		•	
Roundway Down	1643	UK			
Cropredy Bridge	1644	UK			•
Naseby	1645	UK	•		
Linton	1648	UK			
The Dunes	1658	France		•	
Sedgemoor	1685	UK			•
Oudenaarde	1708	Belgium			
Fontenoy	1745	France		•	•
Roliça	1808	Portugal	•		•
Corunna	1809	Spain	•		•
Sorauren I and II	1813	Spain			

monument, to Cromwell, lies completely off the battlefield, in the village of Naseby itself and much closer to the position of the Parliamentary baggage train which was looted by Royalist cavalry: from here no view of the battlefield can be had. While a contemporary monument stands upon the battlefield itself at Roliça, in the form of the cross to Colonel Lake on the high ground above Columbeira (Plate 49), a larger memorial occupies the centre of Roliça: a ceramic representation of the battle stands at a point from which there is a good view of the French second position. At Corunna, the contemporary monument to the British commander stands at the point where he fell, but the more recent memorial on the external wall of Elviña church (Plate 48) – although located in what was the village of Eiris – overlooks the battlefield valley and the slopes of the hills beyond.

Other memorials located within the vicinity of battle sites do not offer views. The nineteenth-century obelisk to Bouvines is located at the roadside in the centre of the village, invisible from the hill above, where the fighting took place, and providing no view of the site. Behind it is the twentieth-century war memorial and behind that stands, on rising ground, the imposing twentieth-

48. *Corunna/Elviña: memorial plaque raised on the 190th anniversary, Elviña church.*

century village church: it is the church that can be seen from the battlefield. The monument to Stamford Bridge is also located in the centre of the town near where the battle took place. It is nearer to the site of the original bridge than the current roadbridge, but not on the actual site, and lies below the main battlefield. The modern monument to Stoke – a replacement to an earlier stone memorial – sits adjacent to the church wall across the road from the site of fighting. Trees and buildings now block any view of the site from here but it is possible that originally the memorial stone acted as a convenient viewpoint from the churchyard. Memorialisation at The Dunes is largely by the Fort des Dunes, deliberately built into the sandhills with a low profile to protect against twentieth-century gunnery: it sits near but not quite on the battlefield; and the stone carrying the Leffrinckoucke village crest, which also marks the event of the battle, occupies a point on the edge of the village overlooking the beach but invisible from the dunes themselves. As mentioned above and in addition, Batalha Cathedral and the monument at Cysoing are both some kilometres from the sites of the battles they reference, as is one of the monuments at Naseby.

At Aljubarrota the chapel on the battlefield sits directly at the point where defenders met attackers (Plate 1), while the great cathedral at Batalha is entirely out of site of this place (Plate 46). The modern monument at The Vineyards in Tewkesbury (Plate 43) is positioned on the battlefield but also at a point that conveniently overlooks other areas where fighting took place: the same is true of the plaque on Cropredy Bridge (Plate 36), which allows a view into the wider battlefield space. The victory monument at Courtrai (Plate 7), the memorials at Sedgemoor (Plate 50) and the nineteenth-century Irish memorial at Fontenoy (Plate 28), together with the twentieth-century plaque at the nearby cemetery, all sit firmly at the centre of the relevant battlefield space and attract attention not as viewpoints but as objects in their own right. This also applies to the monument marking the death of Richard III at Bosworth (Plate 35), although this is less central to the battlefield: it sits in an area set aside from the main arena. The plaques at Maldon and St Albans (Plate 40) are also located within the battlefield space, but serve a particular purpose: theirs is the function not of memorialising the space so much as of informing those who pass by of the historical significance of the location.

49. Roliça: monument to Colonel Lake.

Unmarked Sites

As mentioned, five of our sites are not marked by the erection of any kind of physical memorial or marker. Three of these are in England, and two elsewhere. One of the English examples is Linton, which, as indicated in Chapter Four, does not count as a battlefield proper and therefore may not warrant any kind of memorial. Northampton and Roundway Down, however, may be considered worthy, since both are remembered as proper battles and are also both included in the English Heritage (1995) *Register*, as well as appearing on Ordnance Survey maps with the familiar cross-swords and italicised date symbol. At Northampton the site was considered to be 'lost' under industrial development and was subsequently disputed until very recently, which may explain a reluctance to mark the site. At Roundway Down the land is in private hands, and the site itself inaccessible to the public, although it can be viewed from locations along public rights of way described in local literature (Colman and Coupe, n.d): specific memorialisation may not therefore have been considered necessary or appropriate.

The reasons for non-memorialisation in our two non-English examples may be different. The space of Oudenaarde is relatively open and uncluttered (Plate 15). Unlike Aljubarrota or nearby Courtrai, no monument marks it as a national shrine; and unlike Fontenoy it is not marked by any of the nations who supplied troops: so far as most people are concerned, it is relatively forgotten. Sorauren is also unmarked by any monument or memorial; moreover, there is very little local memory of it. The site lies on the pilgrimage route to Santiago de Compostela and receives many tourists and pilgrims annually, but no tourist office can provide any information on the battle, and local transport to the villages of Sorauren and Zabaldica – through which fighting took place – is sparse. One reason is that the site lies close to the city of Pampeluna/Iruña, and along the road to San Sebastián/Donostia – one the former capital of the medieval kingdom of Navarre, the other the centre of Basque Spain. Local identities are crucial in this region: local Navarrese seek to reassert their regional identity within Spain and to establish the legitimacy of the local language, while Basque organisations seek to establish an independent Basque nation. In Pampeluna, medieval monuments glorify the independent kings of Navarre; those from the twentieth century celebrate the Spanish Civil War and its aftermath; and the most recent refer to the acts of Basque independence movements. Sorauren and Oudenaarde are therefore battlefields largely forgotten by those who live on or near them. Both actions were fought by people from other places for causes largely alien or irrelevant to the local population, and while Oudenaarde is just more or less ignored, the meaning of Sorauren is overlain by more recent concerns and more recent memories, many of them painful to recall.

Summary: Memorialisation and Meanings

This discussion has demonstrated the variation evident in the marking of historic battlefields. Table 6.4 summarises them in terms of the type of meanings this kind of memorialisation or non-memorialisation may imply.

Table 6.4 *Meanings of memorialisation of some western European battlefields*

Historical Narrative	The Nation Supreme	Shared Heritage	Complex History	Unclaimed and Overlain
Maldon	Courtrai	The Dunes	Bouvines	Linton
Assandun	Aljubarrota	Fontenoy	Sedgemoor	Oudenaarde
Stamford Bridge		Roliça	Corunna/Elviña	Sorauren
St Albans I				
Northampton				
St Albans II				
Tewkesbury				
Bosworth				
Stoke				
Roundway Down				
Cropredy Bridge				
Naseby				

While the majority of our sites – especially those in England – contribute to or emphasise a national story, several others provide hints as to how to overcome a purely national vision of the past. At Fontenoy, the battlefield is shared both by France and by Ireland. At Roliça, the battlefield really belongs to British visitors rather than to Portugal or the Potuguese – especially since the latter are more interested in the place as a natural landscape rather than a cultural one. The Dunes is memorialised by France, but because of the associations made with the events of 1940 – as well as direct involvement by English troops – is also shared by Britain. Corunna is claimed as part of a distinctively local heritage, and yet it too can be claimed by Britain; and by constructing a university on the site, it became a place of contemporary meaning. This sharing of heritage is similar to that at Fontenoy and Roliça, and especially so at The Dunes. It is powerfully expressed at Bouvines, where conflict of the distant past is directly referred to in memorialising more recent war. In doing so, the intimate relations that have historically existed between

France as a political entity and German political forms become clear. At The Dunes, it is the equally volatile relationship between France and England that is highlighted, but here the remembrance focused upon is that of alliance and friendship rather than long-term hostility. At Fontenoy the relationship with Britain is emphasised by the absence of any local reference to Britain's part in the story of that battle; instead, the presence of monuments to Irish involvement make it part of the story of Britain's complex relationship with that nation as well as that of Franco-British rivalry. The construction of the university at Elviña perhaps goes beyond all of these. It is quite clear from local responses that the people of La Coruña are perfectly aware of the relationship between the site and the new construction: that the site was chosen because it carries the local association with an important historic event of which the people of the city, and of Galicia more generally, are very proud. It is very much a local and regional identity that is being asserted here, and in opposition to a national Spanish one: but in a way and through a means that looks to the future rather than to the past. In commemorating the violence of the past they simultaneously assert hope for the future. Oudenaarde and Sorauren are not particularly claimed as sites of historic significance by anyone, leaving them open for future claims or none. None of the countries involved has placed a mark upon them: not Britain, not France, nor yet Belgium or Spain where they were fought.

The meanings of battle sites, as expressed through the physical markers placed upon them, are therefore much more complex than is commonly assumed. This complexity is, perhaps inevitably, more clearly visible in terms of international conflicts, since there is an inevitable sharing of such sites by both victor and defeated. On the other hand, these complexities may be framed within the specifics of local and national ideologies. The co-referencing of conflicts seven centuries apart at Bouvines is done within the framework of an idea of a French nation distinct and indeed saved from German domination. The respective high and low visibility of Corunna and Sorauren both operate within the context of the assertion of local identities over Spanish. The majority of English sites find their place in a narrative of the amalgamation of differences and emerging national unity. The possibility of a challenge to these dominant tales is, however, present at other sites: Sedgemoor illustrates local distinction over national identity in England, Fontenoy and The Dunes celebrate connections between nations, and Roliça recognises alternative claims by failing to incorporate the site within national or local narratives.

We noted at the outset of the discussion the apparent hiatus in terms of monument construction on battlefields between the close of the medieval period

50. Sedgemoor: stone monument on the battlefield.

and the nineteenth century: this does appear to be a real phenomenon rather than the product of our sampling strategy. The UK-based National Inventory of War Memorials identifies few such monuments from the post-medieval period prior to the very late nineteenth century, and of these notes one of the earliest to be a memorial tablet in a church (rather than a triumphant column or statue) dedicated to a particular individual (Hewitt, 2001, 15–16). At the opening of her comprehensive study of monuments to the British heroes of the Napoleonic Wars, Alison Yarrington (1988, vi) emphasises how few monuments were erected to national figures at public expense prior to 1800: her discussion makes it clear how much reliance was placed upon private initiatives and funding (1988, 1–60). Accordingly, the monuments to heroic commanders raised at Roliça and Corunna may fall into the emerging new tradition of public commemoration her work delineates. It seems quite likely to us at this stage of our work that raising memorials to past battles is a further development of this early nineteenth-century practice, one that feeds on but also feeds rising nationalism (Hobsbawm, 1990) and becomes normalised in our own day as a secondary result of the need to commemorate the cataclysmic wars of the twentieth century. Battlefield memorialisation in the form with which we are most familiar is therefore a quite recent development (see also Hobsbawm and Ranger, 1983), and this contributes to current approaches to the management of such sites.

SITES OF BATTLE AND LANDSCAPES OF WAR:
MANAGING HISTORIC BATTLEFIELDS

Although not perhaps highly evident from the discussion so far of the place of historic battlefields in the present, there is a necessary distinction to be made between the construction of memorials and the management of the ground where the battle took place. Some of these locations have been marked out for particular kinds of use in the present, while others have not. Some have passed into some measure of public ownership while others have not. Some have been made specifically available to tourists by various means while again others have not. None of our sites has been entirely inaccessible, even where direct access to the site of fighting itself has not been possible: if it were, it could not count as part of our project. This does not mean, however, that all historic battlefields are universally available to visitors: as our project develops further, these sites will necessarily emerge from the entire set of all battlefields everywhere. At the same time, formal recognition by responsible (and usually official, state-sponsored) agencies of the historic significance of a site does not necessarily imply its development for particular uses, while development can be the product of private rather than public endeavour (Table 6.5).

Designation

There was some preliminary discussion of the formal designation of battlefield sites as places of historic and cultural interest in Chapters One and Two, but such formal recognition is by no means a universal practice: a review of the UNESCO World Heritage List revealed a number of sites on that list that were connected with conflict and especially battles in the past, but none of these had been specifically added to the list as a direct consequence of that connection unless they represented war in the twentieth century. The list of possible official designations for battlefields from the USA given in Chapter Two (see pp. 29–30) indicates that designation of battlefields is most likely in the Anglophone world, but also suggests the lack of clear consensus as to the most appropriate approach to such places. This is further compounded by the fact that it is at the level of the nation state or below that decisions about battlefields are always

Table 6.5 *Aspects of management of some western European battlefields*

Battle	Date	Country	Designation	Public Control	Tourist Access	No Direct Access
Maldon	991	UK	•		•	
Assandun	1016	UK				
Stamford Bridge	1066	UK	•			•
Bouvines	1214	France				
Courtrai	1302	Belgium		•	•	
Aljubarrota	1385	Portugal		•	•	
St Albans I	1455	UK			•	
Northampton	1460	UK	•	•	•	
St Albans II	1461	UK			•	
Tewkesbury	1471	UK	•		•	
Bosworth	1485	UK	•		•	
Stoke	1487	UK	•			
Roundway Down	1643	UK	•			•
Cropredy Bridge	1644	UK	•			
Naseby	1645	UK	•			
Linton	1648	UK				
The Dunes	1658	France			•	
Sedgemoor	1685	UK	•		•	
Oudenaarde	1708	Belgium				
Fontenoy	1745	France				
Roliça	1808	Portugal		•	•	
Corunna	1809	Spain				
Sorauren I and II	1813	Spain				

taken: unlike other types of historic resource there is no common agreement across territorial boundaries as to the correct or most appropriate treatment, nor even the significance, of such sites. Accordingly, of our sites, it is only among those in England that a formal (bureaucratic) system of site designation occurs.

The strength of designation and the degree of protection it affords to sites varies from country to country and system to system. What also varies is the understanding of what kind of object (especially historical or archaeological) the site represents. In England, inclusion on the *Register of Historic Battlefields* (English Heritage, 1995) – such as the sites of Maldon, Stamford Bridge, Northampton, Tewkesbury, Bosworth, Stoke, Roundway Down, Cropredy Bridge, Naseby and Sedgemoor – is a recognition of significance in terms of historical consequences or the presence of a historically important person at the battle. The similarity of the current landscape to that at the time of the event is also taken into account for inclusion, but this is not a critical factor for initial consideration. Any capacity the site may have for archaeological research is not taken into account at all. The *Register* is, accordingly, subject to criticism for treating historic battlefields as landscapes of historical interest rather than as archaeological sites: the level of physical protection is therefore low and there is no provision for preventing the unsystematic and incompletely recorded retrieval of artefacts by unqualified collectors. Direct evidence of the poor level of protection offered to registered battlefields comes from two of our sites: at both Tewkesbury and at Stamford Bridge registration was unable to prevent new building on part or all of the battlefield; at Stamford Bridge this resulted in the entire site where fighting took place becoming buried under new houses and roads (Plate 22).

Despite this variability, however, there are certain aspects of designation that can be considered common to all territories. The application of a particular designation – whether as 'Registered Battlefield', 'National Monument', or 'National Military Cemetery' – is part of the broader process of memorialisation: it marks the site as significantly meaningful to a particular community, and engages that community (which may be an entire national community) in recognition of the site as meaningful to them. By doing so, it also renders less meaningful other similar sites that are not so designated. This is the same process as Schaafsma (1989) noted in relation to the ascription of legal significance to archaeological sites, whereby sites not marked as 'significant' are held to be positively 'insignificant'. The effects of this process can be seen in the community of battlefield archaeologists. On the one hand there are concerted efforts to establish registers similar to that in England in other parts of the UK and nearby, and beyond this to gain for battlefield sites considered particularly important additional safeguards and protection, drawing especially upon the North American model. On the other, the greatest focus of attention in England is upon the sites listed in the *Register* rather than other possible sites of similar interest. Similar processes to these are at work elsewhere, such as the USA, where concerted efforts by interest groups seek to gain formal recognition and protection for particular sites of battle and conflict.

A related issue that arises is that of definition – an issue that has appeared several times so far in our work, most notably in Chapters Two and Four. Particular kinds of designation are reserved for particular kinds of object, so that the English Heritage *Register* only includes the sites of events that can be classed specifically as battles, only sites where the dead are buried can be classed as cemeteries, only those sites containing a built structure can be classed as monuments, and so on. Problems arise, however, where sites of very similar events may be classed differently. In practice, archaeologists interested in battlefields are also interested in the sites of other kinds of warlike activity:

sieges and skirmishes, defensive constructions, military training grounds and supply depots. None of these is strictly a battlefield, and many are not the sites of actual combat. At the same time, the sites of activities not regarded as battle but certainly of violence may become the subject of archaeological interest. Many of the actions against indigenous populations by incoming Europeans and vice versa were on a small scale and may not constitute even skirmishes. They very often took the form of raids which, because of their one-sided nature, subsequently gained the title of 'massacre': the 'Fetterman Massacre' by Native Americans of a US army unit, and the 'Sand Creek Massacre' of Native Americans by the US army were both of this kind (Foote, 1997, 6). Other forms of violence – such as gunfights between rival 'outlaw' gangs – may also excite archaeological interest, such as the 'siege' of a house as part of the so-called Lincoln County 'War' of 1878 in New Mexico (Kirkpatrick, 1997, 243–55). None of these is a battle as such, and many such events are not strictly military. A suitable category of designation is therefore often lacking. Their inclusion in the general category of 'battlefield archaeology' (or 'conflict archaeology'), however, serves to blur any distinction between small- and large-scale fighting and non-military versus military action, and, by a process of association, to raise their perceived historical significance, which in turn demands some kind of formal recognition. In particular, this is the process Shelby Foote has noted, whereby what he terms 'designation' may result ultimately in the 'sanctification' of a site; the latter is often marked by the passage of the site 'from private ownership to public stewardship' (1997, 20).

Public Control and Public Access

Designation of a site does not imply any particular management regime will be applied to it. Foote's (1977, 20) statement quoted above notwithstanding, formal recognition of the site by officialdom does not necessarily imply that it passes from private to public control. Where it does, that public control may take a number of forms. At the same time, while public control generally ensures public access to the site, designation alone may not. Accordingly, access is not limited to those sites under public control, and the form of public access itself varies from site to site. Overarching this, sites may be managed for public access but this is not necessarily related to their historic status.

There are restrictions on direct access to the battlefield site itself at only two of our sites. At Stamford Bridge, the restriction is a purely physical one: the main site of fighting has been completely built over (Plate 22); and the point of first encounter – the bridge itself – is no longer present. If any features from the battle had survived into the present, presumably they would be publicly accessible: the bridge or any successor on the same location would continue to be a public right of way; and other public rights of way such as roads and footpaths would provide access to the main battle site. Public rights of way – or rather, their lack – are the reason why Roundway Down is not directly accessible. Local rights of way such as roads, bridleways and footpaths effectively circle the site of the action: access is available from Devizes to Oliver's Castle and the rear slope of Roundway Hill (Plate 17), across which the panicked Parliamentary cavalry would have ridden to the Bloody Ditch (Plate 31), northwards from there to the foot of King's Play Hill and thence eastwards to viewpoints along the Old Bath Road. From here one can look into the battle site but it cannot be crossed without violating private land rights. This is a very English restriction on access. One of the reasons for such good access at sites in Belgium, France, Spain and Portugal is the different rules of access to land that apply: on the European continent, the assumption is generally in favour of a public rights of way across land rather than the English assumption in favour of the private landowner.

The only site in England subject to direct public stewardship is that of the battle of Northampton: as the location of the municipal golf course (Plate 14) it is owned and managed by the local authority but for leisure activities, not as a historic battlefield site. In similar vein, the hills where Roliça was fought are controlled as an area of natural interest (Plate 16): their status as a historic battlefield is unacknowledged. By contrast, both Aljubarrota (Plate 1) and Courtrai (Plate 7) are marked out as parks specifically because of their battlefield status: the monuments raised there are testimony to this. By virtue of this public control, all of these sites are also available to visitors. At both Northampton and Roliça, the site is a place of ongoing activity: at least during the summer, golfers inhabit one and hillwalkers the other. Aljubarrota and Courtrai are both quieter: on the days we visited neither had any other persons present. The museum at Aljubarrota was closed, which may explain this quietude in part, and at Courtrai it was a workday. As parks, both are relatively small and surrounded by habitations and roads: they form part of a landscape that will become familiar to those who live and work locally and who may simply cease to see them as 'special' places. All four, however, have been specifically landscaped to serve their purpose. Northampton's golf course is a built and shaped landscape designed for a particular game; Courtrai's and Aljubarrota's cut grass, set paths and fixed seats define where it is allowable to move and sit; and Roliça's built facilities, marked paths and established roads define clear routes around the space. In similar vein, the preserved stretch of ancient downland on the side of Roundway Hill (Plate 17) is not entirely open to general use. Public stewardship does not necessarily imply a complete freedom of movement.

At some sites a relatively formal 'tourist experience' may be made available; although this can take different forms, they all represent, one way or another, highly 'managed' experiences. At Bosworth, the only battlefield site in England dedicated to tourists, we are offered the full 'tourist experience' with arranged car parks, a visitor centre with all the usual facilities and a well-marked route around the site: the small railway station just off the main battle site provides another focus of interest. This is a site privately managed specifically for tourist visitors; its battlefield status is paramount and is the reason for the site's existence as a venue. This is the most managed site we have examined, but others also offer a degree of controlled experience. The circular 'battlefield drive' at Sedgemoor and the circular battlefield walk at Tewkesbury are similar in kind if not form: one is for cars and the other for walkers, mainly because of the relative distances to be covered and the kind of access involved. The idea, however, is identical: to reveal to the visitor the story of the event of battle by allowing access to the main locations at which it took place: interpretation is chiefly by information panels placed at each such location. At both these sites, as at Bosworth, the visitor makes their own way around the site. At St Albans, although the occasional blue wall-plaque marks particular points in the battlefield space and it is relatively easy to trace the routes of armies through the battlefields from guidebooks, the main approach to the battles is through guided walks made available from the local tourist office. On these, the visitor is led through the space by an interpreter: the experience is pre-ordered and, rather than discovering the space for themselves, the visitor is directed towards key elements chosen by the guide.

A 'battlefield walk' is also on offer at Maldon, although this is less restricting than some others. It follows the public right of way along the estuary down from the town of Maldon to the battlefield opposite Northey Island. The latter is set aside as a nature reserve, but unlike the site of Roliça the battle is explicitly acknowledged as part of the site's significance; the natural and cultural aspects coincide rather than compete for supremacy. The visitor is, accordingly, free to consider the site as a battlefield or as a coastal wetland or both, and to follow paths on to or away from the site according to interest. This may be something typical of shore locations: the experience at the area around the site of The Dunes is similar. Here, the battle is not at all promoted, although referenced by other features. Most visitors come because it is a seaside location: the impressive Fort des Dunes and the ruined coastal gun emplacement nearby provide points of interest in the landscape and seascape, but it is essentially beach activities that predominate. However, as a leisure area one is free to move through the space in any direction and to experience it as one chooses.

Among our sample of sites, it is generally those least managed – at least from a tourist point of view – that offer the greatest freedom to explore. This is not to say that there are no limitations on doing so, since private property rights and claims to privacy must be respected, but that the lack of a controlled and organised 'tourist experience' provides a sense of greater ability to explore the site on the visitor's own terms. These sites are almost all in rural locations, the exceptions being Linton and Fontenoy, both of which are in part urban. The lack of formal management as a 'heritage site', however, does not prevent Cropredy Bridge, Naseby and Stoke from inclusion in the English Heritage *Register*, while the formal marking of these sites and those such as Bouvines and Corunna with monuments does not make them any more tourist-orientated. These sites among all of our examples exemplify the general lack of correlation between formal designation, official preservation, monumentalisation and a tourist function. At both options for Assandun, at Oudenaarde and at Sorauren none of these apply and yet (as seen in Chapter Five) they rank high on the standing of a 'sense of place'. So far as historic battlefields are concerned, it may be that the more managed the experience, the less it becomes an experience of the place and the more it becomes a particular preordained experience.

Interpretation

Specific provision for tourist access implies also some effort at explanation and description. This is not to say that no other locations offer interpretive material, merely that at sites dedicated to tourist access it is generally more present. The forms of interpretation, as with other aspects considered here, however, are variable and only partly related to issues of formal designation and type of public access. The most common form of on-site interpretation is that of the outdoor free-standing information board containing details about the site. Similar boards can be located elsewhere, especially inside buildings such as churches which may be on or near the site or more distant. Museum displays tend to be well away from the site itself. The interpretations offered on battlefield walks are inevitably offered on-site. An aspect of interpretation rarely discussed relates to one of the issues evident from Chapters One and Two: the focus on the battle as an event over that of the battlefield as a place. This is reflected in the mode of interpretation offered.

Information boards are variously sited on battlefields, but often stand on good points of view of the entire battlefield space. This is true at Naseby, where it is located adjacent to the monument overlooking the valley where the battle took place; at Sedgemoor, where it is located immediately in front of the monuments marking the battle site; and at various points in the Bosworth route from which key locations in the story may be seen. The Bloody Meadow at Tewkesbury is the site for the main plinth for that battle: the view from it is only of that small portion of the battlefield space, but this is generally considered to be an important location for understanding the course of events. Information about Fontenoy stands outside the gate to the chateau at Antoing, sharing space with information about the chateau itself. At Stamford Bridge, information on the battle is included in the monument raised in the town square (Plate 51). Other key locations for such information are inside major buildings on or adjacent to the battlefield, especially in churches. The small church at

51. Stamford Bridge: modern monument to the battle.

Aljubarrota contains a board explaining the archaeological investigations of the early 1960s and their findings, and how these relate to the site as subsequently set out. The churches at Bouvines, Stoke and Westonzoyland near Sedgemoor all contain descriptions of the battle for visitors to read. At Cropredy, this is also the case, together with a small display of contemporary arms and armour in memory of those killed (now replaced by replicas after the theft of the originals).

The museum displays of Corunna and Courtrai are both off-site. Of the two, Corunna provides the fullest coverage, having an entire room dedicated to it in the city museum located in one of the buildings in the Castle of St Antonio. Here are displayed images in the form of paintings and prints, including general views of the action, maps and a picture of the death of the British commander in suitably heroic style. There are also artefacts on display, including a captured French artillery piece brought into the city and left on the evacuation of the British army. It signals the significance of the event to the locality and the importance of the battle as an event in local history. It does not, however, make any reference to current uses of the space of the battle, especially the construction of the new university there despite the clear association between the battle and the building recognised by local residents. Other rooms are dedicated to other aspects of the history of the town, including social and economic history. In the grounds of the castle yet other aspects are emphasised, in particular a reconstructed prehistoric burial cairn. The Groeningeabdij Museum in Kortrijk is also a general museum of local history and culture, specialising in the economic aspects of the city's life. The battle is represented only on the model of the city as it was in a fourteenth-century heyday, by showing the positions of forces in relation to the city walls and gates. A view of the actual site in comparison with this suggests – although this may be a misleading comparison – that the area covered by the battle as shown on the model is somewhat exaggerated. Any such exaggeration may, however, reflect the significance of the event in local and national narratives and therefore a kind of 'truth'.

Offering 'truths' is what John Jameson (1997) suggests can be achieved through archaeology by a specific interaction with the wider public. In the case of the Little Bighorn fight of 1876 (Scott, 1997, 234–42) and a gunfight in which Billy the Kid was involved from 1881 (Kirkpatrick, 1997, 243–55) it is specifically events of violence that are the object of interpretation. In both cases, the focus is upon an event in the past, although closely connected to a particular place: the Little Bighorn Battlefield National Monument (Foote,

1997, 325–7; Scott, *et al.*, 1989; Scott, 1997, 234–42) and the site of the McSween House in Lincoln, New Mexico (Kirkpatrick, 1997). But it is as events that these interpretations treat them: as Kirkpatrick puts it, visitors left the site of the McSween House 'with a better understanding of Billy the Kid as a person [and] the Lincoln County War as a political and economic event' (1997, 255). Our own sites reflect this concern with treating historic battlefields as the locations of events rather than specifically as landscapes with a historic significance. Off-site interpretations, perhaps not unexpectedly, are particularly prone to do this: at Stamford Bridge the monument in the town square emphasises the event rather than the location, as do the museum representations at Courtrai, Corunna and Tewkesbury, and the church explanations at Bouvines, Aljubarrota, Stoke and Cropredy. The Fontenoy information board also takes this approach: any emphasis on place is reserved for discussion of the role of Antoing and its chateau. Accordingly, such emphasis is more likely to be found in those locations where interpretation is offered directly at the place of action. This applies particularly to the information boards at Naseby and Sedgemoor – where one is looking directly at the point of action as one reads – and in those locations where more active engagement with the landscape takes place, such as guided walks at St Albans or the self-led walk at Tewkesbury.

SUMMARY: BATTLEFIELDS AS MANAGED SPACES

It is clear that the types of management regime that can be applied to historic battlefields – at least as represented by the sample examined here – are a varied collection. At one extreme there is no formal management at all of the site as a historic place: among our sites, this will include both potential sites for Assandun as well as Bouvines, St Albans, Stoke, Roundway Down, Cropredy Bridge, Naseby, Linton, The Dunes, Sedgemoor, Oudenaarde, Fontenoy and Sorauren. Such a lack does not necessarily correlate with any other management factor, since among these only Assandun, Linton, Oudenaarde and Sorauren are unacknowledged as battlefield sites, and of the remainder all but one of the English examples are designated as significant by their inclusion in the English Heritage (1995) *Register*. In theory, such registration does provide a modicum of protection by marking the sites as factors to be taken into account for development control purposes: as we have noted in respect of Tewkesbury and Stamford Bridge, however, such protection is not guaranteed. Only a few of our sites are subject to any direct public control or custodianship; this does, however, correlate very closely with their reshaping for other purposes. At

Northampton, the site is used for sporting and other leisure activity; at Aljubarrota and Courtrai they have been marked out as formal parks; and at Roliça the area is made available for hill walking and nature study. Having said this, the lack of formal management of sites specifically as battlefields does not mean that they are not otherwise subject to environmental management regimes. To some extent, all our sites are managed, whether as rural farmland or as urban spaces: there are inevitably limitations placed upon the possible use and on possible changes to the shape of the space. Others are subject to more direct management intervention. Maldon, for instance, is managed like Roliça as a nature reserve, and a patch of land on Roundway Down is preserved as ancient pasture; Courtrai, St Albans and Linton are historic towns in their own right, battles notwithstanding; Sedgemoor sits in a protected wetland zone; and Sorauren sits astride the historic pilgrimage route to Santiago de Compostela, protected under European legislation.

Among our sites, only Aljubarrota is specifically dedicated to memorialisation, although this is also evident at other places by the erection of monuments. This distinction between the site itself and any monuments erected upon it is perhaps also worth emphasising: it may go some way towards explaining the frequent erection of such monuments away from the site itself. Because, as described above, it is so often the event of battle that is considered significant – rather than including in this significance the place itself – it may be considered allowable to commemorate it at places other than the specific location where it took place. In Britain the erection of monuments to distant wars (as recorded by Yarrington, 1988; and the National Inventory of War Memorials: Hewitt, 2001, 13–22) is testimony to the emphasis so often placed in modern culture upon events rather than places. This, in turn, may be part of a general attitude to landscapes that treats them as places to look upon rather than to experience. Where an experience of the site is made directly available by opening it up to tourists in particular, it is so often a highly managed experience that is offered rather than allowing visitors to interpret the place for themselves. An interesting paradox that arises is our finding (and discussed in Chapter Five) that it is so often the least formally managed sites that speak so readily to us of their history.

CONCLUSION: HISTORIC BATTLEFIELDS IN THE PRESENT

This chapter has been a contribution to the study of places that carry historic significance in the present, as part of our modern 'heritage'. Picking up on

52. Stoke: battlefield church.

aspects of the experience of being in such places described in Chapter Five, we considered the changes these landscapes have undergone over time, which have sometimes been considerable. We then considered the placing of monuments and other forms of memorialisation at these places or nearby; and then turning to their consideration specifically as landscapes, we looked at the various ways in which these places are managed. Together, these different but related elements provide a picture of how we think about and treat the sites of past war in the present. What emerges is the wide range of different treatments available to such places, and the manner in which one type of treatment does not necessarily correlate closely with others. This, in turn, suggests that there is not yet any clear consensus internationally, or even within nations, as to the proper way to treat such sites. From the perspective of our own approach, however, it was clear that the least managed sites provided the most interesting insights and the clearest experience of the past.

Although firmly located in the present, what this chapter has not done is to attempt to link the past of the sites we have studied to their present. Together with an overview of the Bloody Meadows Project so far, and a consideration of its future, this is the topic for Chapter Seven.

SEVEN

GOING FORWARD

As we hope we made clear at the beginning, this book represents not the end of the Bloody Meadows Project but a stage in its development. The purpose has been to outline (as we did in Chapters One and Two) the origins of the project and the particular way it represents of looking at sites of battle in the past. We used twenty-three examples of sites we have visited in several countries, from different periods of history, spanning nearly 900 years (reported on in Chapter Three) to outline how we approach such places and the kinds of understandings of them our approach will generate. We offered in particular an approach that sought to combine an interest in the past with the study of heritage sites in the present, by looking at them specifically as landscapes (partially achieved in Chapter Five), and drawing upon recent methods developed in our home discipline of archaeology. What we have not yet done is to truly combine those interests into a single statement: Chapters Four and Six each looked closely at our sites in terms of either the past or the present, but we reserved an attempt to link them until this chapter. We shall attempt to make this link in the next section, and use this to consider what our approach has shown it can offer. We will then close the chapter and the book by looking to see where the project needs to go in future, and by returning to some of the concerns of Chapter One to a short review of the relation of our work with work deriving from other fields.

WHAT WE THINK WE HAVE LEARNED . . .

. . . about battlefields

It is clear from previous chapters (especially Chapters Four, Five and Six) that the places where people fought in the past are subject to changes in the type of use and appropriation they experience. In the past, particular types of people came with a particular purpose in particular sets of circumstances. The memory of that past event has since been used to support contemporary causes and to create modern meanings (and for some American examples, see Foote, 1997). The memory and the event are connected but are not the same; and the form of the memory often does not reflect the form of the event at all. In visiting battlefields today, one can look at these issues as changes in three areas: the ownership (or claimed ownership) of the site; the realm of modern discourse within which the treatment of the site is located; and the modern experience of being at the site (Table 7.1).

Ownership

The majority of battles involve the active occupation of ground and a determination to hold it against assault; on occasion this also includes the construction of physical barriers to assault. In an 'encounter' battle – where forces meet by happenstance rather than by planning – the ground itself is disputed as both sides move to occupy it simultaneously. Regardless of types of combatants – whether professional soldiers, civilian rebels or volunteer soldiers – the act of claiming possession of a piece of ground is central to the act of battle. It is the subsequent outcome of the battle that may determine the ownership – or at least recognised and acknowledged claims of ownership – today. Frequently, where victory was achieved by the forces of the state in whose territory the battlefield is located, it is that nation state which makes the claim, using the event as part of its own claim to legitimate existence. Where national forces were defeated, the battle may not be adopted by the host nation, but by others: at Fontenoy the claim is made instead by another state from which combatants were drawn. Where the battle was fought between forces from places alien to the host territory, a more local and regional association may be forged, although at some such sites no particular claim of ownership is made. Where all the combatants were natives of the home state (especially in civil conflicts) a local claim seems to be the most common, and this kind of association may also be made where there was a specifically local involvement in the battle. Bosworth is an exception to this general rule, but Bosworth has particular associations with dynastic rivalry, and it is this alienation from the modern sense of what it is legitimate to die for that perhaps makes it ripe for specifically private ownership and exploitation.

Discourse

The notion of 'discourse' was introduced in Chapter Two. It is defined as 'the communicative practice in a specific domain of knowledge' (Gray, 1997, 95), so that rules of discourse 'establish who can be listened to, and who can't, as well

Table 7.1   *Some western European battlefields from past to present: from event to memory*

Battle	Past			Ownership/Claim	Present	
	Conflict and Battle Type	Combatants	Landscape Type		Discourse	Experience
Aljubarrota 1385	International, attack on prepared position	Professional	Open, high, rural, defences	National	Nationalist	Monumental
Assandun 1016	International, mutually agreed	Warriors	Open, riverside	None	N/A	Historical
Bosworth 1485	Civil war, mutually agreed	Professional	Open, high, rural	Private	Commercial	Tourist
Bouvines 1214	International, mutually agreed	Professional	Open, high, rural	National	Trans-historical	Monumental
Courtrai 1302	Rebellion, mutually agreed	Volunteers, professional	Open, low, urban	Local and national	Nationalist	Monumental
Coruna /Elviña 1809	International, mutually agreed	Professional	Featured, high, rural	Local and regional	Future-orientated	Monumental
Cropredy Bridge 1644	Civil war, encounter	Volunteers	Open, low, rural	Local	Historical	Tourist
The Dunes 1658	International, attack on prepared position	Professional	Open, coastal	Local	Trans-historical	Monumental
Fontenoy 1745	International, attack on prepared position	Professional	Open, low, rural, defences	Other national	Nationalist	Monumental
Linton 1648	Rebellion, attack on prepared position	Volunteers, professional	Urban and rural	None	Historical	Historical
Maldon 991	International, mutually agreed	Warriors	Coastal	Local and National	Historical	Tourist
Naseby 1645	Civil war, mutually agreed	Professional	Open, low, rural	National	Historical	Tourist
Northampton 1460	Civil war, attack on prepared position	Professional	Open, low, near town	National	Historical	Historical
Oudenaarde 1708	International, encounter	Professional	Open, low, rural	None	None	Historical
Roliça 1808	International, attack on prepared position	Professional	Featured, high, rural	Visitors	Common	Natural
Roundway Down 1643	Civil war, mutually agreed	Volunteers	Open, low, rural	Local	Historical	Natural
Sorauren I and II 1813	International, attack on prepared position	Professional	Featured, rural	None	None	Historical
Sedgemoor 1685	Rebellion, attack on prepared position	Rebels, professional	Open, low, rural	Local	Memorialisation	Memorial
St Albans I and II 1455/1461	Civil war, attack on prepared position	Professional	High, urban	Local	Historic	Historical
Stamford Bridge 1066	International, attack on prepared position	Warriors	Open, high, rural	Local and national	Historic	Monumental
Stoke 1487	Civil war, mutually agreed	Professional	Open, high, rural	National	Historic	Historical
Tewkesbury 1471	Civil war, mutually agreed	Professional	Open, low, near town	National	Historic	Monumental

as conventions that mark out permitted areas for discussion, and those [that are] forbidden, and rationales that allow certain questions to be asked but not others' (1997, 95–6). In the context of the study of war, these rules need not limit themselves to words: what 'warriors and soldiers do with their bodies is more important than what they say. Weapons, rituals, traditions and techniques are all parts of the discourse of war' (Gray, 1997, 95–6). In terms of looking at battle, these rules concern who may take part and how they should be treated, and where it may take place and in what form. These things – which were particularly addressed in Chapter Four – are the content of a particular 'discourse' of battle.

In the past, on the day of the battle, the realm of discourse within which the site was located was always that of war; and the site chosen reflected what was expected and allowed in terms of the rules dictating warfare practice at that time. As discussed in Chapter Four, our research indicates that in medieval times the preference was for sites either on high ground, or adjacent to or even within urban centres, or both; that in the seventeenth and eighteenth centuries the preference was for sites on low ground away from major settlements; and that in the early nineteenth century the preference was for sites containing a number of different kinds of feature. Once the battle is transferred to the realm of memory, however, as discussed in Chapters Five and Six, the appropriate realm of discourse is no longer that of past war but of contemporary purposes. Where a straightforward national ownership is claimed the discourse is generally that of nationalism. A variation is rung on this theme at Fontenoy where the Irish claim on the site is a nationalist one, but the site itself is inside the territory of France. At Bosworth the site is treated as a place for commercial interaction, while Roliça and Maldon are also for visitors but the focus is far less commercial. Sedgemoor is a site occupied by memorials to the dead of all wars, while other sites have been forgotten except as past events, thereby relegated to history. These contrast with those places where the forging of specific links with later events at that place renders the discourse one that works across historical periods. At Corunna, the identification of the battle site with a place for the education of future generations not only crosses historical periods but takes us beyond our own time into that of the future.

Experience

The experience of battle is one of violence and terror: physical features in the battlefield, if any, are examined in terms of the potential threat or possible safety they offer. By contrast, the experience of that place today will be one of peace and safety: features will be examined for their aesthetic appeal or historic interest. Nevertheless, due to the different claims of ownership made upon the place and the modern field of discourse in which it is located, the modern experience of the historic place of battle will vary from site to site. For many sites, the modern experience is that of confrontation with a monumental past, frequently represented by one or more built monuments. This is particularly the case where one is dealing with nationalist sites or where links to other historical times are being asserted (and see Herzfeld, 1991, 5–9) At Sedgemoor, the monumental experience is transformed into one primarily of memorialisation by the presence of monuments specifically to the dead. Where commercial or visitor interest is paramount, the experience is very much one of tourism, although occasionally – as at St Albans – the experience can also be one of transportation through different historical periods. At others the site has lost its close historical associations and will be experienced primarily as a natural landscape.

. . . about our approach

It will be clear that we think our approach (in some sense) 'works'. By focusing on sites of battle in the past specifically as landscapes we believe we are accessing a resource for understanding aspects of the past generally left untapped. We believe that our results so far – as set out in Chapters Four, Five and Six and summarised again in Table 7.1 – represent types of knowledge that others interested in battlefields, and indeed historic landscapes generally (who use different techniques and approaches), have not been able to acquire. In particular, this relates especially to the patterning of landscape choices made in different periods of history and the range of current treatments deemed appropriate for such sites in the present. On the basis of this, we believe that our approach is reasonably consistent in its application, that it allows us to understand aspects of places and events widely different in space and time, and that in doing so it allows us – as we began by wishing to do – to make meaningful comparisons between one site and another and different sites from different historical periods. We believe that it is a relatively easy approach to take, allowing it to be used not only by ourselves but also by others interested in battlefields as historic landscapes. This means that the project as a whole can grow by being taken up by other people, and that it can also be used in conjunction with other techniques of battlefield investigation. There is no reason, for instance, why archaeologists concerned with the study of artefact patterning on sites or with the excavation of mass graves (e.g. the kind of work reported on in Freeman and Pollard, 2001) should not also be able to apply our approach to understanding the locations where these are found. At the same time, geologists more concerned with understanding the role of the physical terrain of battlefields (e.g. Doyle and Bennett, 2002) should also cast their eyes up and around them as well as below their feet. In terms of the ways in which sites are marked, memorialised and managed, our work may help elucidate some of the issues addressed by responsible agencies (e.g. English Heritage, 1995; Hewitt, 2001, 13–22).

We believe that any value our work contains is due to its three key aspects: that it represents an entirely material culture-based approach; that in taking such an approach it applies ideas from phenomenology without bogging itself down too heavily in philosophy; and that it uses this basis to consider its objects of enquiry in a comparative frame of reference. As is evident from the discussions in Chapters Four and Six, we are less concerned to relate what we encounter to the literature of the battles fought there, than to identify those features present and absent and especially their physical relations to one another. Chapter Five gave an indication of how the totality of the site acts as an experience of place, which is the 'phenomenological' aspect of the approach, but we have so far avoided the need so often assumed by archaeologists to dwell upon the complexities of thought of phenomenological philosophy. In particular, we have seen no use to our work in going into detail about what figures such as Martin Heidegger may have meant or the application of his thought for archaeology (cf. Thomas, 1996). Although taking a broadly phenomenological approach, however, we are not constrained by its limitation to the specificity of so many 'post-processual' archaeologies (see Hodder *et al.*, 1995, 5). Instead, by considering those places we study, the objects they contain and the relationships between them in an overtly comparative frame of reference – of site with site, and of period or geographical region with other periods or geographical regions, and especially in terms of differences of apprehension between periods, regions and today – we are able to come to more general statements about what these places are like and how they may have been understood in the past.

Having said this, we also believe that our approach must be applied with a concern for specifics. It is not sufficient to take in the general lie of the land or rely on contemporary testimony of battlefield observers as to significant features. Instead, the approach relies upon a capacity to 'see' the space very clearly for oneself, to identify features that are present, and to distinguish what is present today from what was present in the past. Where sources are used, as indeed they will be, it is important not to be 'reading' the landscape in their terms but in one's own: it is the difference between an experience by a present visitor and that of the past that allows an understanding of the site to develop. This experience is not limited to the visual. It is necessary to use all of the senses so far as possible, and to approach the site from a number of different directions, in order to gain a sense of the space from various locations within it and from the perspectives of those in the past who may have passed through it in differing ways and with differing purposes. Since we rely heavily upon our own cultural norms to 'read' the space, the approach is relatively simple, but because of the need to be constantly alert to the difference of a modern reading from past readings, and indeed differences in reading by different individuals in the present, it is not necessarily easy. This is one reason we advocate repeat visits to sites and taking time to explore them (as set out in the appendix to Chapter Two, see pp. 33–4): as the project develops we may need to revisit some of the sites covered here, to note new developments and to reconsider them in the light of further work.

What We Do Not Yet Know . . .

One of the key activities of research is always to review its own progress and to reconsider earlier findings in the light of new data or alternative explanations. In the same way, one of the main purposes of research is always to generate new sets of research questions and reconsider old ones. In the case of the Bloody Meadows Project, this means a constant review of our aims and methods, and taking our approach into new areas and new historical periods.

. . . about battlefields

This book offers only a small sample of the total number of known sites of battle across the globe: a mere 23 out of an estimated 7,000 (approximately 0.33 per cent). It also covers only one small transect of the globe, from England through Belgium and France to Spain and Portugal, and a relatively short period of human history, spanning only 900 years or so. Any broad conclusions we have reached – about sites, about ideologies of war, about understandings of landscape, and about memorialisation and remembrance – must remain provisional until more work has been done. This further work will be developed at two interacting levels. At one level, we shall be extending our range of periods and geographical regions investigated: accordingly, work from 2002 to 2004 focused upon battlefields from the periods of the classical civilisations of Greece and Rome, most of them in Greece (Carman and Carman, 2005a, 1:1). At the other level, we shall be extending and deepening our understanding of battlefields within particular periods of history. Both will add to our database as it grows and will also provide at once new data and confirmation or denial of previous ideas. The more sites the project is able to study, the greater confidence we can have in its findings and the more useful those findings will be to other students of war in the past.

An issue that we have not yet encountered as a serious problem (so far as we are aware) but may emerge as the project develops, is that of identifying clearly the location of the events in which we are interested. To some extent we have already addressed this in looking at alternative sites for Assandun, and in noting the revision of ideas about the precise location of the battle of Northampton: similar issues may well emerge over Bosworth. Otherwise all our sites have been firmly identified. Where they are not, however, the question must arise as to what we can say about them: if our examination is based upon a place that is not in fact the place of fighting, then any statements we make about the choice of that location will be misleading. From a purely 'military historical' point of view, this may be considered a significant flaw in our approach. On the other hand, since we inevitably rely on the work of others in identifying such places, we perhaps cannot be too strongly blamed; and – more significantly from the point of view of our concern to reveal cultural understandings and assumptions about landscapes – it does tell us something about how modern researchers apprehend what a battlefield site should be like. To this extent at least, mistaking a battlefield site can still contribute to our work.

All our sites have so far been limited to western Europe, where a high degree of cultural interaction can be both assumed and demonstrated: any patterning we can infer is likely to be the result of that cultural interaction. It is also, of course, our own cultural background that we have been investigating: certain of the assumptions we make – and of which we may be unaware – can therefore be relied upon to hold true. We can perhaps expect that this will not be the case with battles fought elsewhere and under very different political and cultural conditions. This is one of the issues that Jeremy Black (1991; 2000; 2002) has concerned himself with, and in particular the Eurocentricity of much of the discussion of military affairs (referred to also in Chapter Four). If the 'culture of war' changes over time within a relatively small geographical zone (as from our work it seems to) then presumably the changes will be consequently greater over wider geographical space and larger spans of time. In particular, the style of fighting in colonial or other contexts may well turn out to be very different from that in Europe. This is an aspect we have yet to explore. The problem may be compounded if the attitude towards war taken in that region is also significantly different from that in Europe (e.g. those drawn upon by Keegan, 1993).

. . . about our approach

We have yet to fully develop our merging of interests in both landscapes in the past and their role as heritage in our present. As is evident from Chapters Four and Six, these remain quite separate in terms of the issues covered and the manner of approaching them. Although Chapter Five essayed a kind of merger of these aspects by a consideration of the present experience of these places, one or other aspect tended to dominate our response: accordingly, while some were of interest because of the perspective they gave on battle in the past, others offered insights into contemporary attitudes to historic places. Other researchers are also interested in places as various kinds of historic landscape, however, and it may be possible for us to combine some of our interests with theirs to the benefit of both. One approach in particular may prove enlightening: modern 'heritagescapes' (Garden, forthcoming) are considered in terms of three parameters – those of boundaries, cohesion and visibility – which have some affinity with aspects of our own work. One of the interesting aspects of such a 'heritagescape' approach is its ability to distinguish 'places [with a sense of] the past' from 'places apart' (from the rest of modernity); these differences are assessed in terms of the experience they offer. This will clearly offer something to our own work as it develops; it may also serve to address other areas of uncertainty as they emerge.

The Idea of 'Battle'

A question that may arise as we extend our coverage into new regions and periods concerns how we should cope with cultures of war that do not involve battles as we understand them. We voluntarily exclude from our coverage actions such as civil disorder, sieges and military manoeuvre without fighting, as well as issues of logistics. If, however, we encountered a cultural context where these were the only types of warlike activity, it would hamper our ability to make any comment upon it apart, perhaps, from noting the lack of battles. To some extent we have already gone beyond our own bounds, by including in our coverage so far the fights at Courtrai, Linton and the first battle of St Albans, all of which were actions fought as part of uprisings rather than battles as more conventionally understood: as discussed in Chapter Four, two of these were nevertheless ascribed the status of 'battle' but Linton remains merely 'battle-like' in our own designatory scheme. We were able to include them because of the prior designation of battle to Courtrai and St Albans, and because Linton demonstrates the characteristics of a battle regardless of its non-designation as such. We can incorporate other such events into our scheme on the same basis: instead of relying on others' recognition of an event as a battle – whether in the past or more recently – we can use our own definition (set out in Table 2.1 on p. 15) to identify those historic events that fall within our purview.

A specific example of where this issue may particularly emerge as we extend our geographical coverage is in the military history of China. Among others, Tao Hanzhang has discussed the military theory of Sun Zi in relation to specific examples from China's ancient history (Tao, 2000). The 'battles' he discusses are very large in geographical scale and involve actual fighting only as part of much wider manoeuvres: in the Western tradition these would more likely be referred to as 'operations' or even as 'campaigns' rather than as battles proper. Quite how we would deal with them in our scheme is problematic. As an issue it is one that must remain open and the questions it raises unanswered for the time being. It may be that we shall be reduced to acknowledging the fundamental difference of the ancient Chinese approach to war from the European tradition, and that therefore we shall have nothing to say except that no events that we can call battles took place. Otherwise we may be able to identify those war-making activities that are not battles as we define them but involve fighting and are yet not sieges, skirmishes or responses to civil disorder. In this respect, we would be identifying those activities which perform the same functions as battles in the Western tradition and treating them accordingly.

Both these solutions to perceived problems will technically take us beyond our chosen parameters for the project. But in doing so it will, we believe, enhance the value of our work by distinguishing areas of war-making practice that would otherwise be subsumed under a single overarching category in a manner that may conceal rather than reveal significant differences. By opening them up for scrutiny, they will become available for comparative analysis.

Battlefields as 'Heritage'

Part of the transformation of battlefields to 'heritage' places, as discussed in Chapter Six, is often a process whereby they become memorialised in some manner: this is most obvious by the erection of a physical structure on or near the place of battle to mark it as significant. Where this takes place – either soon after the event or later in the site's history – we have been able to comment upon it in terms of its form, its location relative to the site of battle, its dedicator and its dedicatee. Where no such structure exists, however, we have been able to do little except note its absence in comparison with those more formally marked. Shelby Foote, in his discussion of American sites of tragedy and violence, calls this process of non-marking 'rectification', whereby the site gains only 'temporary notoriety' and is then reabsorbed into the everyday:

> Associations with the . . . event eventually weaken, and the site is reintegrated into the activities of everyday life. . . . [Rectification] frequently produces the least activity at the . . . site. . . . Sometimes neglect and abandonment ensue before the site is put to a new use, but changes are little noted and rarely discussed. Rectification is . . . the rule for the vast majority of sites . . . of violence. These are the sites of events that fail to gain the sense of significance that inspires sanctification or designation and lack the shameful connotations that spur obliteration. Rectification . . . is the most common outcome when . . . violence is interpreted as senseless (1997, 23).

The problem that exists for our approach, however, is knowing whether such sites achieved even temporary notoriety in any meaningful sense. Instead, it may be that the armies in the past moved in, fought, and moved away without noting in particular the location where they met, and without leaving behind them any feeling of the significance of their passing. 'Rectification' in Foote's (1997) sense of the term requires a measure of notoriety or fame, however short-lived after the event that inspired it. Rectification is for him one of a set of responses that assumes sanctification, designation and deliberate obliteration as legitimate and proper responses to places of trauma: rectification is the positive absence of these. We have noted, however, battles from periods where it seems memorialisation (whether sanctification or designation in Foote's terms) is not a norm. Accordingly, battles from the seventeenth and eighteenth centuries (in particular) that remain unmemorialised and unmarked may represent something other than 'rectification' in the sense used here. In our age, and in the centuries preceding early modernity, the marking of battlefields as special places seems to have been a cultural norm: the form differs in the medieval period from the modern, and most probably the specific audience and purpose, but there is some similarity of practice. Such places do not appear to require any kind of marking in the intervening period, however, suggesting that a very different set of cultural imperatives are at work. Without any material legacy to consider, it may prove difficult, if not impossible, for us to say very much about those very different cultural traditions of remembrance.

For us to study battlefields as a part of our heritage it is necessary for them to be treated as part of that heritage. Where remembrance is lacking, that 'heritage' status is effectively withheld. Modern attitudes to sites of historic conflict are different from those in the past, but inevitably include the evidence for those past understandings. Where no such evidence exists, it is possible that we shall need to be silent apart from noting the lack of remembrance, and leave it to others to consider the specifics of that particular cultural choice.

CONCLUSIONS

This chapter has been a short but critical review of the work of the Bloody Meadows Project so far. It has reviewed our results and points towards those areas we need to address further as the project continues. It has suggested areas where the project may not be able to make any clear statements about the objects of enquiry we specifically address. What we also cannot comment upon – and nor, strictly speaking, is it our role to do so – is the reception this work will be given by those who also have an interest in our areas of research. We believe there are three main areas of such interest.

The main students of historic battlefields are military historians and military, battlefield or conflict archaeologists (the term used to describe them varies). Our work derives directly from the latter concerns and it is to these that the most direct contribution can be made. We think our work may have three distinctive values, all relating to the limitations of the standard military historical discourse which we discussed in Chapter Two. First, we represent an approach to battlefields neither grounded in nor deriving from military history but instead directly from archaeology. We think this matters because it allows us to say things about battles and battlefields that a military historian simply cannot. This is not to demean military history as such, but we believe that an over-reliance on military history as a source discipline prevents the emergence of the full value of the material culture approach that is central to archaeology.

Second, we believe that our work may have some predictive value where scholars are seeking to locate a battle from the past: by using our 'typology' for that period some places may appear more likely and others less so. Third, because we highlight not functional rationality in decision-making but the unstated assumptions that lie behind choices in the past, we also help to undermine the contemporary myth of war as a rational activity and an appropriate response to perceived threat. Our work goes some way towards demonstrating that the way wars are fought is not grounded in rationality but in cultural beliefs, and that these vary across time and across space. Our work reveals some of this variation for further investigation by both military historians and military archaeologists.

Our second audience is students of landscapes from the past, especially those in our host discipline of archaeology. We believe that our work demonstrates the utility of an approach to landscapes based upon phenomenology; moreover, by applying this approach to historic landscapes we show the usefulness of the approach beyond the study of prehistory. Our approach is based entirely upon the notion that attitudes towards and expectations of landscape in the past were different from those held by people in the twenty-first century: if they were not different we would have nothing to say. We believe our approach seeks out and identifies those differences by using an explicitly Western mode of investigation of space and comparing that with the use of that space made by people in the past. It is from noting the manner in which objects are used, or any failure to use them as we would today, that these differences emerge. We can also compare the uses of space in one historical period with those of another, revealing other differences in attitude and expectation. Where objects that were present in the past and would be available for use in the present – especially for military purposes, such as facilitating or impeding movement, for concealment or for protection – were not used for these purposes, it can be inferred that the objects were not seen as useful. This, in turn, indicates a measure of difference between the past and the present. We believe that choosing to examine landscapes that were used for a very particular kind of purpose in the past makes the identification and examination of these differences in attitude and expectation as revealed by differences in use more reliable, and that they therefore reveal real differences between various periods of history. These can then be taken up by others who are interested in understanding the use and attitudes towards space of people in the past.

As students of the remembrance of historic places, we aim to contribute to studies of modern 'heritage' and of social memory. Here, we record the actual means by which places were marked and memorialised in the present and in the past: where no such marking is evident, we record that too. Accordingly, unlike so many of those interested in these areas, we do not start from the premise that the marking and commemoration of battlefields (among other places) is a universal cultural norm, but that to do so is one form of cultural practice in which we can be interested. From our work the differences in style of marking between the medieval and modern periods emerge; as does also the apparent hiatus in commemoration from the end of the medieval period to the nineteenth century. This is something apparently not remarked upon by other researchers (see Borg, 1991; Hewitt, 2001; Yarrington, 1988). Our work therefore serves to assist those who wish to challenge the assumptions so often made about what is right and proper in relation to social memory, and instead to establish the forms of that memory as an object of study in their own right. It offers to us as something strange our own cultural practices and accepted norms of behaviour. It may serve to raise questions about our own modern attitudes to war and remembrance in the same way that work such as ours raises questions about the rational basis for decision-making in war.

Ultimately, as is so common with much contemporary research work, our project is not really about the past but about our own attitudes and understandings in the present. It lays before us our beliefs and practices as a set of ideas that do not hold true in all times and places, and are different from those in the past. It causes us to question our values and expectations by revealing how historically shallow those values and expectations are. As our work progresses, we hope it will tell us more about the past, but we also hope it will tell us more about the present and give indications to a different, perhaps better, way of thinking about issues of war and violence more generally. We certainly hope it will encourage our readers to think about these things.

REFERENCES

Ashplant, T.G., Dawson, G. and Roper, M. (2000). 'The politics of war memory and commemoration: contexts, structures and dynamics' in T.G. Ashplant, G. Dawson and M. Roper (eds), *The Politics of War Memory and Commemoration*. London, Routledge

Barnes, R. (2004). *The Obelisk: a Monumental Feature in Britain*. Norwich, Frontier Press

Barnett, C. (1974). *Marlborough*. London, Eyre Methuen

Barrett, J. (1991). 'Towards an archaeology of ritual' in P. Garwood, R. Skeates and J. Toms (eds), *Sacred and Profane: proceedings of a conference on archaeology, ritual and religion*. Oxford, Oxford University Committee for Archaeology

Barrett, J. (1994). *Fragments from Antiquity: an archaeology of social life in Britain 2900–1200BC*. Oxford, Blackwells

Bender, B. (ed.) (1993). *Landscape: politics and perspectives*. Oxford, Berg

Bennett, M.J. (1985). *The Battle of Bosworth*. Gloucester, Alan Sutton

Bennett, M.J. (1987). *Lambert Simnel and the Battle of Stoke*. Gloucester, Alan Sutton

Black, J. (1991). *A Military Revolution? Military Change and European Society 1550–1800*. Studies in European History. London, Macmillan

Black, J. (2000). *War Past Present & Future*. Stroud, Sutton Publishing

Black, J. (2002). *European Warfare 1494–1815*. London, Routledge

Bois, J.P. (1992). *Maurice de Saxe*. Lille, Fayard

Borg, A. (1991). *War Memorials: from antiquity to the present*. London, Leo Cooper

Brodie, B. (1973). *War & Politics*. London, Cassell

Brooke, R. (1854). *Visits to the Fields of Battle in England of the Fifteenth Century*. London, John Russell Smith (reprinted 1975, Dursley, Alan Sutton)

Brooks, F.W. (1956). *The Battle of Stamford Bridge*. York, East Yorkshire Local History Society

Burne, A.H. (1950). *The Battlefields of England*. London, Methuen

Burton, P., Evans, M.M. and Westaway, M. (2002). *Naseby 1645*. London, Pen & Sword

Bushaway, B. (1992). 'Name Upon Name: the Great War and Remembrance' in R. Porter (ed.), *Myths of the English*. Cambridge, Polity Press

Carman, J. (1996). *Valuing Ancient Things: archaeology and law*. London, Leicester University Press

Carman, J. (ed.) (1997a). *Material Harm: archaeological approaches to war and violence*. Glasgow, Cruithne Press

Carman, J. (1997b). 'Introduction: approaches to violence' in J. Carman, *Material Harm: archaeological approaches to war and violence*. Glasgow, Cruithne Press

Carman, J. (1997c). 'Giving archaeology a moral voice' in J. Carman, *Material Harm: archaeological approaches to war and violence*. Glasgow, Cruithne Press

Carman, J. (1998). 'Object values: landscapes and their contents' in M. Jones and D. Rotherham (eds), *Landscapes – Perception, Recognition and Management: reconciling the impossible?* Landscape Archaeology and Ecology 2. Sheffield, Landscape Conservation Forum

Carman, J. (1999a). 'Beyond the Western Way of War: ancient battlefields in comparative perspective' in J. Carman and A. Harding (eds), *Ancient Warfare: archaeological perspectives*. Stroud, Sutton Publishing

Carman, J. (1999b). 'Bloody Meadows: the places of battle' in S. Tarlow and S. West (eds), *The Familiar Past? Archaeologies of Later Historical Britain*. London, Routledge

Carman, J. (1999c). 'Settling on sites: constraining concepts' in J.M. Brück and M. Goodman (eds), *Making Places in the Prehistoric World: themes in settlement archaeology*. London, UCL Press

Carman, J. (2001). 'Paradox in Places: 20th-century battlefields in long-term perspective' in J. Schofield, W.G. Johnson and C. Beck (eds), *Matériel Culture: the archaeology of 20th-century conflict*. London, Routledge

Carman, J. (2002). *Archaeology & Heritage: an introduction*. London and New York, Continuum

Carman, J. and Carman, P. (2001). 'Beyond military archaeology: battlefields as a research resource' in P. Freeman and T. Pollard (eds), *Fields of Conflict: progress and prospects in battlefield archaeology, proceedings of a conference held in the Department of Archaeology, University of Glasgow, April 2000*, BAR International Series 958. Oxford

Carman, J. and Carman, P. (2005a). 'Ancient Bloody Meadows: fieldwork in Greece and France 2002 to 2004', *Journal of Conflict Archaeology* 1:1, 19–44

Carman, J. and Carman, P. (2005b). 'War in prehistoric society: modern views of ancient violence' in M. Parker-Pearson (ed.), *Warfare, Violence and Slavery in Prehistory and Protohistory: proceedings of a conference held at the University of Sheffield, 2nd–3rd February 2001*, BAR International Series, 217–24. Oxford, Archaeopress

Chaliand, G. (1994). *The Art of War in World History from Antiquity to the Nuclear Age*. Berkeley and Los Angeles, CA, University of California Press

Chandler, D.G. (ed.) (1989). *A Guide to the Battlefields of Europe*. Ware, Wordsworth Editions

Chandler, D.G. (1995). *Sedgemoor 1685: from Monmouth's Invasion to the Bloody Assizes*. Staplehurst, Spellmount

Churchill, W.S. (1967a). *Marlborough: his life and times*, vol. 1. London, Sphere

Churchill, W.S. (1967b). *Marlborough: his life and times*, vol. 3. London, Sphere

Clausewitz, C. von (1976, first pub. 1832). *On War*, ed. and trans. M. Howard and P. Paret. Princeton, NJ, Princeton University Press

Cleere, H.F. (ed.) (1989). *Archaeological Heritage Management in the Modern World*. London, Unwin Hyman

Cline, E.H. (2000). *The Battles of Armageddon: Megiddo and the Jezreel Valley from the Bronze Age to the Nuclear Age*. Ann Arbor, MI, University of Michigan Press

Colman, P. and Coupe, B. (n.d.). *Devizes in the Civil War: the battle of Roundway*. Devizes, Wiltshire County Council

Cooper, J. (ed.) (1993). *The Battle of Maldon: fiction and fact*. London, Hambledon Press

Creasy, E. (1908, first pub. 1851). *The Fifteen Decisive Battles of the World. From Marathon to Waterloo*. London, Macmillan

Cunha, E. and Silva, A.M. (1997). 'War lessons from the famous Portuguese medieval battle of Aljubarrota', *International Journal of Osteoarchaeology* 7

Daniel, G. and Renfrew, C. (1988). *The Idea of Prehistory*. Edinburgh, Edinburgh University Press

Darvill, T. (1987). *Ancient Monuments in the Countryside: an archaeological management review*, English Heritage Archaeological Report 5. London, English Heritage

DeVries, K. (1999). *The Norwegian Invasion of England in 1066*. Woodbridge, Boydell

Doyle, P. and Bennett, M.R. (eds) (2002). *Fields of Battle: terrain in military history*. Dordrecht, Kluwer

Duby, G. (1973). *Le Dimanche de Bouvines: 27 juillet 1214*. Paris, Gallimard

Duffy, C. (1987). *The Military Experience in the Age of Reason*. London, Routledge

Dupuy, R.E. and Dupuy, T.N. (1970). *The Encyclopaedia of Military History from 3500 BC to the Present*. London, Macdonald and Jane's

Elliot, G. (1972). *Twentieth Century Book of the Dead*. Harmondsworth, Penguin

English Heritage (1995). *Register of Historic Battlefields*. London, English Heritage

Fiorato, V., Boylston, A. and Knusel, C. (2000). *Blood Red Roses: the archaeology of a mass grave from the Battle of Towton AD 1461*. Oxford, Oxbow

Foard, G. (1995). *Naseby. The Decisive Campaign*. Whitstable, Pryor Publications

Foard, G. (2001). 'The archaeology of attack: battles and sieges of the English Civil War' in T. Freeman and A. Pollard (eds), *Fields of Conflict: progress and prospects in battlefield archaeology, proceedings of a conference held in the Department of Archaeology, University of Glasgow, April 2000*, BAR International Series 958. Oxford, Archaeopress

Foote, S. (1997). *Shadowed Ground: America's landscapes of violence and tragedy*. Austin, TX, University of Texas Press

Freeman, T. and Pollard, A. (eds) (2001). *Fields of Conflict: progress and prospects in battlefield archaeology, proceedings of a conference held in the Department of Archaeology, University of Glasgow, April 2000*, BAR International Series 958. Oxford, Archaeopress

Fuller, J.F.C. (1970). *The Decisive Battles of the Western World and their Effect upon History*, 2 vols, ed. J. Terraine. London, Paladin

Garden, M.-C. (forthcoming). 'The heritagescape: landscapes of heritage', in D. Hicks, L. McAtackney and G. Fairclough (eds), *Landscape Archaeology: Global Perspectives. One World Archaeology*. London, UCL Press

Gairdner, J. (1975). *The Battle of Bosworth*. Upminster, Richard III Society

Garlan, Y. (1975). *War in the Ancient World. A Social History*. London, Chatto and Windus

Gray, C.H. (1997). *Postmodern War: the new politics of conflict*. London, Routledge

Green, H. (1976). *The Cockpit of Europe: a guide to the battlefields of Belgium and France*. London, David & Charles

Guest, K. and Guest, D. (1996). *British Battles: the frontlines of history in colour*. London, HarperCollins

Hadengue, A. (1935). *Bouvines: victoire créatrice*. Paris, Plon

Haecker, C.M. and Mauck, J.G. (1997). *On the Prairie of Palo Alto: historical archaeology of the U.S.–Mexican War battlefield*. College Station, TX, Texas A&M University Press

Halsall, G. (1989). 'Anthropology and the Study of Pre-Conquest Warfare and Society: The Ritual War in Anglo-Saxon England' in S.C. Hawkes (ed.), *Weapons and Warfare in Anglo-Saxon England*, Oxford University Committee for Archaeology Monograph 21. Oxford, Oxbow Books

Hanson, V.D. (1989). *The Western Way of War. Infantry Battle in Classical Greece*. Oxford, Oxford University Press

Hanson, V.D. (ed.) (1991). *Hoplites. The Classical Greek Battle Experience*. London, Routledge

Haraway, D. (1985). 'A manifesto for cyborgs: science, technology and socialist feminism for the 1980s', *Socialist Review* 80

Hardy, R. (1992). *Longbow: a social and military history*, 3rd edn. Sparkford, Stephens

Hawkes, S.C. (ed.) (1989). *Weapons and Warfare in Anglo-Saxon England*. Oxford University Committee for Archaeology Monograph 21. Oxford, Oxbow Books

Herzfeld, M. (1991). *A Place in History: social and monumental time in a Cretan town.* Princeton, NJ, and Oxford, Princeton University Press

Hewitt, N. (2001). 'The National Inventory of War Memorials: profile of a national recording project' in J.-M. Teutonico and J. Fidler (eds), *Monuments and the Millennium: proceedings of a joint conference organised by English Heritage and the United Kingdom Institute for Conservation.* London, English Heritage

Hibbert, C. (1961). *Corunna*, British Battles Series. London, Batsford

Hobsbawm, E. (1990). *Nations and Nationalism since 1780: programme, myth, reality.* Cambridge, Cambridge University Press

Hobsbawm, E. and Ranger, T. (eds) (1983). *The Invention of Tradition.* Cambridge, Cambridge University Press

Hodder, I., Shanks, M., Alexandri, A., Buchli, V., Carman, J., Last, J. and Lucas, G. (eds) (1995). *Interpreting Archaeology: finding meaning in the past.* London, Routledge

Holmes, R. (1996). *War Walks: from Agincourt to Normandy.* London, BBC Books

Hutton, W. (1999). *The Battle of Bosworth Field.* Stroud, Tempus

Inglis-Jones, J. (1994). 'The Battle of the Dunes 1658: Condé, War and Politics', *War in History* 1.3

Jameson, J. (ed.) (1997). *Presenting Archaeology to the Public: digging for truths.* Walnut Creek, Altamira Press

Jones, S., (1980). 'Institutions of violence' in J. Chafas and R. Lewin (eds), *Not Work Alone. A cross-cultural view of activities superfluous to survival.* London, Temple Smith

Keegan, J. (1976). *The Face of Battle.* London, Hutchinson

Keegan, J. (1993). *A History of Warfare.* London, Hutchinson

Keegan, J. (1996). *Warpaths: travels of a military historian in North America.* London, Pimlico

Keeley, L.H. (1996). *War before Civilization. The Myth of the Peaceful Savage.* Oxford and New York, Oxford University Press

Kendall, P.M. (1972a). *Richard III.* London, Sphere

Kendall, P.M. (1972b). *Warwick the Kingmaker and the Wars of the Roses.* London, Sphere

Kirkpatrick, D.T. (1997). 'The archaeology of Billy the Kid' in J. Jameson, (ed.), *Presenting Archaeology to the Public: digging for truths.* Walnut Creek, Altamira Press

Knox, M. and Murray, W. (2001). *The Dynamics of Military Revolution 1300–2050.* Cambridge, Cambridge University Press

Laffin, J. (1995). *Brassey's Battles: 3,500 years of conflict, campaigns and wars from A–Z.* London, Brassey's

Lazenby, J. (1991). 'The Killing Zone' in V.D. Hanson (ed.), *Hoplites, The Classical Greek Battle Experience.* London, Routledge

Lipe, W.D. (1984). 'Value and meaning in cultural resources' in H.F. Cleeve (ed.), *Approaches to the Archaeological Heritage*, 1–11. Cambridge, Cambridge University Press

Lynn, J.A. (2001). 'Forging the western army in seventeenth-century France' in M. Knox and W. Murray, *The Dynamics of Military Revolution 1300–2050.* Cambridge, Cambridge University Press

McGimsey, C.R. and Davis, H.R. (eds) (1977). *The Management of Archaeological Resources: the Airlie House Report.* Washington DC, Society for American Archaeology

McLynn, F.J. (1999). *1066: the year of the three battles.* London, Pimlico

McPherson, J.M. (1990). *Battle Cry of Freedom: the American Civil War.* London, Penguin

Montgomery, Field Marshal Viscount, of Alamein. (1968). *A History of Warfare.* London, Collins

Murray, W. and Knox, M. (2001). 'Thinking about revolutions in warfare' in Knox and Murray, 2001

Naylor, J. (1960). *Waterloo*, British Battles Series. London, Batsford

Newman, P. (1981). *The Battle of Marston Moor*. Strettington, Anthony Bird Publications

Nosworthy, B. (1992). *The Anatomy of Victory. Battle Tactics 1681–1763*. New York, NY, Hippocrene Books

Nosworthy, B. (1995). *Battle Tactics of Napoleon and his Enemies*. London, Constable

Ober, J. (1991). 'Hoplites and obstacles' in V.D. Hanson (ed.), *Hoplites. The Classical Greek Battle Experience*. London, Routledge

Oman, C. (1898). *A History of the Art of War: the Middle Ages from the fourth to the fourteenth centuries*. London, Methuen

Oman, C. (1902a) (1995). *A History of the Peninsular War*, vol. I. London, Greenhill

Oman, C. (1902b) (1995). *A History of the Peninsular War*, vol. II. London, Greenhill

Oman, C. (1902c) (1995). *A History of the Peninsular War*, vol. VI. London, Greenhill

Oman, C. (1924). *The Art of War in the Middle Ages*, 2nd edn. London, Methuen

Oman, C. (1953). *The Art of War in the Middle Ages AD 378–1555*, revised and edited by J. Beeler. Ithaca, NY, Cornell University Press

do Paço, A. (1962). 'Em tormo de Aljubarrota. I-O Problema dos ossos dos combatentes da batalha', *Anais da Academia Portugesa da História* II(12)

Parker, G. (1988). *The Military Revolution: military innovation and the rise of the West 1500–1800*. Cambridge, Cambridge University Press

Parker Pearson, M. (1982). 'Mortuary practices, society and ideology: an ethnoarchaeological study' in I. Hodder (ed.), *Symbolic and Structural Archaeology*. Cambridge, Cambridge University Press

Parkinson, R. (1973). *The Peninsular War*, The British at War. London, Hart-Davis MacGillan

Pearson, M. (1998). 'Performance as valuation: early Bronze Age burial as theatrical complexity' in D. Bailey (ed.), *The Archaeology of Value: essays on prestige and the processes of valuation*, BAR International Series 730. Oxford, Archaeopress

Pereira, W.D. (1983). *The Battle of Tewkesbury*. Cheltenham, Line One Publishing

Perrett, B. (1992). *The Battle Book. Crucial conflicts in history from 1469 BC to the present*. London, Arms and Armour Press

Petty, G. and Petty, S. (1993). 'A geological reconstruction of the site of the Battle of Maldon' in J. Cooper (ed.), *The Battle of Maldon: fiction and fact*. London and Rio Grande, Hambledon Press

Prestwich, M. (1996). *Armies and Warfare in the Middle Ages: the English experience*. London and New Haven, CT, Yale University Press

Pujo, B. (1995). *Le Grand Condé*. Paris, Albin Michel

Reichstein, C. (1984). 'Federal Republic of Germany' in H.F. Cleere (ed.), *Approaches to the Archaeological Heritage*. Cambridge, Cambridge University Press

Roberts, M. (1967). *Essays in Swedish History*. London, Weidenfeld & Nicolson

Robins, K. (1991). 'Tradition and translation: national culture in its global context' in J. Corner and S. Harvey (eds), *Enterprise and Heritage: crosscurrents of national heritage*. London, Routledge

Rodwell, W. (1993). 'The battle of Assandun and its memorial church: a reappraisal' in J. Cooper (ed.), *The Battle of Maldon: fiction and fact*. London, Hambledon Press

Saunders, N. (2001). 'Excavating memories: archaeology and the Great War 1914–2001', *Antiquity* 76

Savage, A. (ed.) (1983). *The Anglo-Saxon Chronicles*. London, Heinemann

Schaafsma, C.F. (1989). 'Significant until proven otherwise: problem versus representative samples' in H.F. Cleeve (ed.), *Archaeological Heritage Management in the Modern World*, pp. 38–51. London, Routledge

Schofield, J., Johnson, W.G. and Beck, C. (eds) (2002). *Matériel Culture: the archaeology of 20th-century conflict*. London, Routledge

Scott, D.D. (1997). 'Interpreting archaeology at Little Bighorn' in J. Jameson (ed.), *Presenting Archaeology to the Public: digging for truths*. Walnut Creek, Altamira Press

Scott, D.D., Fox, R.A., Connor, M.A. and Harmon, D. (1989). *Archaeological Perspectives on the Battle of the Little Big Horn*. Norman, OK and London, University of Oklahoma Press

Scovill, D.H., Gordon, G.J. and Anderson, K. (1977). 'Guidelines for the preparation of statements of environmental impact on archaeological resources' in M.B. Schiffer and G.J. Gumerman (eds), *Conservation Archaeology: a handbook for cultural resource management studies*, Studies in Archaeology. New York, NY, Academic Press

Seymour, W. (1975). *Battles in Britain*, 2 vols. London, Sidgwick & Jackson

Shapiro, M.J. (1997). *Violent Cartographies: mapping cultures of war*. Minneapolis, University of Minnesota Press

Skeates, R. (2000). *Debating the Archaeological Heritage*. London, Duckworth

Smurthwaite, D. (1993). *The Complete Guide to the Battlefields of Britain with Ordnance Survey Maps*. London, Michael Joseph

Stone, P. and Molyneaux, B.L. (eds) (1994). *The Presented Past: heritage, museums and education*. London, Routledge

Sutherland, T. (2000). 'The archaeological investigation of the Towton battlefield' in V. Fiorato, A. Boylston and C. Knusel (eds), *Blood Red Roses: the archaeology of a mass grave from the Battle of Towton AD 1461*. Oxford, Oxbow

Sutton, J. (2000). 'The Linton Uprising 1648' in T. Kirby and S. Oosthuizen (eds), *An Atlas of Cambridgeshire and Huntingdonshire History*. Cambridge, Anglia Polytechnic University

Swagg, D.G. (ed.) (1981). *The Battle of Maldon*. Manchester, Manchester University Press

Tao, General Hanzhang (2000). *Sun Tzu's Art of War: the modern Chinese interpretation*, trans. Yuan Shibing. New York, NY, Sterling Publishing

Tarlow, S. (1999). *Bereavement and Commemoration: an archaeology of mortality*. Oxford, Blackwell

Thomas, J. (1991). *Rethinking the Neolithic*. Cambridge, Cambridge University Press

Thomas, J. (1996). *Time, Culture and Identity: an interpretative archaeology*. London, Routledge

Tilley, C. (1994). *A Phenomenology of Landscape*. Oxford, Berg

Tomasson, K. and Buist, F. (1962). *Battles of the '45*, British Battles Series. London, Batsford

Toynbee, M. and Young, P. (1970). *Cropredy Bridge: the campaign and the battle*. Kineton, Roundwood

Trevelyan, G.M. (1965). *England Under Queen Anne*, vol. 3: *Ramillies and the Union with Scotland*. London, Fontana

Tuchman, B.W. (1978). *A Distant Mirror: the calamitous 14th century*. London, Macmillan

Turney-High, H. (1971, first pub. 1949). *Primitive War: its practice and concepts*. Colombia, University of South Carolina Press

Verbrüggen, J.F. (2002). *The Battle of the Golden Spurs: Courtrai 11 July 1302*, trans. D.P. Ferguson. Rochester, NY, Boydell Press

Walsh, K. (1992). *The Representation of the Past: museums and heritage in the postmodern world*, The Heritage: Care, Preservation, Management. London, Routledge

REFERENCES

Walton, J. (1998). *The Battle of Bosworth 1485: an account of the battle.* Lincoln, Freezywater

Wedgwood, C.V. (1957). *The Thirty Years War.* London, Pelican

Wedgwood, C.V. (1966). *The King's War 1641–1647.* London, Fontana

Weigley, R.F. (1991). *The Age of Battles: the quest for decisive warfare from Breitenfeld to Waterloo.* Bloomington and Indianapolis, IN, Indiana University Press

Weller, J. (1992, first pub. 1962). *Wellington in the Peninsula.* London, Greenhill

Winter, J. (1995). *Sites of Memory, Sites of Mourning: the Great War in European Cultural History.* Cambridge, Cambridge University Press

Woolrych, A. (1966). *Battles of the English Civil War*, British Battles Series. London, Pan Books

Yarrington, A. (1988). *The Commemoration of the Hero 1800–1864: monuments to the British victors of the Napoleonic Wars.* New York, NY and London, Garland Publishing

INDEX

References in **bold** are to black and white plates in text.